Cyber Crime, Security and Digital Intelligence

For Dad

Cyber Crime, Security and Digital Intelligence

MARK JOHNSON

Routledge
Taylor & Francis Group

LONDON AND NEW YORK

First published 2013 by Gower Publishing

2 Park Square, Milton Park, Abingdon, Oxfordshire OX14 4RN
52 Vanderbilt Avenue, New York, NY 10017

Routledge is an imprint of the Taylor & Francis Group, an informa business

First issued in paperback 2020

British Library Cataloguing in Publication Data
A catalogue record for this book is available from the British Library.

The Library of Congress has cataloged the printed edition as follows:
Johnson, Mark, 1959–
    Cyber crime, security and digital intelligence / by Mark Johnson.
        pages cm
    Includes bibliographical references and index.
    ISBN 978-1-4094-5449-6 (hardback : alk. paper) — ISBN 978-1-4094-5450-2 (ebook) – ISBN 978-1-4724-0365-0 (epub)
    1. Computer crimes. 2. Cyberterrorism. 3. Computer security. 4. Computer networks – Security measures. I. Title.

    HV6773.J64 2013
    658.4'78–dc23

                                                                        2013008805

ISBN 13: 978-1-4094-5449-6 (hbk)
ISBN 13: 978-0-367-60546-9 (pbk)

Contents

List of Figures

List of Tables

About the Author

Mark Johnson first became involved in high-technology risk management in the late 1980s when he joined Cable & Wireless as a communications fraud manager. Prior to this he had served as a military officer engaged in narcotics enforcement operations in the Caribbean.

At Cable & Wireless, Mark designed and managed the development of one of the Telecom industry's first fraud management software solutions and oversaw the system's installation at over a dozen sites worldwide. This experience led to him being engaged by a number of leading high-tech firms, including Alcatel, Nortel and Ericsson. In 2001 Mark set up his own consulting business, The Risk Management Group, and with his associates he has been providing consultancy, product design, training and awareness raising services via that channel ever since, addressing risks and countermeasures in both online and telecommunications services.

Mark lives in Cambridgeshire with his family. In his books he attempts to demystify topics that are often riddled with jargon and therefore obscure to the layman. Mark is about to start work on his third book which will tackle the subject of e-Crime.

Preface

Let me start with a confession: the Internet liberated me. Prior to discovering that I could work profitably and globally for clients from the top floor of my home using just a website, email, Skype and various social media tools, I was trapped in a stultifying corporate role, spending long hours commuting and working for people who, in many cases, annoyed me as much as I annoyed them. Perhaps it's just me, but the sense of being trapped was very real. Today, I am free; free to pick my clients and hours of work, to collect my children from school, take them to the doctor when necessary, or spend time with them in the early afternoon, as I please.

Consequently, I fear any cyber threat to my online business more than I fear recession, competition or cancelled contracts. These other challenges can and have been overcome several times in the lifetime of my firm, but a cyber attack that brings online services to a halt, even for a few days, would obliterate my means of seeking business, doing the work, delivering the results and securing payment. Extended over a longer period, it would also make the majority of my services and publications irrelevant. Like many in today's digital marketplace, my stake in the evolving online technologies is therefore both commercial and deeply personal. I quite literally need a secure and reliable digital environment in order to survive in the physical world. I frankly have no idea what I would do without it.

Most people who use online or Internet-enabled systems will occasionally have a vague sense of the innumerable processes that take place outside their field of vision, of the speed with which data now flies around the globe and of the sheer number of people connected to the global network at any particular time. But few will have any inkling of the fact that every hour of every day, hundreds of thousands of cyber attacks are deflected by the security systems and administrators quietly doing their jobs in computer rooms and back offices scattered all over the planet.

The simple fact is that any corporate or public sector information technology (IT) system is a large ship sailing through a churning sea of malware and other attacks. Your home PC is at best a dinghy. It is not only the occasional shark that you need to worry about, but the ceaseless roiling of the poisonous soup through which you sail. Security is your hull and as you read this your Internet service is fending off another automated hacking attack, your email server is in the process of blocking one of a ceaseless flood of root login attempts, and your Firewall is fighting ubiquitous malware infections and other intrusions on a non-stop basis. In fact, looking at the Internet from this perspective, it is hard to see how we manage to have a network at all, so awash is it with viruses, Botnets, Rootkits and myriad other attack tools.

In the autumn of 2012 the mighty super tanker that is the US financial services sector suffered an unprecedented series of cyber attacks launched by tens of thousands of individuals who had been inspired to act by the Hacktivist group Anonymous. The favoured attack weapon was the freely available Low Orbit Ion Cannon (LOIC) which is an open source application designed to launch what is known as a Denial of Service (DoS) attack. The LOIC does this by flooding a target server with messages once the user has inserted the target's IP address. If this flood of messages reaches a sufficiently high volume, the targeted system is unable to cope and it may go offline. Police in the UK reported that 34,000 LOIC downloads in that country occurred over a period of only three days. For those lacking the knowledge, videos had been placed on YouTube that provided lessons on how to use the LOIC tool effectively.

This attack came close to causing what Leon Panetta, the US Secretary of Defense, described as a 'Cyber Pearl Harbor'. He was alluding to the possibility that a successful cyber attack could one day bring down the US financial system and potentially the global economic system. This isn't mere scare mongering. The cybercrime and security threat is getting more sophisticated at the same time as our dependency on cyber technologies becomes more absolute and Panetta was describing in macro-level terms exactly what scares me in relation to my own firm.

Given the speed of technological progress, no book on cybercrime and security can provide more than a snapshot of today's risks and contermeasures. For example, as I write this on my big, noisy, clunky box of a PC, my son is sitting on the floor beside me, playing with my iPad. Even the iPad has started to look old and I know that by the time he is a young man, all of the state-of-the-art tools I am using will look as ancient to him as a mechanical gramophone looks to me today.

Nevertheless, criminals' motives, the general techniques they employ and their methods of exploitation tend to follow broadly consistent paths and I am reasonably confident that if my children should leaf through this title 30 or 40 years from now, the deeper essence of what I will describe here will still hold true, whatever their future world might look like.

An important aspect of the risk we face is widespread ignorance. Carl Sagan once said that we live in a society exquisitely dependent on science and technology, in which hardly anyone knows anything about science and technology. He was speaking many years ago, but he could easily have been describing our relationship with current communications technologies. The dependence on the Internet and its related systems and processes that I have already alluded to is unprecedented and yet very few understand either the technology or its associated risks. Even the attackers often require training of their own, via sites like YouTube or through online forums, before they can competently execute their tasks. This means that, though most cyber security risks are entirely manageable, there is a dearth of people ready and able to do the managing, and even fewer sufficiently well informed to willingly allocate the funds and make the necessary management and policy decisions.

It is with this perspective on current risks that I have set out to demystify three major topics with this book in the hope of making them more accessible to a wider, non-technical audience:

- The current nature of cyber security risks and threat actors.

- The scope and type of controls needed to counter those risks.

- The opportunities now available for investigators and analysts via online sources, this last being as much a risk as an opportunity, as I shall attempt to explain.

These are big, complex subjects but I have tried to avoid, or at least clarify, any jargon. I will also utilise a number of simple illustrations in order to explain key points or technical concepts.

Cyber attack models

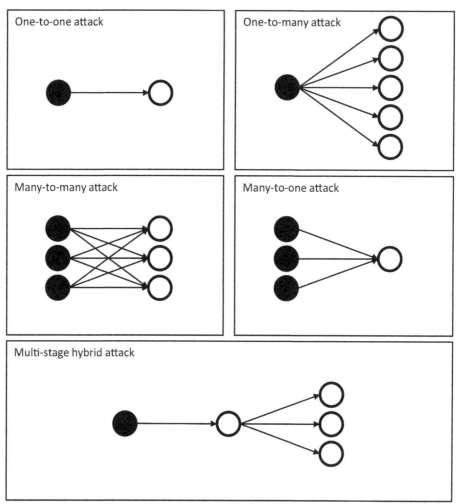

Figure P.1   Cyber attack models

The Threat

The Distributed Denial of Service (DDoS) attack that was the LOIC event represents one of several attack patterns that have evolved over time. Because I tend to think graphically, and because the Internet, its connected devices and its users are all real physical entities, I try to construct graphical models (see Figure P.1) for the often complex attacks, many of which I struggle to properly understand myself. At the lowest level, we can group most cyber attack scenarios into one of five types, or class them as hybrids:

- one-to-one

- one-to-many

- many-to-many

- many-to-one

- multi-stage hybrid

Each LOIC attack on a given bank was an example of a many-to-one attack. If someone was to socially engineer you out of your credit card details that could represent a one-to-one attack, depending on the technique they used. Some attacks have multiple stages, perhaps employing a one-to-many approach to infect a large number of devices before triggering a many-to-one attack from those devices against a single target. We will return to these alternative models at points throughout the book.

> *The ability to respond to the evolving cyber-threat environment is not a destination but rather a journey. There is and always will be a permanent race in cyber space between attackers and defenders. Unfortunately, at the moment attackers are one step ahead. In this race it is impossible to know and, finally, to beat the opponents without understanding their attack methods. Hence, understanding threats is a vital element towards protecting cyber assets that needs to be in the focus of information security professionals.*[1]

This rapid evolution of cyber security threats is in part a result of a process of convergence, illustrated in Figure P.2, below. The technological shift has facilitated the emergence of the 'many-to-one' model in which cyber attack capabilities are widely distributed in order to support large-scale organised attacks, often with acquisitive motivations, against precisely specified targets. Convergence has also had the effect of bringing different types of criminal together in one space; financial fraudsters, communications service fraudsters, hackers, spies and extremists all cross paths online in a manner that is unique

---

1   ENISA: Threat Landscape Published, http://www.enisa.europa.eu/activities/risk-management/ evolving-threat-environment/ENISA_Threat_Landscape (accessed 22 March 2013).

The product of convergence

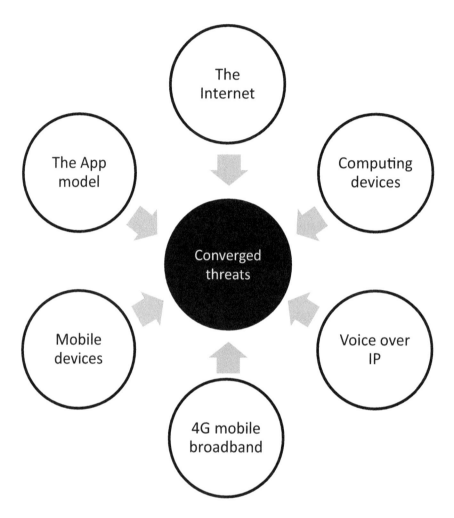

Figure P.2   The role of convergence

in the history of civilisation. This convergence of threats demands a converged response, both at the organisational level and above, and we can no longer afford to think in terms of different types of security or risk control – everything is interrelated and interdependent.

As we shall see, the sophisticated new threats (often described collectively as the emerging or evolving 'threat landscape') can threaten the very survivability of large commercial firms and even of market sectors. Effective audit and cyber security control mechanisms are now essential and they cannot remain the purview of a small number of backroom experts. They must become topics that receive the attention of management and users at all levels.

One important challenge is that there remains a very widespread lack of understanding of cyber security risks and solutions and this is made worse by the confusing and all encompassing definitions for cybercrime, e-Crime and cyber security that abound at all levels. Many regard any unauthorised act involving even the most minimal use of IT or communications technology as some form of 'cybercrime'. In today's high-tech society, this means that the vast majority of crimes are deemed to have a 'cyber' element.

A crime deserves to be described as a 'cyber security crime' if the primary mechanism by which the crime was committed involved the use of the Internet, and/or World Wide Web, and:

1. the primary target of the attack was data, code or other digital material stored on an Internet connected device; or

2. the primary motive of the attack was to disrupt remote systems or services, or the Internet itself.

We can see from Figure P.3 that there is a distinction to be made between cyber and communications crime on the one hand and 'e-Crime' on the other. In my suggested use of the terms, e-Crime is *facilitated* by technology but it might merely involve someone sitting at your PC without your permission and stealing your bank details, or using your credit card fraudulently to make an online purchase, having obtained the card by picking your pocket. In such cases, neither the data nor the network is the real target; they are simply tools or avenues of attack and the target was your money.

The distinctions between what constitutes a cyber crime and what constitutes an e-Crime can seem vague, even arbitrary, so why bother to make them? The answer is that most high-tech attacks have at least two phases – an access phase and an exploitation phase. Cyber and e-Crime access phases are often indistinguishable (they may both involve hacking, for example) but the exploitation phases can differ hugely; taking R&D data for its intrinsic value

Cyber crime is...

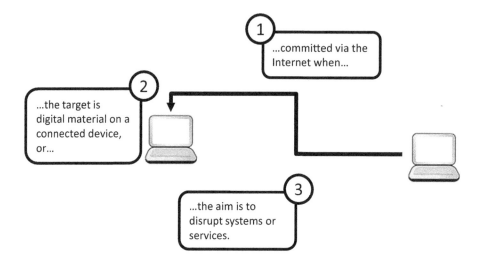

Cyber Security is all of those efforts designed to prevent, avoid, mitigate, detect, deter, investigate and punish cyber crime.

Figure P.3   What is cybercrime?

in a 'Cyber' case, or using stolen payment data to perpetrate a subsequent financial fraud in the case of an 'e-Crime'. It is the wide variation in *exploit* techniques that is important here. One set of controls can potentially address both Cyber and e-Crime access attempts, but very different types of controls, detection mechanisms and investigative skills are needed to deal with Cyber and e-Crime *exploits*. Cyber security experts will rarely understand the e-Crime exploit and conversely financial crime experts will rarely understand the cyber crime exploit technique. This is where we can most clearly see convergence in action as very different types of crime management skills and investigative techniques are brought to bear on a single incident.

One unique feature of the Internet is that it has grown to become a communications technology the evolutionary direction of which is largely determined by consumer demand rather than by rational corporate and governmental decision making. So, we find corporate and government organisations, most of them directed by people with only a limited understanding of emerging technologies and services, jumping on the Internet bandwagon in order to keep pace with their stakeholders. As these bodies have recognised the cost-savings that can also be achieved through the use of the Internet, their reliance on the technology has only grown, with the result that many vital services are now delivered or controlled almost exclusively online.

Today's 'cyber' technology is also a product of the convergence of several communications and information technologies on a single point – the 'IP' network. Your morning paper, the television news, the journey to work, the traffic light that delayed you, your cup of coffee, the report you browsed, the phone call you made, even this book, were all delivered to you via or with a major contribution by cyber technology. While cyber is not the only way in which such goods and services can be delivered, it has become the de facto mechanism for delivery, with the result that other solutions, such as manual or paper-based operations, are largely redundant and there is now no readily available fall back system for most of the cyber technology operations that now govern or facilitate our daily lives and our shared dependence is absolute. As I intend to explain, high levels of dependency on a vulnerable resource equate to high levels of risk.

The Cost of Cybercrime

The United Kingdom Threat Assessment produced by the Serious Organised Crime Agency (SOCA) now includes cybercrime and related crimes as key threats.[2] Meanwhile the 2013 report by the European Network and Information Security Agency (ENISA), referenced earlier, lists sixteen top cyber threats and describes the current trend for eleven of them as increasing, while five are stable and only one (Spam) is said to be declining. My personal experience would lead me to question the decline of even the one. So, why do we still face huge cyber security challenges in what is a very mature market for solutions? One possibility is that large, complex and diffuse systems are much more costly to defend than to attack. The defender must succeed everywhere, all the time, while the attacker only needs to succeed at one point, once. This is the case with the Internet and all of its associated or dependent systems and networks; cyber attack is the ultimate form of asymmetric warfare.

---

2   http://www.soca.gov.uk/threats (accessed 20 July 2012).

In a paper titled *Measuring the Cost of Cybercrime* (2012) by Ross Anderson, Michael Levi and others, the authors report that:[3]

> *We distinguish carefully between traditional crimes that are now 'cyber' because they are conducted online (such as tax and welfare fraud); transitional crimes whose modus operandi has changed substantially as a result of the move online (such as credit card fraud); new crimes that owe their existence to the Internet; and what we might call platform crimes such as the provision of Botnets which facilitate other crimes rather than being used to extract money from victims directly. As far as direct costs are concerned, we find that traditional offences such as tax and welfare fraud cost the typical citizen in the low hundreds of pounds/Euros/dollars a year; transitional frauds cost a few pounds/ Euros/dollars; while the new computer crimes cost in the tens of pence/ cents. However, the indirect costs and defence costs are much higher for transitional and new crimes. For the former they may be roughly comparable to what the criminals earn, while for the latter they may be an order of magnitude more. As a striking example, the Botnet behind a third of the spam sent in 2010 earned its owners around US$2.7m, while worldwide expenditures on spam prevention probably exceeded a billion dollars. We are extremely inefficient at fighting cybercrime; or to put it another way, cyber crooks are like terrorists or metal thieves in that their activities impose disproportionate costs on society. Some of the reasons for this are well-known: cybercrimes are global and have strong externalities, while traditional crimes such as burglary and car theft are local, and the associated equilibria have emerged after many years of optimisation. As for the more direct question of what should be done, our figures suggest that we should spend less in anticipation of cybercrime (on antivirus, firewalls, etc.) and more in response – that is, on the prosaic business of hunting down cyber-criminals and throwing them in jail.*

As you have read, many leading thinkers and agencies have identified cybercrime as one of the main threats to the global economy. This is a challenge that affects all modern economies and while the true cost of high-technology crimes is difficult to calculate, the number of reports and news media stories appearing daily on the topics of hacking, data loss and online fraud serves to support the notion that this class of risk is indeed of special importance. Given the scale of the problem and the dependencies mentioned, cyber security

---

3   http://weis2012.econinfosec.org/papers/Anderson_WEIS2012.pdf (accessed January 2013).

awareness should be one of society's top priorities, but it isn't even close. Our educational, governmental and corporate management systems all need to be much better engaged so as to ensure that this critical risk receives the attention it needs and that the necessary management skills are available in abundance because in an era of absolute dependence on the cyber technologies for most economic, commercial, political and social systems and processes, attacks or exploits that target or transit these technologies, and which may deliberately or accidentally bring said services to a halt, represent an existential threat to our globalised systems of trade, supply chain management, finance and the financial markets, governance and security.

Cybercrime at a Glance

You will recall that by 'Cybercrime' I refer to any crime involving the use of a computer connected to the Internet, or to an equivalent network. The motives may be political, commercial, anarchical or other, but the basic attack and intrusion techniques generally remain the same regardless of motive. Cybercrime is becoming increasingly complex, reflecting both the increased complexity of our cyber technology and services mix, as well as ongoing improvements in security.

It has been reported that an increasing number of cyber attacks are being launched via 'Malnets'[4] (malware networks) and a sharp rise in such attacks has been described by Blue Coat, a leading solutions provider with whom I have no association. While statistics provided by security solution vendors must always be treated with caution, the examples cited by this firm are compelling and the particular trend they describe appears to be consistent with the evolution of the online threat in general.

Blue Coat defines Malnets as 'distributed infrastructures within the Internet that are built and maintained for the purpose of launching a variety of attacks against unsuspecting users over extended periods of time. They gather users, typically when they are visiting trusted sites and route them to malware, via relay, exploit and payload servers that continually shift to new domains and locations.' Blue Coat claims to be tracking more than 500 unique Malnets although they admit that not all 500 will be active on any given day. The actual

---

4   http://bluecoat.com/sites/default/files/documents/files/BC_2012_Security_Report-v1i-optimized.pdf (accessed 10 December 2012).

size of each Malnet varies from day to day depending on the current level of malicious activities and attacks.

Typical cybercrime attack methods also include:

- **Hacking,** or breaking into computer systems and networks using highly skilled 'manual' techniques.

- **Code injection** attacks designed to access logon data tables of user names and passwords, such as those allegedly perpetrated against Sony Online Entertainment[5] in 2011.

- **Cross-site scripting (XXS)** attacks that launch attacks on a target site via a malformed web page.

- **Man-in-the-middle** (and man-in-the-browser) events wherein an attacker interposes themselves between two parties in order to intercept their communications.

- **Spyware** that captures key strokes, personal data and logon information.

- **Trojans, Worms, viruses** and other malware that can deliver a payload or disrupt and even damage systems, such as Gauss,[6] or the Stuxnet and Flame attacks centred on Iran over recent years.

- **DoS attacks** that attempt to bring down selected services or even whole networks, normally by flooding them with traffic or signaling messages.

- **Botnet exploits** involving networks of thousands, or even millions, of infected computers that might broadcast SPAM or be used to facilitate distributed DDoS attacks.

The list goes on and we will explore these techniques in greater detail in later chapters, but my point is that increasingly complex technologies are, by their very nature, exposed to increasingly complex sets of risks. Many of these risks can

---

5   http://www.channel4.com/news/sony-networks-hacked-again (accessed 10 August 2012).
6   http://www.guardian.co.uk/technology/2012/aug/09/stuxnet-gauss-virus-kaspersky (accessed 10 August 2012).

manifest themselves in combination, with one case involving, for example, a code injection attack designed to compromise root passwords and gain administrator rights, followed by the insertion of a Worm to infect a system or network in order to then exfiltrate confidential data and send it back to the attacker.

Social Media Risks

Notwithstanding the potential for an increase in complexity at one end of the spectrum, many of today's risks are remarkable for their simplicity. Indeed, we have seen a large proportion of them before and we ought to be able to deal with many of them quite easily. Take social media for example.

Social networking is an Internet within the Internet. Now the communications tool of choice for billions of users, social media services such as Facebook[7] provide unprecedented access and communications capabilities at almost zero cost. They also introduce a new dimension to some very old risks, including but not limited to:

- **Data protection risks** in relation to user's account and profile information, which often includes dates of birth, addresses and telephone numbers. LinkedIn recently suffered a hacking attack[8] that is thought to have exposed 6.5 million user names and passwords.

- **Identity verification risks,** demonstrated by the ease with which fake social media accounts can be created and 'friends' found. In tests conducted by my own firm, using eight fabricated test Facebook accounts and one test LinkedIn account, we were able to attract an average of 120 online 'friends' per account and over 950 friends in one notable instance, simply by using an attractive photograph. We also demonstrated possible vulnerabilities in the security controls provided by both sites.

- **Harassment, grooming and targeting,** whereby criminals and others are using social media to identify, locate and investigate potential victims.[9]

---

7   www.facebook.com (accessed 4 June 2012).
8   http://www.bu.edu/today/2012/linkedin-hacking-what-you-need-to-know/ (accessed 14 December 2012).
9   http://www.legalandgeneral.com/_resources/pdfs/insurance/digital-criminal-2012-report.pdf. (accessed March 2012).

- **Brand and reputational harm,** particularly from events such as 'Twitter Storms' where users target a brand and generate thousands of negative messages that are read by millions of consumers in a very short period of time.

In the 1940s, Allied messages to citizens on the home front often included the phrase 'Loose lips sink ships', implying that by carelessly talking about vessel movements, or other sensitive information, people could accidentally pass information to the enemy. In the social media domain it's more a question of loose clicks, but the impact on personal relationships, reputations and trust can be dire nonetheless.

Annecdotal evidence, our own tests and the experiences of clients indicate that a good proportion of malicious incidents in cyber space now occur within or via social networking sites and the ENISA report cited indicates that seven of the top threats undergoing an increase are seeing part of this increase as a result of risks introduced via social technology.[10] This problem is compounded by the ease with which anyone can create and use a fake user profile on almost any of the social media services. Facebook claims to have 900 million users, but many in the sector, including yours truly, question the basis for this claim. In fact, in disclosures[11] made in its filing to the US Government prior to the recent Facebook initial public offering (IPO), the firm admitted that approximately 4 per cent of all accounts are known to be either fakes or duplicates. The true figure may well be much higher, although Facebook in all probability can't assess this accurately. However, an unknown percentage of fake accounts equates to an unknown percentage of worthless data.

Mobility and Bring Your Own Device (BYOD)

Firms are increasingly allowing staff to use their mobile devices for work, both in the office and when working remotely. According to Gartner,[12] personal device usage will be the hottest topic for IT Managers for the next ten years. This is likely to add a number of risks as users engage in the following activities:

---

10 ENISA Threat Landscape report, Table 1, p. 3 , http://www.enisa.europa.eu/activities/risk-management/evolving-threat-environment/ENISA_Threat_Landscape/at_download/fullReport (accessed March 2013).

11 http://www.sec.gov/Archives/edgar/data/1326801/000119312512325997/d371464d10q.htm#tx371464_14 (accessed 27 November 2012).

12 http://www.gartner.com/it/page.jsp?id=2048617 (accessed 16 June 2012).

Blurred usage boundaries

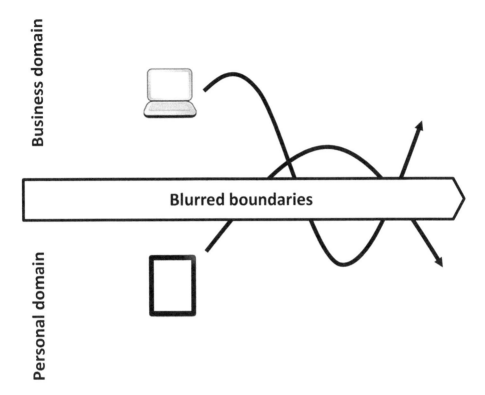

Business domain

Personal domain

Blurred boundaries

Figure P.4   **The blurred boundaries between personal and corporate device use**

- use of a single device for both personal *and* business purposes, with use by children becoming increasingly commonplace;

- use of devices across public, home and corporate networks, with increased potential for man-in-the-middle attacks;

- transportation of devices to and from work and on personal trips;

- storage of sensitive corporate data on personal mobile devices;

- access to corporate Cloud storage via remote personal devices.

These behaviours already occur and laptops have long been a source of what IT support teams sometimes refer to as 'Malware Mondays' as devices come back onto the corporate network after having spent the weekend being used at employee's homes, but as BYOD becomes standard practice, the risks arising can be expected to become even more commonplace. Figure P.4, above, illustrates how the boundaries are becoming increasingly blurred.

4th Generation Mobile Broadband

4th Generation mobile broadband, or '4G', is the latest manifestation of the mobile data revolution and it looks set to accelerate the blurring of boundaries described above. Unlike 3G, which took several years to get off the ground, 4G enters a market already dominated by smart phones or PDAs (Personal Digital Assistants), laptops and tablet devices such as the iPad.

Mobile broadband has two effects that drive risk:

- it increases the pressure for BYOD to be permitted, as workers become increasingly reliant on a plethora of devices that the corporate employer hesitates to purchase for them and that are therefore the user's personal property;

- it increases the scope for remote working and working while in transit, thus exposing ever more corporate data to interception and other forms of cyber attack, or to intrusions, while simultaneously delivering huge increases in productivity and relative competitive advantage.

Network Security

Communications service providers (primarily telephone operators and Internet Service Providers (ISPs)) have long struggled with internal and external fraud challenges. Figure P.5 shows that, as everyone goes online and as the boundaries between different types of network and service also become blurred, the security issues that once remained hidden within homogeneous networks now become shared issues.

Who secures your users' networks?

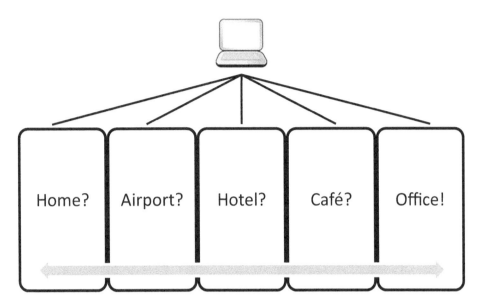

In today's networked world, you provide security for only a fraction of the time your user spends in cyber space.

Figure P.5   Who really secures the networks your users access?

Of particular relevance are:

- the communications interception risks already mentioned, which are compounded when a single call or data session passes across local WiFi, then the Internet and finally across a corporate IT network;

- the risk of remote database access, attacks that bypass authentication (for example, 'man-in-the-browser' attacks) and malware-triggered DoS attacks, each of which we will examine later in the text.

The Cloud

The Cloud introduces yet another set of issues. Firms may unknowingly share platforms with competitors. Auditors and IT managers need to establish where data is stored and how data classification schema should be applied in relation to remote storage or data processing. Third-party employees need to be trained and vetted to standards that comply with those of the business responsible for data protection. Cyber security controls also need to be operating at the same level. Cloud services don't only 'virtualise' computing and data storage; they 'virtualise' cyber security risks and risk management but without removing your accountability for data protection, as depicted in simplified form in Figure P.6 and explored in more detail within later chapters.

The basic Cloud concept

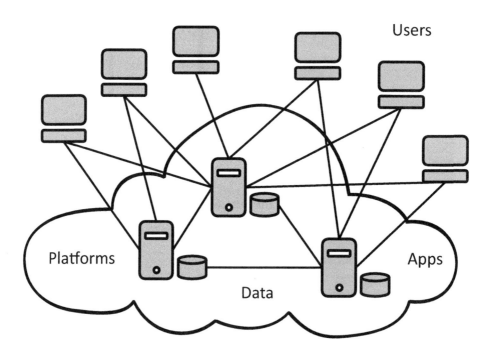

The Cloud revolutionises computing, transforming the network into the machine, but could Cloud services merely be the manifestation of a takeover of the Internet by a few large corporations?

Figure P.6   The concept of the Cloud

Online Freedoms

In November 2012, web information company Alexa listed the world's top 15 websites in descending order as:

1. Google

2. Facebook

3. YouTube (owned by Google)

4. Yahoo

5. Baidu.com (China)

6. Wikipedia

7. Windows Live (Microsoft)

8. Twitter

9. QQ.COM (China)

10. Amazon.com

11. Taobao.com (China)

12. LinkedIn

13. Blogspot.com

14. Google India

15. Yahoo! Japan

The criteria used for this assessment were:

- **Global reach** – percentage measuring the number of Internet users around the world who visit a particular site.

- **Global page views** – percentage measuring the number of page views on a particular site, compared to global web traffic.

- **Sites linking in** – the number of links sending users to a certain websites from other, outside web pages.

Previous studies from 2011 revealed that in January, 73.5 per cent of the world's Internet users either visited Google's main page or that of its video-hosting subsidiary YouTube. Now, none of this is necessarily bad, but when viewed alongside the role of major corporate firms in developing the Cloud, and when the workings of search engine indexing systems are considered, it does paint a picture in which control of what users see and experience, and where their data is held, is now concentrated in a very small number of hands, primarily in the US and China. How this will impact users' choice and their online freedoms in the longer term remains to be seen, but net citizens are generally unaware of just how constrained their search results are today. We explore this in much more depth in the chapter on Digital Intelligence.

Cyber Dependency

As I have already stated, our collective dependency on a single set of technologies for the operation of a very broad set of essential activities constitutes a serious risk in its own right. It is certainly not an exaggeration to say that any catastrophic cyber event that resulted in a long-term (meaning days rather than hours) termination of cyber services at a national or continental level would have the potential to trigger a global economic collapse.

If our dependency on ICT/cyber is the most important risk factor we face today, then the security of our ICT/cyber infrastructure, systems and processes should become our top managerial and political priority.

Cyber Warfare

One of the most likely scenarios for the widespread disruption to, or termination of, cyber services is a cyber warfare attack. Conventional thinkers sometimes describe this in terms of a form of 'cyber bombing raid' on the enemy's systems, akin to a Second World War strategic bombing campaign against centres of production and 'worker's housing'.

As with any attack of this kind, however, whether kinetic or digital, the potential for collateral damage is immense. Amongst the numerous challenges facing cyber warriors are two that deserve special mention:

- **Entanglement** – in our globalised world, separating one part of the cyber infrastructure from another might prove challenging. How can any protagonist be sure that in a wholesale cyber war the collateral damage caused will not do as much harm to the globalised economy of the home nation as to its enemies?

- **Attribution** – given the capacity for sophisticated state-sponsored cyber attackers to mask their true location and the origin of an attack, or even to route their attacks through a third country, those responding to such incidents will face difficult choices when it comes to attributing any attack to a particular source. It has been alleged,[13] for example, that North Korea routes many of its frequent cyber attacks on South Korea and other nations via IP addresses in China, or via virtual addresses that appear to be Chinese, in order to shift the blame for these incidents. My personal belief is that this kind of masking is more the rule than the exception (after all, it hardly requires a huge intellectual leap to adopt such a defence) and that many, even most, allegations regarding the national identities of cyber attackers published in the media are therefore inaccurate.

A number of other challenges exist and it seems possible that a major cyber warfare event will not necessarily be a clean affair, characterised by precision attacks on pin point targets, but that it has the potential to cause widespread harm to friend, foe and innocent bystander alike.

Particular Concerns for Regulated Firms

Regulated firms face a particular set of additional issues as a result of the increasing level of cyber security risk. Operating in a very tightly regulated space, while simultaneously touching networks and technologies that are often inherently vulnerable, Financial Services ('FS') firms need to be especially wary about cyber security as their exposure is three-fold; they will suffer all the harm that a cyber security breach can bring to any business, but they may also be

---

13 http://www.reuters.com/article/2013/03/22/us-cyber-korea-idUSBRE92L07120130322 (accessed 22 March 2013).

exposed to regulatory fines or other measures and their account holders can suffer massive harm at the same time. This distinguishes them from, say, a manufacturing plant or a software developer.

Furthermore, because consumer confidence is such an important consideration in FS, and because the particular customer data held is so sensitive, the scope and impact of potential reputational harm is also multiplied several times over when compared to most other sectors.

Modern communications technologies introduce two more challenges in terms of adherence to regulated firms' mandated responsibilities[14] for spotting and reporting suspicious financial transactions:

- **Big Data**. Big Data refers to data sets that are too large to be efficiently processed by conventional data-processing platforms. As increasing numbers of financial transactions go online, driven in large part by the evolution of the mobile data service mix, the volume of transaction records that will need to be collected and assessed is also rising. We have already experienced this in the conventional telecoms sector, where daily traffic volumes across all services have risen dramatically around the world over a twenty year period. The Big Data challenge is likely to affect FS teams over the coming years, leading to requirements for new and bigger data-processing solutions and new approaches to timely data analytics.

- **Unregulated payments**. The unregulated payments sector (Bit Coin and others) poses an additional challenge, if not for FS firms directly, then for their regulators, although this is more e-Crime than cybercrime.

Online banking and credit card service providers are particularly exposed to online crime. The risks they face include:

- **Card not present fraud**, when payment card details are stolen and then used for online transactions.

- **Man-in-the-browser attacks** in which infected web pages hijack online banking sessions after customers have logged in and

---

14 http://www.worldcompliance.com/en/resources/white-papers/third-eu-directive.aspx (accessed 9 March 2013).

authenticated themselves, in order to change the amounts and destination accounts of payments and transfers.

- **Phishing attacks** that target the personal data of bank's customers.

- **DoS attacks** designed to bring down bank services.

- **Database intrusions,** intended to steal, edit or delete sensitive data, possibly in order to facilitate fraud or market abuse, or merely to damage the firm by hindering its business operations and damaging customer confidence. Economic warfare is another likely motive.

Although Chip and Pin, combined with other emerging authentication technologies, have reduced some types of payment card fraud, the general trend towards more and more remote transactions is likely to keep this class of risks alive.

The evolution of the SIM card inside the mobile handset that sees it slowly becoming a payment card in its own right will further complicate the picture. In fact, it is this convergence (that word again) of financial services and mobile communications, plus Internet services, which will probably act as the main driver for both cybercrime and e-Crime over the coming decade.

A Summary of the Main Cyber Security Responses

As you can see, cyber security is a huge subject but here is a selection of a few key concepts and developments in the area of controls and other responses. All these and many more are described in greater depth in Part II.

AWARENESS AND A RISK MANAGEMENT MINDSET

Everything falls apart if we are not risk aware, but in this interconnected, mobile world, it is not sufficient simply to educate employees; we need to educate their families, including children, many of whom will be sharing the portable device that the employee brings, or will soon bring, into the workplace.

CYBER HYGIENE

'Cyber hygiene' is the next big initiative being discussed in senior cyber circles. The IT Law Wiki defines Cyber hygiene as 'steps that computer users can take to improve their cyber security and better protect themselves online. It may include reorganizing the IT infrastructure, hardware and devices; patching authorized software and removing unauthorized software; continuous monitoring, training and awareness; and formalizing existing informal information security controls'

A related conversation addresses the responsibilities of Internet Service Providers (ISPs). Many feel that they should bear a greater burden of corporate responsibility for cyber security risks and incidents. But Neira Jones, a prominent cyber security thinker, has some concerns about this mindset. 'What should we be making ISPs responsible for?' she asks. 'In the car industry, a manufacturer is responsible for making sure that equipment is safe for the road, judged against some kind of agreed baseline, but the driver and owner are responsible for the maintenance and safe *usage* of the vehicle. A line had to be drawn there, purely on the basis of common sense, and responsibility is shared between corporate suppliers and consumers. Another parallel is seen in the online shopping sector. If a retailer develops their online service in a shoddy way and ignores the published security standards, data protection rules and so forth, then they must be accountable for their failure, but if a consumer misguidedly surrenders their personal information during a Phishing attack, it is the consumer, not the ISP or the online retailer, who is to blame.'

In the short term, adds Jones, there are challenges that make it difficult to apply such a common sense standard. For example, if a small shop wants to go online today and the owner Googles the term 'web hosting', a long list of options will be displayed. One web host might offer a basic 'bronze' service that provides little or no security, as well as a 'gold' package that includes a security certificate. Most small retailers, unaware of either the risks or the security alternatives, will take the cheapest option. The question Jones asks is why any host is allowed to offer online retail services that don't include these basic security protections. 'Cyber hygiene' must address issues along all parts of the spectrum, from the ISP through service providers, device manufacturers and corporate users, down to small and medium enterprises (SMEs) and individual consumers.

ADDRESSING THE SHORTAGE OF SKILLS

The simple fact is that even in today's high-tech world, information security experts are in very short supply. Nothing taught in primary school or secondary school, opines Jones, either prepares or encourages anyone to enter this essential field of study. Once students enter university they are presented with options to go into highly technical fields such as cryptography, but it is almost impossible to deliberately pursue an information security career and many of today's practitioners only found their way into the field by accident. Information security is also misunderstood and has far too technical a facade, making it off-putting for most potential candidates. In reality, as Jones says, most information security activities are about common sense rather than technology.

'We have built a funnel of unaware people,' says Jones. 'We should start teaching security at nursery level. There are already some excellent resources out there for children, parents and teachers, for example the "Digi Duck" story,[15] but these have to be produced by willing individuals or charities at present. Not enough is being done globally to educate tomorrow's users and leaders in a coordinated fashion, (although this is changing for the better, at least in the UK). Behaviour is much more important than technology, especially in the era of social media.'

SOCIAL MEDIA POLICIES

New social media challenges require organisations to develop workable social media guidelines that reflect real world conditions while still helping to keep the firm secure. The matter of good user habits must underpin any solution, yet few users have the faintest idea about the risk inherent in the design of social media services.

We will explore some of the issues and responses later, but Neira Jones again has some valuable points to make on this subject. 'Embrace Social Media; it will happen regardless of the policies you put in place so you need to make sure that you are in a position to guide the process. I am not a believer in adding a new policy for every new technology, but social media best practice guidelines should be incorporated in all existing policies because it's a new

---

15 http://www.kidsmart.org.uk/teachers/ks1/sourcesDuck/index.htm (accessed 9 March 2013). Also see http://www.trmg.biz/the-a-to-z-guides/ (accessed 9 March 2013) for teacher's and parent's guides to child online safety and safe social media use.

xxxviii   CYBER CRIME, SECURITY AND DIGITAL INTELLIGENCE

dimension of communications. We also need to stay in touch with developments elsewhere, for example, there is a new law[16] being enacted in three US states limiting employer's access to employee's social media network data and what happens legislatively in the USA tends to happen here eventually. Our policies and practices need to be sustainable and they must be based on and widely accepted principles.'

AUTHENTICATION

In today's environment, traditional user name and password techniques are no longer effective and many firms have already moved away from them. User names and passwords can be intercepted or retrieved from insecure tables, they are frequently written down, and in some cases they are reused on other sites, such as social media pages, by people who don't want to have to remember more than one logon combination in their lives.

Enhanced approaches normally involve what is known as two or three factor authentication; something you *know* (perhaps a password), plus something you *have* (such as a security dongle) and something you *are* (such as a biometric measurement). Even this approach is likely to evolve and 'five factor' solutions have already been developed that take authentication to even higher levels.

DEALING WITH MALICIOUS APPS

Ross Anderson lists[17] three important steps that need to be taken to address the threat of malicious applications, particularly those targeting mobile payments systems:

- *'Remove bad apps quickly from app stores'* – this implies that App stores must take responsibility for the goods they retail to consumers..

- *'Instrument the network to spot malware quickly'* – so as the close down risky Apps before they spread.

- *'Delay payments to suppliers'* – in order to give consumers a chance to detect and report concerns.

---

16 http://leginfo.legislature.ca.gov/faces/billNavClient.xhtml?bill_id=201120120AB1844 (accessed 4 January 2013).
17 Risk and Privacy Implications of Consumer Payment Innovation, Prof. Ross Anderson, 2012, http://www.cl.cam.ac.uk/~rja14/Papers/anderson-frb-kansas-mar27.pdf (accessed 9 March 2013).

DATA CLASSIFICATION AND ENCRYPTION

As we navigate the ocean of cyber risks in the world of Big Data on BYOD ships of our own choosing, it is important that security does not become an inefficiency that inhibits our operations. What is needed is a good balance between risks and rewards. One tool for achieving this balance is data classification, which involves scoring different types of data based on its sensitivity. Good data classification can support the following:

- **Different authentication levels** for different roles and data types, so that even someone with a sensitive role can quickly logon and view unclassified data, such as an intra-net page, only going through the higher levels of authentication when the type of data to be viewed justifies it.

- **Sound decisions** about Cloud strategies and off-shoring, consistent with compliance rules, risk assessments and other guidelines.

- **Economically sound choices** with respect to data storage, encryption and security in general.

- **Properly conducted risk assessments** that reflect the true value of various data assets and which do not treat all data as equal.

DISASTER PREPAREDNESS

Is your organisation ready to deal with a complete cessation of Internet services over a period of several days or weeks? Can you assure the survival of your business, and those of your customers, in such circumstances? How many readers will answer this question with a confident 'Yes'? If you accept that such a service disruption is a realistic possibility, then Cyber disaster preparedness and business continuity should also be amongst your top priorities going forward.

Conclusion

Risk in the high-technology era, where cyber technology is king, orients itself towards data and towards the systems that hold it, the networks that carry it and the people who use or depend on it. Data is now one of our greatest assets and any risks that affect the security, integrity, completeness or timeliness of delivery of that data are consequently our greatest risks. This is the reality that this book explores.

Acknowledgements

Finalising the acknowledgements for a book is often the most difficult task, particularly when the work is a product of many years of professional engagements, with bits and pieces being learned, forgotten and then relearned. Indeed, I was often struck while doing my research by how little the principles of cyber security have changed over the 20-plus years during which I have been working in the communications sector. Things evolve and complexity tends to increase, but the fundamentals remain largely the same.

I will start by thanking everyone I have worked with over the years who has contributed to my pool of knowledge, or opened my eyes to the need to learn more about a topic, including Mr Camrodeen Khan formerly of Cable & Wireless Jamaica (sadly, now deceased), Alan Kemp who helped me to design our first commercial IT system at C&W UK and Jonathan Day who has worked on numerous data analytics projects with me over many years and in far flung places.

A special word of thanks goes to my researcher, Louise Brozinic. Without her tireless efforts this book would not have been what it is.

Finally, I would like to thank Petra, Cleo and Luca for being so patient while I worked on this project.

List of Abbreviations

AML	Anti-money Laundering
API	Application Programming Interface
APT	Advanced Persistent Threat
ASP	Active Server Pages
BCP	Business Continuity Planning
BI	Business Intelligence
BM	Bandwidth Manager
BYOD	Bring Your Own Device
C&C	Command and Control
CA	Certification Authority
CISO	Chief Information Security Officer
CLC	Closed Loop Confirmation
CNP	Card Not Present
CPU	Central Processing Unit
CSRF	Cross-site Request Forgeries
DDoS	Distributed Denial of Service
DISA	Direct Inwards System Access
DMZ	Demilitarised Zone
DNS	Domain Name Server
DoS	Denial of Service
DPI	Deep Packet Inspection
FIU	Financial Intelligence Units
FTP	File Transfer Protocol
HD	High Definition
HIPS	Host-based Intrusion Prevention System
HTML	Hypertext Markup Language
HTTP	Hypertext Transfer Protocol
IaaS	Infrastructure as a Service
ICT	Information and Communications Technology
IDS	Intrusion Detection System

IM	Instant Message/Messaging
IP	Internet Protocol
IPR	Intellectual Property Rights
IRC	Internet Relay Chat
ISO	Information Security Officer
ISP	Internet Service Provider
LAN	Local Area Network
LOIC	Low Orbit Ion Cannon
MAC	Message Authentication Code
MBR	Master Boot Record
MMS	Multi-Media Service
ODPC	Office of the Data Protection Commissioner
OS	Operating System
OSI	Open Systems Interconnection
OWASP	Open Web Application Security Project
P2P	Peer to Peer
PaaS	Platform as a Service
PABX	Private Automated Branch Exchange
PCI	Payment Card Industry
PCRF	Policy & Charging Rules Function
PHP	Hypertext Preprocessor
R&D	Research and Development
RA	Revenue Assurance
RBS	Royal Bank of Scotland
RDP	Remote Desktop Protocol
RFID	Radio Frequency Identification
SaaS	Software as a Service
SEO	Search Engine Optimisation
SME	Small and Medium Enterprises
SMS	Short Message Service
SNS	Social Network Services
SOCA	Serious Organised Crime Agency
SOE	Sony Online Entertainment
SPI	Software/Platform Infrastructure
SQL	Structured Query Language
SSL	Secure Sockets Layer
SSN	Social Security Number
TCP	Transmission Control Protocol
TLS	Transport Layer Security
TMF	Tele Management Forum

UAV   Unmanned Aerial Vehicle
URL   Uniform/Universal Resource Locator
VOIP   Voice over Internet Protocol
VPN   Virtual Private Network
XXS   Cross-site Scripting

PART I
The Cybercrime Challenge

Introduction

We should all be talking about how we can achieve a holistic globalised approach to cyber security technologies, techniques and awareness. We should be actively debating ways in which cyber security can be adapted to match the threats we face in our interconnected world. We should be thinking deeply on how we can ensure that security controls reflect the asymmetrical character of cyber conflict, the potential for attacks by non-state actors and the fact that an army of one might be able to cause very significant harm to the many. Unfortunately, most people in positions of authority are not talking or thinking about any of these topics in an informed and structured way.

Here are three core issues they might wish to consider:

1. dependency without control equals risk;

2. speed as a barrier to decision making;

3. awareness as a scarce resource.

Dependency Without Control

To compound an already complex security problem, we find ourselves today at a point in history where we have dispensed with most of our printed data backups and manual processes. In the event of a major cyber systems failure, whether as a result of an attack, human error, technical failures or energy security crises, our costly digital backup systems may well prove to be a computerised Maginot Line. After all, what good does it do to process data if you cannot communicate or provide access to the results? Our paper-based systems and records are mostly gone and the great majority of people have little or no training in any alternative manual processes; simply switch off payment card handling and ATM systems for a few hours on a weekday in any major western city and chaos ensues. Disable the cyber technologies and we are a society possessing little more than medieval solutions to twenty-first century problems.

The degree to which we are interdependent when it comes to cyber security is underscored by statistics on Internet usage. In 2013, some 45 per cent of the world's Internet users live in Asia, according to the online analytics firm Smartling. Only 13 per cent live in North America, while 23 per cent are European. The Internet today, while invented in the US, is essentially a Eurasian infrastructure – almost three quarters of the world's users are Eurasian. A corresponding shift can be seen in terms of the languages present on the World Wide Web, with Chinese now overtaking English as the main Web language, while the fastest growing online language is Arabic.

Lesson 1: The West has put all of its physical eggs in one virtual basket and its dependence on cyber technology is now absolute, while its control over that technology, as well as its influence over online debate, is rapidly evaporating.

Speed

After dependency, the next factor to consider is speed:

- the speed of data growth;

- the speed of data processing;

- the speed of human decision making.

SPEED OF DATA GROWTH

As of July 2012 there were an estimated 6.9 billion *indexed* web pages online, according to collated statistics from Internet search providers such as Google and Yahoo. Yet even this vast compilation of human thought accounted for less than 10 per cent of all data actually held online. The estimated total in terms of just publicly accessible data in the so-called Deep Web is another 80 billion pages or more.

Just consider Facebook alone. In the same year, Facebook reported that its data storage was growing by half a Petabyte every two days. Now, one Petabyte equates to 13.3 *years* of high-definition (HD) video, while two Petabytes equals all of the data currently held in US academic research libraries nationwide. The global data mountain, already unimaginably vast, is growing at light speed and there seems to be no stopping it, while the economic and social value of much of the data stored is highly dubious.

SPEED OF DATA PROCESSING

A jumbo jet only travels 50 times faster than a horse and buggy but the fastest modern supercomputer computer processes data millions of times faster than its own forebears. In fact, quadrillions of times faster in at least one case, but if you are reading this book a few years from now then even the fastest of these speeds will probably seem slow to you:

- the 1975 Altair 8800 PC was capable of two million processes per second;

- the 2012 Apple iPad handles upwards of one billion processes per second;

- with 1.5 million processing cores, Livermore's Sequoia supercomputer performs 16.3 quadrillion calculations per second, making it the fastest computing device built to-date.

SPEED OF HUMAN DECISION MAKING

Meanwhile, the human brain, having taken millions of years to evolve to its current state, has changed little (if at all in my case) since the era of wooden hunting sticks. Our brains actually process about 400 billion Bits of information per second, but we are only aware of 2,000 Bits, with most of the processing being related to various metabolic functions. But even 2,000 processes sounds like a lot. Actual conscious decision making involves even smaller amounts of processing per second, perhaps as low as 60 Bits per second in certain circumstances.

It is little wonder that we collectively struggle to comprehend, much less cope with, the speed of modern data processing and computing applications. In fact, computer system output must be slowed to a crawl, or frozen temporarily on a screen, in order for us to process and absorb it. On the other hand, no computer yet built can come close to us in terms of our ability to make intelligent extrapolations and choices most of the time, based on the limited amounts of data we can hold in active memory.

When viewed in the context of cyber security decision making, this mismatch between computing speeds and human capabilities takes on a special significance. Cyber attacks may be conducted in fractions of a second. While automated prevention and detection tools can operate at computer speeds, investigative, incident response and decision processes generally run at human speed, and slow human speed at that, because rational decisions are required that factor in many parameters not easily captured in a data table. The discrepancy is compounded by the fact that in the corporate world our business processes and tools may focus more on the breach of security than they do on the resulting exploitation of that breach, leading to many instances when the attacker is allowed to remain active within the system while the security responses take place, the Advanced Persistent Threat (APT), of which we will hear more later, being one such example.

Lesson 2: In the cyber era, we may lack the capacity to react to crises quickly enough to influence their immediate outcomes and disaster recovery plus business continuity planning therefore take on added significance.

Awareness

The issue of speed provides part of an explanation for why so many leading blue chip firms handle post-cyber security incident responses and communications so badly, but it is further compounded by a profound lack of awareness; the people in charge don't fully comprehend the risks, while very few users understand either the technology they are using or the threats they face.

There is a serious question to be asked about the very capacity of parts of the global user base to take on board even the most basic cyber security lessons. Let's look at a few more statistics, this time showing the percentage of people in the USA, with varying levels of education, who are active online:

- less than high school – 24 per cent;

- high school graduates – 54 per cent;

- some college courses – 78 per cent;

- college graduate – 85 per cent.

Now, 24 per cent is not a small number but that is the percentage of those with less than a high school level of education who are regularly active online in the USA. Although the US has a relatively high standard of education, when compared to large parts of the planet, over 12 per cent of the country's population has not graduated from high school. This amounts to more than 30 million people, of whom 7.5 million are online. A rough extrapolation suggests that at least 175 million Internet users worldwide lack a high school education. This is not to say that they are by any means stupid, but it does speak to their inclination and capacity to be taught about security. And let's not forget that we now have that multi-lingual, multi-cultural InterWeb.

In simple terms, just as things are getting more complex, the Web is getting faster and the decisions are getting tougher, yet our dependence on users is getting greater, while the average user is getting harder to reach and harder to teach. Since these users share the Internet with the rest of us, their awareness is a very big part of any truly effective solution that doesn't involve creating a separate, secure Internet 2.0 for the educated and informed, with restrictions on access, leaving an insecure old Internet for the rest of humankind.

Lesson 3: A lack of awareness at all levels undermines our collective ability to manage cyber risks.

This relationship between increasing levels of risk and falling levels of awareness (or of the capacity to be made aware) can be described by three simple laws:

1.   The number of device owners is inversely proportional to the cost of device ownership; as devices and Internet access get cheaper, more people will buy them.

2.   The overall level of cyber security risk is a function of the number of devices in use and the number of discrete vulnerabilities that exist; more devices equals more risks of infection.

3.   The mean level of awareness and security competence of the user base declines as the user population increases; as less well educated users come online the overall capacity of the user base to be made aware falls.

And just as the mean educational level of the user base starts to decline, in large part as a result of social media take-up, the complexity of the cyber security ecosystem is rapidly increasing. John Naughton opines that this increasing complexity is a function of the density of interconnections and the speed of change and development, both of which are overwhelming even for the informed observer. To expect the growing base of new users to grasp cyber security concepts is to expect a miracle. Consequently, we must move forward assuming that a large and growing segment of the user base will never be made security aware and we must tailor the online environment accordingly.

1

Threats to Key Sectors

Introduction

There are several factors determining the future shape of the cyber security landscape:

- the rise of the machine readable Web, also known as 'Web 3.0';

- increasingly vast data storage;

- computer processing at light speed;

- increasingly advanced and persistent threats;

- slow human decision-making speeds and a general lack of awareness;

- a growing chasm between cyber security decision needs and cyber security decision capabilities.

The only obvious solution to this conundrum is the complete automation of cyber security decision making, but the technology to support that is far from ready.

In the meantime, we need to learn to live with the challenge and find ways to better protect our information assets from attack, theft, exposure, loss or damage. Cyber security and cyber risks are ubiquitous, which is to say that they are everywhere and of importance to any person or organisation using one or more Internet-enabled devices. The importance of security and the potential impact of the risks described in later chapters are primarily determined by the level of dependency that the person or group has on the technology.

Key Sectors

The one word we need to keep in our thoughts is 'resilience'. How resilient are we as a sector, community or nation in the event of a major cyber security event? Some sectors are more sensitive than others and there are also strong interdependencies between key sectors (listed below) which suggests the potential for what is called a 'cascading failure':

- financial services

- energy

- transportation

- supply chain

- defence and security

- government

- communications.

Loss or degradation of service in any one of the above areas is likely to have deleterious effects on the others. This makes these sectors particularly attractive to an attacker as well as making them the most sensitive in terms of accidental failures or natural disasters. Essentially, if you work in any of the areas listed, you should be prepared for the possibility of state-grade cyber attacks and intrusions and you should be putting corresponding state-grade countermeasures in place.

Cyber Security Risks for Financial Firms

As outlined in the introduction, during the late summer of 2012, a number of leading US banks experienced a serious and apparently coordinated series of DoS attacks that lasted for a period of several weeks and in fact, some of the attacks commenced earlier in the year. Senior political figures in the USA, including Senator Joseph Lieberman, chairman of the Senate Homeland Security Committee, reportedly asserted that these attacks originated in Iran, although no evidence to support this statement was put forward in the public domain.

Coincidentally, during the same period the computer systems of the UK's Royal Bank of Scotland (RBS), one of the country's largest financial firms, went down due to what was reported to be an internal software failure following an upgrade. Whatever the facts behind these events, it is now clear that western banking was in crisis mode through much of the year due to various types of cyber vulnerability.

DoS attacks are one thing, but intrusions and data theft are of even more importance. To paraphrase Dr Jerry Hart, a leading risk practitioner and thinker, the distinctions between terrorism, organised crime, fraudsters and data thieves are purely academic when it comes to evaluating the risks of intrusion into financial systems because confidential data is itself more valuable today than ever before. Our online world and the existence of a multitude of remote transaction opportunities make it so. Social media firms have already demonstrated the value of the information asset, with market valuations in the tens of billions of dollars based purely on the user data they hold and the marketing opportunities it supports. So it is with financial services; firms' customer account and transaction data might be the most valuable asset they hold, more valuable even than the cash in their vaults or the customer balances on their electronic systems.

Key cyber security risks, all of which are covered in detail later, include:

- DoS attacks;

- account takeover, for example via man-in-the-browser attacks;

- deletion and corruption of files;

- theft of data and confidential or personal data exposure;

- cyber blackmail;

- reputational harm.

Online Banking and eCommerce Risks

Electronic commerce, (also known as 'eCommerce' or 'online commerce') involves the buying and selling of products or services over communications networks such as the Internet, other computer networks and mobile telecommunications networks. The amount of trade conducted electronically worldwide has grown extraordinarily with widespread Internet usage. Statistics are limited, but in 2009 UK consumers spent an estimated $4bn online, while US consumers spent $30bn.

Cybercrime and e-Crime are constant and growing challenges for eCommerce firms and for consumers. Key eCommerce risks include:

PAYMENT FRAUD

Payment fraud, most frequently involving credit card fraud, is a term often used to describe theft and fraud committed using a credit card or any similar payment mechanism as a fraudulent source of funds in an online transaction. The purpose of the fraudster is to obtain goods or services without paying, or to obtain unauthorised funds from an account. Online identity theft or hacking into account databases is very often a tool used to facilitate this class of crime.

STAFF FRAUD

Staff fraud is one aspect of internal theft that involves the use of deception to steal funds, goods or services, as opposed to simple physical theft of goods or cash. In an eCommerce context, staff fraud can take several forms, including embezzlement and data theft (for example, misuse of online customer details, payment details or the resale of this data to competitors or criminals).

VENDOR OR SERVICE PROVIDER FRAUD

Vendor eCommerce fraud generally occurs when an online seller or service provider defrauds consumers or suppliers. Consumers may be defrauded when payments are taken but no goods and services are delivered, faulty goods are knowingly sold, or counterfeit and stolen goods (including digital media) are delivered. Vendor eCommerce fraud often involves breaches of artist's digital rights in download-able media.

CORPORATE DATA THEFT

Corporate data theft involves the stealing of data, typically from corporate databases or other data storage systems (for example, laptop computers) in order to misuse or resell the stolen data to a third party. The most common eCommerce scenarios involve resale of customer, pricing or product data to competitors (a form of corporate espionage) but fraudsters, other criminals and foreign government agencies are also regularly involved in these cases as recipients of the stolen data.

MONEY LAUNDERING

eCommerce and mobile payments are particularly vulnerable to use as mechanisms for money laundering due to the challenge of validating online identities in many prepaid markets, the speed of transaction processing and the cross-border nature of many payments. Money laundering refers to any action deliberately taken to conceal the proceeds of crime. Money laundering cases often involve a large number of transactions between businesses and via banking houses.

SPAM

Spam refers to unsolicited electronic communications and it is closely tied to eCommerce with the majority of Spam messages promoting products that are only available for purchase online. This is not to say that most eCommerce firms are engaged in Spam. In fact, the number of serious Spammers is believed to be very small with a handful of people accounting for most of the traffic.

All eCommerce firms need to assess and manage these risks effectively, as well as ensuring that effective staff training is regularly carried out.

Risks Facing the Energy Sector

Deny any modern economy access to energy supplies and not only the Internet, but virtually every activity and sector you care to name will come to a halt within hours. So, while cyber-comms security (communications security plus cyber security) is important across the board, it is of strategic importance in energy security terms.

There are several very real high-tech communications and cyber risks facing the oil, gas, nuclear and extraction industries:

- DoS attacks on management systems;

- deletion and corruption of critical files;

- theft of data and confidential data exposure;

- cyber blackmail and other financial costs;

- reputational harm.

An important point to consider is not the immediate effects of the above on any one organisation, but the effects of fear in the market, fear that extraction, processing and transportation might be disrupted by any of these attacks. In any market, fear leads to speculation and prices can rise rapidly and dramatically. Nowhere is this more true than in the energy market and few markets have greater potential to cause serious harm to the global economy.

There have been a number of recent high-profile cyber security breaches affecting the sector and these offer salutary lessons on the effects of a major security breach. Grouped together as the 'Dropper, Reporter and Wiper' infections (see Figure 1.1), the Stuxnet, Flame and Shamoon attacks represent a set of industrial grade malware that might have the capacity to bring whole production and processing lines to their knees.

Cyber attacks are the ultimate expression of a-symmetrical warfare. Just as social media has levelled the political playing field, potentially giving any person on the planet the same reach as the most senior political figure, so have modern technologies levelled the crime and military playing field. In marketing terms we talk now about a 'customer segment of one', referring to the ability of firms to use online data to produce very granular delineations between potential customers. Likewise, in cyber security and cyber warfare terms we need to come to grips with the reality of a 'cyber army of one', or the possibility that the cyber technologies could take personal empowerment and democratisation to their ultimate endpoint.

Transportation and Supply Chain

On the 27 October 2012 the UK's *Manchester Evening News* ran the following item:

> *Counter terrorism police are investigating the theft of powerful land mines from a goods train. Ten packages owned by the Ministry of Defence were snatched from the train when it stopped in Warrington*

Drop, Report and Wipe

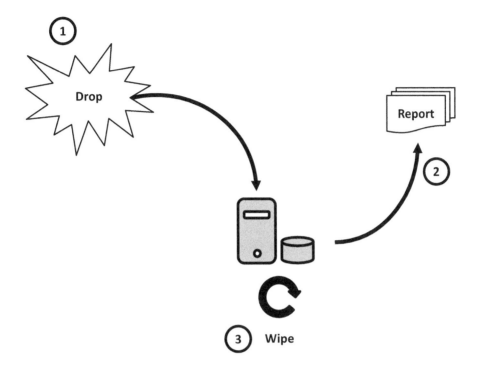

1. The malware is dropped onto the target machine.
2. The malware executes its payload and the extracted data is sent to the attacker.
3. The now wipes itself off the machine, hiding the evidence.

Figure 1.1   **The Dropper, Reporter, Wiper model**

*on its way from Cumbria to Oxfordshire. The freight train had stopped
to observe a red light.*

*Seven of the packages were later found abandoned near the railway
line close to Folley Lane in Warrington. The remaining three, which
contain four plastic cases each, are still missing.*

*It is understood each 4ft-long case is an anti-tank mine used by the
Army in Afghanistan. Police have stressed the missing munitions are
stable 'in their normal condition'. It is believed other components are
required to blow up the explosives. Detectives are treating the theft as
'opportunistic' rather than the work of terrorists.*

How might the above scenario have played out if terrorists had been able to hack into the railway's computer systems and gather information about the train's cargo? What if they were also able to trigger the red light at just the right moment? While this is not what happened in this case, given what we know about the power of tools like Stuxnet and Flame, such a scenario hardly seems farfetched and tracking high-value cargoes and then arranging for them to be interdicted for the purpose of theft or destruction is hardly a novel concept. Since the era of the Phoenician traders, through the piracy of the eighteenth and nineteenth centuries, the partisan attacks on railroads of the Second World War, the U-boat war and even in the modern day piracy and kidnappings off East Africa, we see exactly this pattern of events played out. Cyber risks simply amplify the threat, offering a sophisticated attacker a means to develop better intelligence, or allowing a clever backer to focus his minions on particular targets.

The main cyber security risks facing maritime, air and land transportation operators therefore fall into the following classes:

- account takeover;

- system intrusions and man-in-the-middle attacks;

- theft of data, for example cargo manifests and routing plans;

- alterations to programs or files;

- reputational harm.

In another possibly cyber-related incident in December 2011, an American unmanned aerial vehicle, or 'drone', was seized by the Iranian military in north-eastern Iran. The Iranians claimed that the unmanned aerial vehicle was brought down by its cyber warfare unit which they say broke into the drone's control systems remotely, then commandeered the aircraft and landed it. Some western news sources claimed that the unmanned aerial vehicle been shot down, but the US Government said that it had malfunctioned and crashed. The aircraft was later displayed in Iran TV with no obvious signs of physical damage to its exterior, although it is certainly not beyond Iran's capabilities to effect repairs to the skin of a damaged unmanned aerial vehicle.

Iran has a well-educated population and, reportedly, a very advanced cyber warfare capability, so we should not imagine that drones are going to be commandeered in this fashion by all and sundry, or on a regular basis and, no doubt, the US will have conducted a major review of its drone fleet's communications security controls. However, the rapid move towards remotely controlled and robotic systems, many of which are 'weaponised', does mean that there are ever increasing amounts of hardware out there that could conceptually be hijacked and used. This is certainly not something about which we can afford to be complacent or dismissive.

Finally, we should not forget the dependency factor. Both energy and food security have a heavy dependence on the transport sector, with food security being almost utterly dependent. A system failure or an attack affecting transportation systems has the potential to trigger cascading failures or challenges in the food and energy sectors. Such failures can trigger their own cascades and it this type of dependency-cascade model that should most exercise cyber security planners.

Defence and Security

Not surprisingly, the focus of the nation state in cyber security terms tends to be on attack from abroad by hostile states or their proxies. As a consequence, even those in the private sector often find it easiest to talk about all classes and categories of cyber attack as acts of war, even though the reality may be far more nuanced. Whatever that reality is, in numerous discussions and papers published over recent years on the subject of cyber conflict, 'globalisation' is a key word that seems often to be ignored. Disentangling the globalised economy from the global Internet is probably impossible and it is this single factor that makes a major cyber conflict involving the world's leading powers potentially catastrophic.

One of the greatest risks we run as the cyber warfare arms race gathers pace, is that we fall into the same trap as that met by Europe's major powers at the advent of war in 1914; plans in place, military capabilities refined and ready, enemies identified before the fact, mobilisation and forward movement in progress, all before attribution had been effectively carried out. Preparedness for war and talk of war can often guarantee that war occurs. Even a change as simple as a deliberate rebranding of 'cyber warfare' to 'cyber defence' can make the difference.

Government and Communications

The Internet is a digital spider's web with national governments as the flies trapped in its sticky embrace, not quite understanding their predicament, but powerless to escape their bonds. The Internet was invented by the public sector, but it has been expanded and exploited primarily by the private. The divergence of national political goals and those of globalised corporate entities is nowhere evidenced more clearly than in the structure of the Internet and the uses to which it is being put.

Furthermore, the increasing influence of individual Net Citizens (or 'Netizens') on capacity requirements, infrastructure investments and roll out, as well as on the evolution of Internet services, is shifting cyber power away even from corporate players towards user-consumers at a rapid rate. This is best seen in the rise of social media, infotainment and eCommerce. This all adds up to dependency without control and this is a key marker for our biggest risks.

Our globalised economic system is not the first of its kind, although it is certainly the largest in absolute terms. Nevertheless, the Romans, Chinese, Persians and several other civilisations had equivalent 'globalised' economic models, limited only by the boundaries of their respective expansions. Likewise, a middle class citizen of the British Empire in the late 1800s found it unremarkable to sit down to a breakfast of Indian tea, sweetened by West Indian sugar alongside toast produced from American wheat, while reviewing South African gold prices in the daily papers.

What is truly unique about our modern version of globalisation is its total reliance on a shared and often insecure communications technology; a single point of failure the likes of which we have never previously seen. Globalisation in the twenty-first century is about far more than trade, international finance, free markets and consumerism – it is about a vast, ubiquitous transnational digital network, off-shored customer data, the massive electronic movement of capital and the outsourcing of cyber infrastructures and services in the Cloud. It is this complexity and virtualisation that makes the task of cyber security practitioners particularly daunting.

Conclusion

Whatever the sector, and whatever the true financial cost of cyber crime may be, it is often useful to develop simple harm matrices to express the potential effects and to support debate and decision making.

Table 1.1   A simple cyber crime Harm Matrix

Type of harm	People	Processes	Technology
Financial loss	Job security	Loss of efficiency	Cost of replacement
Denial of service	Ability to work	Loss of services	Loss of access
Customer experience	Customer relations	Customer care cost	Site or call traffic
Data breach	Fraud losses	Audit and investigations	Suspension of use
Employee trust	Confidence and morale	Productivity	System access
Brand and reputation	Confidence and morale	Marketing costs	Trust in systems

The example in Table 1.1, above, is only a model and is not exhaustive, but you can adapt it to match your own organisation, environment and circumstances. As we will see in Chapter 2, there are a many additional factors influencing risk and its effects in cyber space, but if you are familiar with the idea of risk and want to jump straight into cyber security examples, you can choose to skip straight to Chapter 3.

2

Cyber Security Fundamentals

Before we delve further into the details of how cyber attacks occur, let's review some fundamental concepts.

Cyber Security Risks

The term cyber security risk refers to the relationship between the frequency and impact of an attack, normally measured during a 'risk assessment' which is in part a quantification exercise. The effect of controls already in place can also be factored in to this assessment. Quantification is the key point to consider when using the term 'risk'. If it's not quantified, it's not a risk, though it might still be a threat or an actual attack.

So, a 'risk' must not be confused with a 'threat'. I face a *threat* of the Moon crashing into the Earth, but the *risk* of this happening is so low that there is no point preparing for it. Perhaps you disagree? You are entitled to do so if your own risk assessment is different!

Another important characteristic of risk is that it fluctuates constantly. Risk is subject to the effects of chaos theory, or the 'Butterfly Effect', in that small changes in the environment can have big effects on risk scores. Therefore, risk assessments need to be repeated regularly, especially for key assets. Even the definition of what your key assets are needs regular review.

MANIFEST CYBER SECURITY RISKS

Manifest risks are those risks that are assessed on the basis of an attack/threat having a proven frequency and impact in the past (normally the relatively recent past). If your business has been hit by computer hackers recently, that is a manifest risk; its probable frequency and impact are known. If you assess that you *could* be hacked weekly but that this hasn't yet occurred, then this is a risk but not a manifest risk. The focus when we think about manifest risk is on an actual series of events; manifest risks are defined statistically and are not merely conceptual in nature.

INHERENT CYBER SECURITY RISKS

Inherent risks are those risks that have not yet manifested themselves but which have obvious potential due to the existence of one or more key assets. If you walk out late at night wearing an £10,000 Rolex, for example, you face an inherent risk of robbery even if no robberies have ever occurred in that town or city.

Inherent risks can be defined by common sense, even where statistics are not available.

CONTRIBUTORY CYBER SECURITY RISKS

Contributory risks are those risks that arise when control processes or systems fail or people are incompetent, thus creating a new vulnerability. For example, yesterday your network was protected by an Intrusion Detection System, but last night that system went offline and could not be re-started. This constitutes a new vulnerability that increases your risk profile, even though no new threats have been identified and the number or type of attacks has not altered.

INFORMATION SECURITY RISKS

Information security risk refers to threats that impact information assets. We can think of them in terms of causes, events and effects. Typical causes of information security risks include natural, deliberate or accidental occurrences while harmful events may include malware attacks, hacking attacks and 'flooding' attacks, and while typical effects might encompass data breaches, loss of service and brand damage.

A framework for thinking about cyber security risk is provided in Figure 2.1, below, based on the work of Dr Peter Speight at Securitas which I have adapted used with his kind permission.

Cyber risk management framework

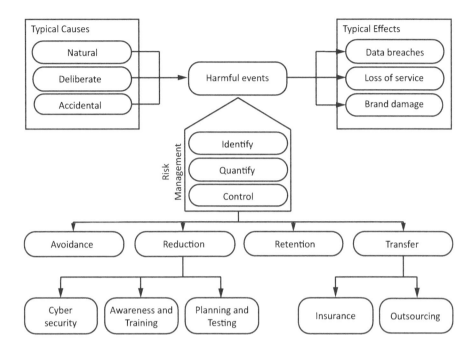

Figure 2.1   What is cyber security risk?

Source: Based on the work of Dr Peter Speight

Access vs. Exploitation

In cyber or information security terms, there are generally two stages to an attack:[1]

- The Access Stage, where attackers gain access to systems or data.

- The Exploitation Stage, where the attackers use their access to steal data for resale or reuse, edit or delete data, harm systems, damage brands or carry out any other harmful or unauthorised act.

---

1   Mark Johnson, 2012. *Demystifying Communications Risk*. Farnham: Gower Publishing.

Information Assets

This is a general phrase that has its roots in a time when information security focused on securing data. Today, with the rise of the Internet, security must focus on a much broader set of assets, including data, resources, quality of service and brand or reputation. However, you will still find the term 'information asset' widely used.

Threats

A 'threat' is something that threatens an asset, organisation, place, idea or attribute (such as a brand) or people. A threat has the potential to act upon the affected thing, but it may not do so. Robbery is a threat. Tsunamis are threats, as are earthquakes. Fire is a threat and so is fraud, but I am not experiencing them as I write – let me just check my bank balance!

THREAT ACTORS

Threat actors are things (almost always people) who cause a threat to act upon a thing. A robber is a threat actor and so is an arsonist. Threat actors are also called 'attackers'.

ATTACK

An attack occurs when a threat actor targets an asset. An attack may be successful, partially successful or unsuccessful. It may also be detected or go undetected.

Vulnerabilities

Vulnerabilities are those factors, including missing controls, poor processes, things or people that provide an avenue or opportunity for a threat and/or threat actor to have an effect upon an asset. Vulnerabilities may be exploited by an attacker. Gaps in controls are examples of vulnerabilities.

Controls

A control is a process, measurement or device (such as a burglar alarm or a fraud detection software tool) that serves to prevent, detect and/or reduce the impact or lifespan of an attack.

Security

Information or cyber security refers to all the processes, controls tools, people, software and ideas engaged in reducing risk in relation to defined information or cyber assets and equipment. This may extend from basic PC security through to preventing reputational harm via Twitter.

How Risk Evolves

To fully understand risk, we first need to understand some simple principles by which risk evolves in any sector. There are obviously many factors that have a bearing on risk, such as the environment, technology, dependency on certain assets or processes, people's awareness, skills and motivations, plus many more. Risk assessments are consequently never anything more than best estimates, often produced with limited information, and they need to be repeated regularly so as to take account of changes occurring with people, processes, technology or the environment.

THE RISK CASCADE

The concept of a risk cascade is based on simple cause and effect ideas. Simply put, each new technological advance (WiFi, for example) triggers new cyber security threats or is exposed to old ones via new vulnerabilities. This in turn cascades down to impact the tools, techniques, teams and training needed to respond. This process is constant and new triggers are constantly resulting in new cascades of risk.

THE RISK 'BALLOON'

Another useful concept is that of a 'balloon' of risk. Imagine that the air inside the balloon represents all the forces acting *for* risk; motives, vulnerabilities, failing controls, and so on. Meanwhile, the skin of the balloon, keeping the air in a limited space, represents all the *controls* and other factors mitigating risk.

Normally, the balloon is in equilibrium and of a certain size. However, if you increase the amount of air (risk factors) without a corresponding increase in the strength or thickness of the skin of the balloon, the total volume of the balloon (amount of risk) will increase.

A second characteristic of this risk balloon is that if you add external pressure in order to reduce risk, without addressing the drivers for risk (the air inside) the balloon probably won't get any smaller. Instead, it will simply expand into any remaining process gaps or into new technologies and services – it will stick out between your fingers.

Most of the time, successful risk management is about keeping the balloon in equilibrium where the volume of risk is known and tolerated by the business. The only way to effectively eliminate all risk is to address the underlying causes, and this generally lies beyond the capabilities or reach of risk and security managers.

THE 'PATH OF LEAST RESISTANCE' THEORY

The action of squeezing the risk balloon may reduce risks, or it may force threats and risks to evolve. My own theory is that threats, and therefore risks, will tend to evolve along the path of least resistance flowing towards assets, in terms of:

- **People** – people 'pull' threats towards them, for example when lack of staff awareness or collusion creates opportunities for criminals to launch attacks that they would otherwise not attempt.

- **Processes** – gaps in processes or poor process design do not merely contribute to risk, they pull risks towards them. In other words, there are likely to be a greater number of discrete risks concentrated around a weak process than there are elsewhere in a system. It is not merely the degree of risk that is affected, but also the *number* of different risks and incidents.

- **Technology** – likewise, flaws in technology or potential exploits act to pull risks towards them. A good example is the old analogue mobile phone system that was hit by cloning, interception, roaming and subscription fraud risks all at once because the technology was fundamentally insecure.

You can use this simple framework to think about and then list emerging or potential risks in your own sector. The Financial Services Authority's 2011 Financial Crime Guide[2] also provides a useful list of good and poor practice examples which illustrate my point regarding the path of least resistance.

By now you will appreciate that cyber security risks are constantly evolving and that many of the latest developments are probably still unknown. Any attempt to classify and categorise these risks is basically an exercise in herding cats, but here is a table that attempts to do just that.

Table 2.1   Classification and categorisation of common cyber security risks

Cyber Security Risk Class	Common Categories
Network and web-facing App Attacks	WiFi penetrations
	Man-in-the-middle attacks
	Sniffing
	Code injection
	Cross-site scripting
Malware Attacks	Spyware
	Adware
	Crime ware
	Attack ware
Social Engineering Attacks	Social media
	Face-to-face
	Phishing
	Pharming
Hacking Attacks	Password cracking
	Cloud side channel attacks
	Access control breaches
	Domain Name Server (DNS) redirects
Denial of Service	DoS flooding
	DDoS flooding
	Wipers and overwrites
	Hostage taking

2   http://www.fsa.gov.uk/pubs/cp/cp11_12.pdf (accessed 21 August 2012).

Cyber Security Risk Class	Common Categories
Advanced Persistent Threats	Botnets
	Malnets
	Cloud nets
	Rootkits
	Industrial Worms

We will examine each of these in turn, but for now it is sufficient that you recognise the range of attack methods commonly employed while also noting the fact that there are different types of attacker, each of which can and will employ several of the methods listed. This all adds up to a complex picture that needs to be broken down into its component parts.

3

Cyber Attack Fundamentals

Introduction

As cyber technology evolves, the number of tools available for launching cyber attacks also increases. Countermeasures have had to become increasingly sophisticated. This, in turn, means that the attackers have upped their game, making for a complex, evolving situation and a long list of possible attack techniques, a number of which are often used in tandem.

Only last week, as I was completing the edits for this chapter, some parts of the world experienced a marked slowdown in the speed of Internet services. This was blamed on a series of flooding attacks, a concept I will explain later, directed at the servers of a Dutch online security firm apparently in revenge for the fact that that firm had fingered another company as a security risk. However, this was an attack with a difference. Instead of targeting the company's servers directly, the attackers managed to fool a number of Internet domain name servers in such a way that they sent a flood of lookup responses to the target when in fact no actual domain name requests had been made. This provided an excellent example of an increasingly sophisticated tandem attack technique.

Having said that, many of the older techniques are still in use and a few of these techniques are almost as old as the Internet. Other 'new' techniques are merely variants of older ones and it is important that we understand both the old and the new. This chapter provides descriptions and examples of the most common online attack tools and techniques.

A serial technology entrepreneur, Richard Harris has a track record as a C-level executive, building and transforming early-stage technology companies. He has been involved in various high-profile enterprises, operating at

Board level, and he is now the CEO of Ensygnia Limited, a UK business that focuses on authentication technologies:

> *Perhaps the most important characteristic of the modern world is that we are now more interconnected than we have ever been. This has a number of implications, one being that cyber crime exploits can be replicated en masse in ways that cannot be easily duplicated in the physical world. We see frequent examples of this, for example when cyber thieves steal millions of username and password combinations in a single attack using techniques that have been recorded and posted on sites like YouTube. Of course it's not just criminals that are a threat, Hacktivists and state-sponsored Cyber-warfare represents a real and present danger.*
>
> *In the corporate world, this increased threat level can be managed to an extent, but consumers are likely to use much less secure passwords and to reuse them across many systems and processes, from PC and tablet logins to online banking. Some forms of service provider are exacerbating the problem as they seek to make logging in as painless as possible. The default username based on a new user's email address in most social media services serves as another good example.*
>
> *Or consider your credit card which has your full name, account numbers and bank sort code embossed on the front, with your signature on the back. How much of this personal data really needs to be visible on the card, given today's technologies which offer the opportunity to conceal all of this information digitally on a chip? The whole nature of identity is thrown into question by the approaches to identity verification being pursued by many large organisations.*
>
> *In my view, identity and authentication are today's key security issues, as it is easier to steal an identity than to create one. Therefore, the focus of work on responses to security and fraud challenges should be on protecting personal data more effectively, as a preventative measure, and on developing much more sophisticated mechanisms for authenticating identity, using data that cannot be easily fabricated. Examples include the use of an individual's digital history, including transactional and behavioural data, that offers a better basis for assessing identity risk and authenticity than a PIN or password ever will.*
>
> *Events have patterns and they leave traces across a range of systems. The effort involved in creating a realistic pattern of events across the range of systems required would probably exceed the rewards for the crime and be exceptionally difficult to do undetected. Behaviour*

is also hard to fake as a fraudster needs to follow your purchasing habits and geo-location. If a system detects unexpected behaviour then an additional security question or factor is used (like Verified by Visa); inconvenient to you perhaps but a block to the criminal.

Dependency is another critical risk factor and the potential for cascading service failures, whether resulting from accident or deliberate attack, should be a very real concern for all. It is questionable whether we, as a society, have the wherewithal to manage a widespread and prolonged cyber technology failure, in terms of managing key infrastructures and services, transporting food or maintain communications. Contingency planning and disaster recovery strategies need to include not only isolated and independent technological systems but also manual process and procedures for use in the event of a total technological failure. Technology should be an enabler for better living; we should not allow ourselves to become totally dependent on it.

We are where we are, so how are businesses responding, or what should they be doing? We are evolving naturally to a higher level of security, and despite recent high-profile cyber technology failures (such as the RBS computer system problems or the O2 mobile network failure in the UK) we don't seem to have wildfire problems, so existing controls are probably doing a reasonable job overall. However, this is not to say that our risk exposure is low. On the contrary, those cases that have occurred demonstrate just how serious the risks are. Criminals, in particular, respond to new controls with technological answers of their own and we have to plan accordingly.

My top list of priorities is as follows, although we are really talking about common sense and good practice here, with only a few really new ideas added to the mix:

- *better vetting of employees – criminals will attack the weakest link and that includes your staff;*
- *avoidance – not allowing employees access to data they don't need. For example, call centres – the agents need to know that a transaction is authorised or declined, they need to be able to tell the customer why and what to do if it is declined. They do not need your card data, date of birth and so on, and if they know it they can be and are targeted by criminal gangs;*
- *anti-virus, including on the mobile device;*
- *Firewalls;*
- *deep packet inspection solutions;*

- *improved business processes;*
- *regular penetration testing including ethical hacking (White-hat);*
- *better authentication – replace username and password and current two-factor authentication with more sophisticated methods;*
- *awareness;*
- *secure devices – current security at the end-point is weak. The Virtual Private Network (VPN) protects the comms channel but very little is done to make the device safe to use.*

The BYOD movement mandates all of the above, with better user awareness and enhanced authentication that doesn't slow business processes or reduce efficiency emerging as essential considerations.

In the area of authentication, we now need to start talking about the choice between single sign on vs. the data classification model. There is a need to assign assets and access rights to risk profiles in tiered hierarchical models, so that a user has limitations imposed in terms of the kind of data that simple single sign-on username and password techniques will give him access to. More sensitive systems or data should require enhanced sign-on levels.

Such a hierarchy ensures that most users are not negatively affected by security controls most of the time, while key users accessing key systems, though having to go through a more rigorous authentication process, are made to understand why that is necessary. Indeed, this more rigorous process can become a badge of merit, in the sense that 'if you don't need biometrics to access the system, then you ain't saying nothing!'

So what does the future of authentication look like? We already have encrypted data channels using VPN and secure sockets (https), the natural evolution is to extend that security to the device using techniques such as browser hardening to allow any device to become a secure thin or even thick client, dynamically on-the-fly. Some technologies such as this also enforce communication between known end-points eliminating threats from spoofing, man-in-the-middle and man-in-the-browser, augmenting VPNs and certainly reducing if not removing the requirement to use them in many cases. When combined with out-of-band authentication and Closed Loop Confirmation via mobile devices, this is not only secure and hard to hack but it is a pleasure to use and it also delivers significant benefits to merchants and *e-tailers as well. Such approaches have the added benefit of removing the need for a password file, thus eliminating the risk of code injection of cross-site scripting attacks, which are very common today.*

In summary, the magic mix includes several ingredients, including data about each user's history and background, plus biometric data combined with secret things that only the user will know, such as a PIN, to provide multi-factor, multi-band or 'omni' authentication as I call it. The identity of the device used and its location and the introduction of digital credentials that the user does not even know and cannot communicate or divulge, which can be generated on a secure mobile handset, for example, based also on the user validating their identity to the handset, will almost certainly be central to our thinking as we develop the next line of defence.[1]

Computer Networks

A computer network is simply a collection of computers or similar devices that are connected to each other by some kind of communications link. Even if you only have two computers linked to each other, they are described as being in a network.

Networks can be small and simple or they can become hugely complex and the Internet is a vast network-of-networks connecting billions of devices. The network at your place of work is likely to be quite complex in its own right, even though it may be relatively small in global terms.

In any computer network, one or more technologies must be used to connect the networked devices to each other. These are generally broken down into two classes:

- **Wireless technologies** – such as various forms of radio, satellite systems and microwave.

- **Wired technologies** – old fashioned copper wire, heavier duty coaxial cables or more modern fibre optic cables.

Most of us are aware of the communications satellites overhead, but did you know that the world is embraced by a vast network of massive undersea

---

1   From author's interview with Richard Harris, 2012.

communications cables that connect every major country? These cables are laid and maintained by specialised ships and the first transatlantic copper wire cables were laid over one hundred years ago. Today's cables are almost all made of fibre optic materials that transmit signals using light.

Computer networks have both positive and negative sides (see Table 3.1). Computer networks bring important risks with them, as well as having potentially negative effects on the way we work and socialise.

Table 3.1   Computer networks have both positive and negative sides

Positives	
Facilitate communications	Messaging, phone calls, email, video calls and video conferencing, social media messaging...
Permit information sharing	Remote access to stored data, sharing of files, images...
Allow sharing of network resources	Printers, scanners, storage, Cloud applications...
Negatives	
Security vulnerabilities	Expose connected devices and users to hacking, malware, data theft or identity theft and manipulation.
Dependence	Expose us to new risks should network operations be halted for any reason as we have lost the ability or knowledge to run many processes manually.
Complexity and cost	Networks can be expensive to build and maintain, particularly when backup and redundancy requirements are added.

The Anatomy of an Attack

As with any type of crime, most cyber attacks on computing devices, or on the networks that connect them, will conform to certain patterns. At the most basic level, an attack requires some form of access to the targeted system (via a device, an application or a network) and this is normally followed by some kind of exploit. Exploits can range from popping up a message, through installing Spyware all the way up to DoS. Not every attack follows this pattern, of course, but it is still a useful baseline model. It is not uncommon for victims of attacks to focus solely on the access side of the equation, never asking what the exploit or motive might have been. Oversights of this nature are what facilitate 'persistence' – the state that exists when an attacker is still active on your systems even after you have detected the intrusion.

THE ACCESS AND EXPLOITATION PHASES

The Access Phase can be broken down further into two forms:

- attacks that require some kind of user action or error of omission;

- attacks that are executed automatically, without any use action being needed to facilitate them.

The Exploit Phase may also include a 'Wiper' activity, in which all evidence of the attack is deleted from the system. Effects of the Exploit Phase can include:

- data breaches:
    - unauthorised access to data;
    - exfiltration of data;
    - destruction of data or systems;
    - disclosure of data;
    - modification of data;
    - DoS;

- brand damage;

- fraud and other e-Crimes;

- market abuse.

THE TYPICAL ATTACK LIFE CYCLE

Every cyber attack will have a life cycle, often conforming with the example in Table 3.2 to some degree:

Table 3.2   A generic cyber attack life cycle

Attack Phase	Description
Reconnaissance	The attacker scopes the target (or the target type) and develops his plan of attack.
Penetration or Access	The attacker gets into the target system or network.
Installation	The attacker installs attack software on the target.
Obtain credentials	The attacker obtains root or administrator privileges.
Lateral movement	The attacker moves from the access point into other systems or databases.
Data exfiltration	The attacker extracts the data found.
Maintain persistence	The attacker may maintain a presence on compromised systems or install 'back doors' that allow repeated access in future.

When assessing the impact of an attack, it is often useful to draw an attack time line to plot the above activities. This not only helps you to understand what the attacker has done, as well as when and where, but it also triggers key questions such as 'What did they take?' or 'Are they still here now?'

Penetration Attacks

Penetrations, or 'hacking' attacks, are access techniques and the manner in which they are then exploited, for example via lateral movement, can vary widely. Attackers are human and they live, breath and think just like you do. While you are dealing with a penetration, there is every chance that the hacker is watching you operate, responding to your moves, wiping evidence and exfiltrating data in parallel.

'Hacking' is a disputed term that is used to refer to several different types of activity and individual. 'Hacker' can describe:

- a person with expert skills;

- who attempts to access a computer system;

- without authorisation;

- by circumventing or cracking its security.

Another type of hacker is the ethical hacker who is paid by organisations to test their security controls. We will look at ethical hacking and penetration testing in more detail in Part II.

Hobbyists who play around with hardware and software, sometimes writing their own code, are also commonly referred to as hackers, and just to confuse matters, any quick code fix implemented to patch over a problem may occasionally be called 'a hack'.

The following example (Table 3.3) describes a typical cyber attack timeline, derived from several reported by various victims and security firms.

Table 3.3   Timeline of a typical cyber attack

Day	Events
1	Attacker installs Day 1 malware on target machines and creates back door
30	Victim detects and removes the Day 1 malware
32	Attacker installs new Day 32 malware via the Day 1 back door
35	The victim removes data from the known compromised systems
38	Attacker exfiltrates the now empty directories
39	Attacker pushes Day 1 malware to new systems
41	Attacker pushes Day 32 malware to new systems

The game of chess being played between the attacker and the victim in such scenarios is quite gripping. The point to remember is that, while the attacker is clearly aware of the steps the victim is taking, the victim may well be completely ignorant of the fact that he is being observed and also of what the attacker is doing next.

There are several points for consideration when looking for evidence of compromise during such events. These can be used to form the checklist shown in Table 3.4.

Table 3.4   Considerations when looking for evidence of compromise

Number	Question
1	Is there evidence of the malicious use of valid user accounts?
2	What other remaining evidence and partial files have been discovered?
3	Are command and control activities still in progress?
4	Have any known or previously unknown forms of malware been identified?
5	Is suspicious traffic taking place that points to possible data exfiltration?
6	Are there any valid programs running that might be used maliciously?
7	What files and programs could have been accessed?

Gary McKinnon is a British (or to be precise, Scottish), computer hacker who was accused by the US authorities of hacking into 97 US military and NASA computers over a 13-month period in 2001 and 2002. Although McKinnon claimed that he was only looking for information on UFOs and other matters of public interest, US authorities relentlessly pursued his extradition on charges that could have led to a lengthy prison term. The extradition case ran for more than ten years but in early 2013 a decision was made not to extradite and McKinnon continues to reside in the UK.

The US alleged that McKinnon's hacking activities left them vulnerable to attack in the wake of the events of 9/11. McKinnon refuted this charge by stating that while he was surfing the military net without authority he encountered many other hackers doing the same thing and that he is merely a scapegoat.

SCRIPT KIDDIES

'Script Kiddie' is a pejorative phrase describing supposedly young (although in fact they can be any age) and less-skilled persons who utilise programs (thus executing software scripts) created by expert hackers to attack computer systems and websites.

Script Kiddies may obtain their hacking programs from Internet sites and are often not aware of who the program's creator was or what the full implications of their actions might be. Therefore, Script Kiddies represent one useful channel for malware or attacks that can be exploited by organised hackers while keeping the actual attacker one step removed from the crime.

Reliable statistics are rare but experts estimate that a majority of malware attacks (excluding Adware and Spyware) are channelled via Script Kiddies. There are believed to be relatively few truly expert criminal hackers in cyber space and Script Kiddies are the active foot soldiers who are responsible for much of the problem.

MAN-IN-THE-MIDDLE ATTACKS

A man-in-the-middle attack involves an attacker positioning himself between two parties (A and B) who wish to communicate, without the knowledge of either party. So, the man in the middle (C) tricks party A into believing he is party B. He then tricks party B into believing he is in fact party A.

In this fashion, C handles all communications between A and B without them realising this fact and he can copy or alter any messages sent, as depicted in Figure 3.1. In Internet terms, this means that passwords, user names, addresses, attachments, email and message content and all manner of confidential information can be captured.

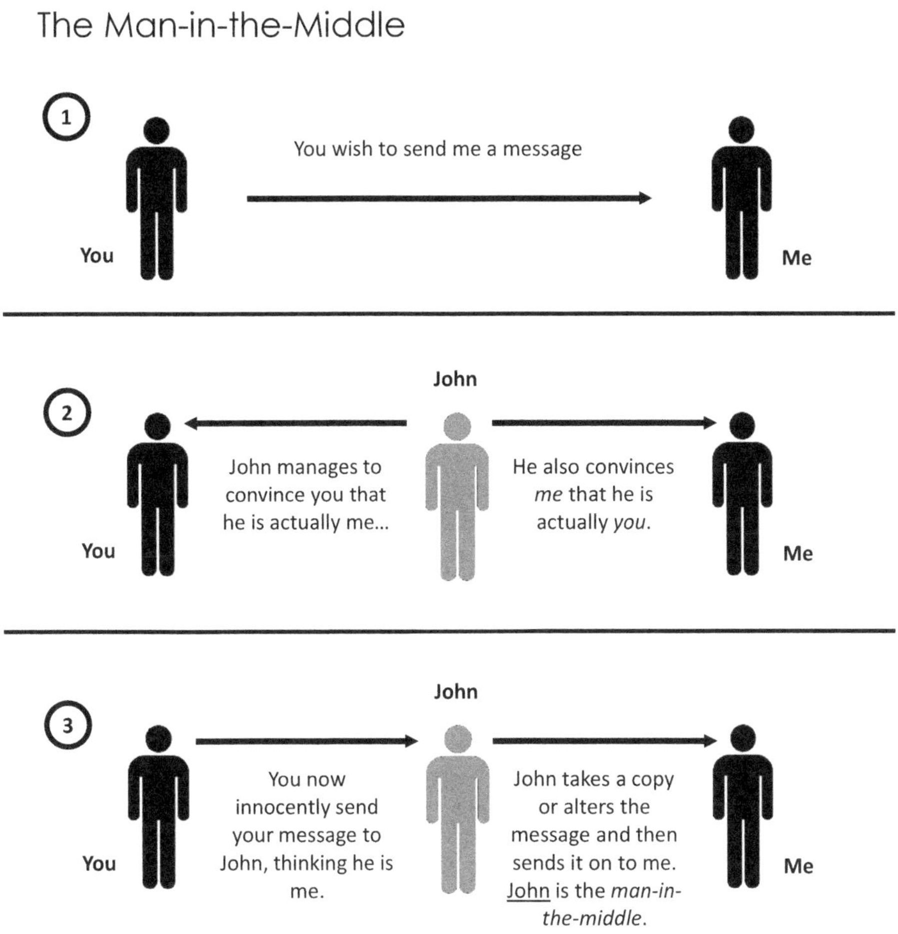

The Man-in-the-Middle

Figure 3.1   A man-in-the-middle attack

Man-in-the-middle WiFi attacks

In recent years, WiFi services have been a common target for man-in-the-middle attacks. The attacker selects a popular public WiFi network, for example in a coffee shop, and sets up his own separate WiFi network using specialised attack tools, but gives it the same name (Joe's Coffee Shop Network, for example).

Users who logon to the fake network do not realise that all of their communications are now passing through the attacker's devices, which are running special software to capture all content. The users receive the Internet services they expect and have no reasons to suspect that any of their activities have been intercepted.

Man-in-the-browser attacks

Man-in-the-browser attack techniques have been reported since 2005 and are considered an important risk for online banking services. During a typical Man-in-the-browser attack a piece of malware infects a web browser by taking advantage of vulnerabilities in browser security to modify web pages, transaction content or to secretly insert additional transactions. This is hidden from the user and the host web application.

During an Internet banking transaction, such as a funds transfer, the customer will always be shown the exact payment information as keyed into the browser. The bank, however, will receive a transaction with materially altered instructions, that is, a different destination account number and often a different amount. This attack takes place after the customer has authenticated themselves with the bank – the attack is executed from the browser *after* a successful account login.

'Out-of-band' communications are often employed to defeat this type of attack (for example confirmation of the transaction via SMS) and some attackers have added man-in-the-mobile attacks to spoof the SMS message received. This requires an attacker to infect both the browser and the mobile device and it is therefore relatively challenging.

BRUTE FORCE ATTACKS

The term 'brute force attack' refers to attempts to obtain logon credentials by guessing usernames and passwords. Some risks exist for services that allow remote access, although basic security controls should detect most attacks of this nature.

Brute force attackers use password guessing tools and scripts containing default password databases, dictionaries, or 'Rainbow Tables' that contain commonly used passwords, and they may also try all combinations of a character set. Rainbow Tables reduce the difficulty in brute force cracking a single password by creating a large pre-generated data set of hashes from nearly every possible password.

Brute force attacks are typically one-to-one attacks executed by an expert attacker against selected targets.

PORT SCANNING

In order for communications to flow between computers, it is necessary for each packet to be delivered to the correct address, process or thread within the receiving device. Under the IP protocols, these addresses are a combination of an IP Address and a port number. The port number in this case refers to a software construct within the operating system (OS), correctly known as an Internet Socket Port.

This defines what services and protocols can be handled via that route and it should not be confused with a serial port, which is a *physical* communications connection that allows the transfer of data in or out of a device one 'Bit' at a time, or 'in series'; the port on the back or side of your computer that connects to a monitor or projector is one example of a physical serial port.

A port scanner is a software application designed to identify available Internet socket ports on a device. During a port scanning attack, the attacker sends client requests to a range of server port addresses on a host, with the goal of finding an active port and exploiting a known vulnerability of that service. Port scanning attacks are one-to-many attacks in which the attacker usually scans multiple potential targets in search of vulnerabilities.

PACKET SNIFFERS

A Packet Sniffer (also known by several other names) is a program or hardware device that intercepts and logs traffic passing over a network. As data flows via the network, the sniffer intercepts and reads each packet, showing the values of each field in the packet. It then analyses the contents of the packet based on various rules and settings.

Sniffers have many legitimate uses, primarily related to monitoring intrusions and network performance, but they are also used by attackers to gather user names and passwords, or other sensitive packet content, particularly where weak encryption is used. On physical networks (for example, Local Area Networks (LANs)), and depending on the type of network, a Packet Sniffer can capture traffic on all or part of the network or from a single device using the network. On wireless networks a sniffer can capture traffic on a particular channel, or on several channels.

Sniffing attacks may be one-to-one attacks directed at a specific target, or they might represent more random one-to-many attacks against a range of targets all sending packets via the same network.

TCP/IP SESSION HIJACKS

Communication and inter-networking between devices on any computer network is governed by sets of rules. These are known as 'protocols'; a set of commonly agreed rules that all parties accept and obey. This distinguishes them from, say, a rule that applies only in your house and which requires guests to do the washing up. The accepted *protocol* would be that *you* do the dishes and I leave with an extra bit of pudding in a plastic tub you lend me, regardless of what your unilaterally derived rule states. The most common classes of protocol governing computer network communications are:

- Ethernet; used on many LANs (for example, in your office building).

- The Internet Protocol Suite (often called TCP/IP for Transmission Control Protocol/Internet Protocol); a set of protocols (or a 'protocol stack') that governs how communications between devices occur across the Internet. TCP/IP primarily governs four major network activities:
  - email;
  - file transfer;
  - remote sign on to other devices;
  - web access to myriad other locations and services.

TCP/IP is actually much more than that, but we don't need to dig any deeper for our purposes. Suffice it to say that TCP/IP is what holds most networks and the Internet together – a sort of digital glue, so to speak. Just think for a moment about the huge range of networked devices we interact with every day and then you'll see how important it is to have a common set of rules that everyone uses in order to make sure that each device can 'talk' to the others.

TCP/IP hijack attacks

TCP/IP session hijacking is a targeted one-to-one attack. During an active session the attacker sniffs valid client IP addresses and Client Port Numbers. The attacker then spoofs or mimics those identities so that he can inject his own packets into the data stream. Having done this, the attacker's commands are processed as if he was the authentic session owner.

Broken down, the attack stages for a TCP/IP session hijack are:

- monitor a session (by sniffing the network or by using malware installed on the targets);

- desynchronise the session:
  - packet sequence prediction is conducted by reading the ACK (acknowledgement) packets which contain that information;
  - the attacker will then 'Bump' the real client's next packet by injecting an attacker packet bearing the expected next packet header in the sequence;
  - the next genuine client packet will bear the same ID as the previous fraudulent packet and it is consequently treated as 're-sent' and ignored by the receiving device;

- having hijacked the session the attacker can now inject commands into the packet stream which will be obeyed by the target system.

Typical exploitation events for hijacked sessions include:

- malware or code injection (see below);

- financial fraud – the attacker injects fraudulent financial transaction instructions;

- data theft – the attacker instructed the target to send back confidential data;

- data deletion – the attacker instructs the target to delete tables or files;

- extortion/hostage taking; the attacker takes control of the target and demands payment from its owner.

CODE INJECTION

'Code injection' refers to efforts to exploit security weaknesses in systems that allow an attacker to inject code that can bypass controls and cause a computer system to act in a way that was not intended. This is a very broad definition and there are various ways in which this could be manifested, as shown in Table 3.5.

Table 3.5   Common types of code injection

Type of Injection	Remarks
Structured Query Language (SQL) injection	Exploits SQL syntax in order to attack a badly designed website, or any SQL database, in order to read or modify a database or table.
File injection	Injects remotely hosted files containing exploits or executes malicious code contained in a file already injected.
Shell injection	A more advanced form of injection that exploits the use of UNIX shells.
Hypertext Markup Language (HTML) script injection	Also known as 'cross-site scripting', this may alter the content of an html page, or even read html code while in transit, thus supporting Phishing attacks (see later).
Active Server Pages (ASP) or Hypertext Preprocessor (PHP) injection	Other types of code injection attack that follow similar principles as those above to inject code to the server side scripting engine.

Expert hackers can change the way systems work and extract secret data by injecting commands remotely. When security controls are weak, such commands can extract user name and password tables or access other confidential data. Web-facing applications often store user name and password combinations, sometimes along with other sensitive data, in tables that are queried whenever a logon is attempted through the web interface. In certain cases, even major corporate firms have left themselves vulnerable to an attack based on entering ('injecting') SQL commands in place of user names and passwords or within other fields such as 'guest comments' (see Figure 3.2).

Over several months in early 2011 hackers executed a series of successful SQL Code Injection attacks against the servers of Sony Online Entertainment, reportedly exposing the personal data of 100 million Sony Online Entertainment customers and costing Sony Online Entertainment a reported figure of $178 million in the process, primarily through lost business resulting from downtime.

The Sony Online Entertainment attack was an example of a many-to-one attack scenario in which an unknown number of attackers appear to have gained access to Sony Online Entertainment's systems. The data potentially exposed during the Sony Online Entertainment incident included user names, passwords, names and addresses and credit card information.

Code injection example

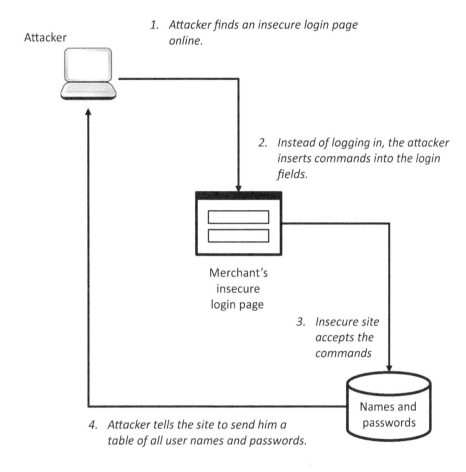

Figure 3.2   A SQL Code Injection attack

BUFFER OVERFLOWS

Buffers are device data storage areas, which generally hold a set amount of data. A buffer overflow occurs when a program attempts to store data in a buffer but the data is larger than the size of the available buffer. This extra data can overflow into adjacent memory locations and corrupt valid data or change execution paths and instructions.

The ability to exploit a buffer overflow allows an attacker to inject arbitrary code into the execution path. This arbitrary code can allow remote system-level access to occur, giving unauthorised access to not only malicious hackers, but also to replicating malware.

The overall goals of a typical buffer overflow attack are to subvert the function of a privileged program so that the attacker can take control of that program and, if the hijacked program is sufficiently privileged, control the host. Buffer overflow attacks typically target a root program. The first major reported example of a buffer overflow attack was Code Red, a Microsoft systems attack against web servers that was first detected in July 2001.

The Code Red Worm defaced hacked websites with a message, 'Hacked by Chinese' and had infected 359,000 machines within a week of its release. Although relatively benign, Code Red demonstrated the speed with which this form of infection could spread online.

CROSS-SITE SCRIPTING (XSS)

Cross-site Scripting (XSS) is a term that refers to forms of Code Injection that exploit the trust relationships established between users and particular websites. One example would be between you and your bank. Once you and your browser have decided to trust the bank's website, your browser will typically accept anything it receives from that domain.

If an attacker can inject malicious code into the bank's web pages by attacking and compromising the bank's web server, then he can use those infected but trusted pages as a channel for delivering that code to your device via your browser. He has sent you malicious scripts 'cross-site'.

XSS attacks:

- exploit vulnerabilities often found in web applications;

- may allow an attacker to hijack a user's session and/or steal their Cookies and confidential data;

- allow the attacker to inject malicious code into a trusted website being viewed by the user;

- let the attacker conceal their own identity from the target.

XXS attacks accounted for 80 per cent of all security breaches reported by the security firm Symantec in 2007. As with all such matters, the security community responded and other forms of attack have become more prominent, but the XXS issue has not gone away.

JAVA APPLETS AND PLUG-INS

In the early days of the Web, pages were inflexible things. A user read the content and then clicked on another link and read some more. Pages didn't allow users to input much data at all and no calculations could be made locally during the session. This was a problem, for example, for those online commerce sites whose owners wanted users to be able to enter data in a form and have calculations made quickly and locally on the user's PC.

The features of the new Java programming language (named in recognition of the development team's coffee habit) meant that it was an effective tool for writing small applications ('Apps') that could be designed to run inside the user's local web browser so that computations and other functions could actually be housed there. This had the effect of personalising the user experience while also supporting a wide range of uses.

These small Apps (that is, 'app-lets') are one of the main things supporting the myriad ways in which the modern Web can be used to provide users with diverse services and experiences, instead of merely going to the virtual library. Other well known plug-ins include QuickTime and Adobe Flash Player, but there are literally thousands of third-party plug-ins available for most web browsers. These have the advantage of keeping the browser application software small and allowing users to choose the additional tools and features they want.

On the risk side, the fact that most plug-ins are developed by third parties means that there is always the potential for them to contain malicious code – to act as Trojan malware. Worries about Java security have been increasing and in late 2012 Apple removed a Java plug-in from all OS X web browsers because of a security concern.

COOKIE THEFT

Many websites, and your web browser itself, can collect and store your web browsing history. One reason for doing this is to build a picture of your habits so that targeted advertising can be directed to you; car ads for people who spend a lot of time looking at car sales sites, for example. The key tool for doing this is the Cookie.

Cookies are files containing small amounts of information that may be downloaded to your device when you visit a website, although within the EU you now need to give consent before this happens. Cookies may then be sent back to the originating website on each subsequent visit, or to another website that recognises that cookie. Cookies are useful to site owners because they allow each website to recognise each user's device and preferences. Cookies do many different jobs, such as letting you navigate between pages efficiently, storing your preferences, and generally improving your site experience. They can also help to ensure that the content you see online is relevant to you. Other Cookies are essential to enable you use certain website features, such as accessing secure areas as an account holder, or performing a secure purchase transaction from an order page.

Tracking Cookies are the tools used to track your online activities, particularly the web pages you visit, by maintaining a log of all Uniform/Universal Resource Locators (URLs) you navigate to. Cookies may also record user's preferences for any given site, in order to restore those the next time he or she visits.

The key point to bear in mind when thinking about Cookies is that Cookies are often transmitted between the user and the originator and this means that:

- they can potentially be intercepted by a third party who (in a process known as 'eavesdropping') will then learn your browsing habits, preferences and even logon details;

- they can be placed on your device by or on behalf of third parties ('third-party Cookies') in order to gather data for Adware or Spyware purposes.

Cookies won't harm a system in and of themselves, but they might create vulnerabilities that can be exploited by a third party. These concerns are what lie behind the new Cookie policies being introduced by some authorities.

WAR DIALLING

War dialling is basically a one-to-one brute force attack in which an attacker cracks a communications platform's password, such as a PABX (Private Automated Branch Exchange, often also called a 'PBX'). If you work in an office, then your office telephone system is very likely to be a PABX rather than a set of direct service provider lines.

Once into the PABX platform, the hacker can then dial outbound, making calls in high volumes to expensive destinations such as Premium Rate Services or international numbers. The cost of this traffic is often borne by the platform owner and cases have occurred in which these figures ran into millions of dollars.

The main breakout techniques involve:

- voicemail breakout;

- DISA (Direct Inwards System Access) feature breakout.

Malware

During 2010 and 2011, the Russia-based Dogma Millions group advertised widely on public boards and in chat rooms for people interested in earning 'easy money'. All the interested parties had to do was to push Dogma's software solutions via their own pages or websites in order to receive a fee per download. As it turned out, Dogma was using this channel to deliver a malware attack via its 'partner programme'.

As John Naughton states in his book *From Gutenberg to Zuckerberg*, 'Once PCs began to be connected to the Net in large numbers, we entered a world in which millions of computers – most of them operated by technically naive users with little or no understanding of security issues – were connected to a global network. And this in turn created a perfect environment for the rapid dissemination of malware of all descriptions.'

Malicious software, or 'malware', is a product of the very open nature of the Internet. Malware has become a very serious problem for Internet users of all types and it probably has the potential, if not effectively controlled, to bring Internet activities to a standstill. Indeed, the software security firm, McAfee, reported for the third quarter of 2012 that online financial fraud attacks have spread worldwide, that malware which extorts money from its victims became one of the fastest growing areas of cybercrime, that the number of malware specimens in the 'zoo' topped 100 million, and that data breaches have reached an all-time high.

Malware comes in many shapes and sizes but the most important categories are:

- viruses

- Worms

- Trojans

- Rootkits.

VIRUSES

Viruses are software programs developed by expert coders that replicate across multiple computer systems in a one-to-many model. The spread of the infection is often dependent on certain user actions, such as opening an email attachment that then executes an unwanted process. These processes can be malicious or benign. Although the phrase is often used to refer to many other forms of 'malware', only malicious code that has this reproductive capability is correctly called a 'virus'.

While older malware programs could infect thousands, or even millions of machines, this actually made them easier to detect. Many modern malware Apps are designed to infect only a few hundred machines before they evolve into a new form, thus making the job of anti-virus practitioners harder than ever. This period during which their existence is unknown is called the 'Zero Day Risk' period or the 'Oh-Day' period.

Computer virus infections can occur in a variety of ways, such as a user clicking on a link and downloading an infected file, using a USB memory stick that contains a virus, or opening infected email attachments. Historically, infections have been more likely to spread in networked systems where they infect files that are commonly accessed by many users. More recently, the increasingly common use of short URLs (for example, 'video') to link to files, thus concealing the full details of the actual URL from the user, has increased susceptibility to virus and other malware attacks. Some viruses have also used cross-site scripting to spread infections via web pages.

Viruses can harm a system's performance or the data stored within it. The effect on users depends on the type of virus involved and many virus infections have no obvious impact. As with clinical epidemiology, there are various mathematical models for computing or expressing the rates of viral infection and the effectiveness of defences or controls. Some of the key parameters include:

- the rate at which external computers are connected to the network in question;

- the recovery rate of infected computers due to the anti-viral capabilities of the network;

- the rate at which one infected computer is removed from the network;

- the rate at which, when having a connection to one infected computer, one additional susceptible computer can become infected;

- the speed with which the virus mutates to another form, creating new Zero Day risks.

WORMS

Similar to viruses, Worms are also self-replicating but are able to send themselves to other machines on a network without user intervention.

Worms operate independently and, unlike viruses, they do not need to be attached to another program or file. While not all Worms carry a 'payload' (a piece of code designed to do something other than merely spread the Worm) security professionals generally regard all Worms as malware. Worms can operate in one-to-one or one-to-many mode, depending on how targeted the attack is designed to be. The Stuxnet Worm, for example, was configured to target very specific systems that are used in nuclear facilities, as we will see later when we look at APTs.

Worm Payloads can be designed to do a wide range of things, but recent examples include:

- crashing the computer;

- taking control of the computer;

- deleting files;

- modifying files to change their content;

- downloading unwanted files;

- uploading files from the target machine (data theft);

- encrypting files as part of a crypto-viral extortion attack – the owner of the files must pay to get them decrypted;

- installing a software 'back door' to allow the author of the Worm to take over the target machine;

- changing the way computer programs work, as was the case with the Stuxnet Worm, described later in this section;

- using the attacked machine as part of a 'Botnet' (as explained in a later section);

- logging and report keystrokes for Phishing or espionage purposes;

- watching the user's PC screen and allowing the attacker to monitor all activity.

Worms use a variety of exploits to infect different systems on a computer network. They can operate on an industrial scale and may target large industrial or commercial systems. The Loveletter Worm of May 2000 sent an 'I LOVE YOU' message that was opened by an enormous number of people which led to many company email servers going into meltdown. The Worm copied itself to all of the contacts in a user's address book once the attached file was opened.

The Mydoom Worm of January 2004 used texts that imitated the technical messages issued by the mail server, while the Swen Worm passed itself off as a message from Microsoft, masquerading as a patch to *remove* Windows vulnerabilities. Many people took Swen seriously and tried to install the 'patch', much to their regret.

In November 2005, a version of the Sober Worm falsely informed users that the German police were investigating people who had visited illegal websites. This message was read by one man who used to frequent child pornography sites and he promptly obeyed orders and turned himself in to the Police, even though he was not actually a suspect.

Trojan attacks

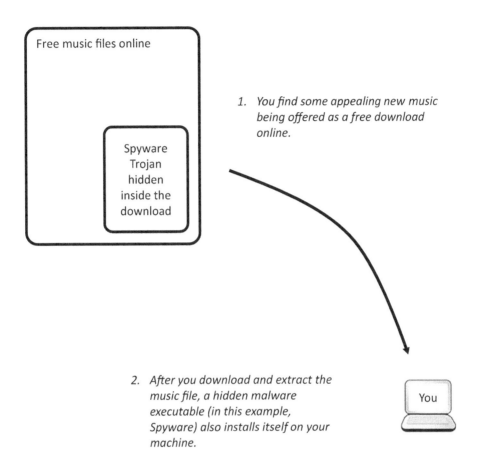

Free music files online

Spyware
Trojan
hidden
inside the
download

1. *You find some appealing new music being offered as a free download online.*

2. *After you download and extract the music file, a hidden malware executable (in this example, Spyware) also installs itself on your machine.*

You

Figure 3.3   A Trojan attack

TROJANS

A Trojan ('Trojan horse') is a piece of malware that appears to perform a useful function, but which simultaneously facilitates malicious activities. Essentially, as shown in Figure 3.3 it hides inside another innocent looking program, such as:

- a useful App;

- a free game;

- a video file.

A Trojan may replicate itself in one-to-many mode like a virus and it can perform any of the tasks already attributed to Viruses and Worms.

The Zeus Trojan has been around since 2007 and is described as one of the most powerful, sophisticated and evasive malware Apps ever created. Designed to steal bank login credentials, Zeus was delivered via an email message containing a link to an infected website. The site infected visitors with a 'drive-by' malware download that worked as a Spyware Key Logger.

With the rise of mobile banking, Zeus gave birth to ZitMo, standing for 'Zeus in the Mobile'. ZitMo can reportedly intercept SMS communications between banks and account holders and may expose confidential data, although its true impact seems less clear than that of Zeus.

Users are accustomed to the need to sometimes install a new video codec to use multi-media and Malware authors sometimes offer up malware as a fake codec Trojan. If you are still reading, you should by now have updated and run every security utility installed on your devices!

ROOTKIT ATTACKS

Rootkits are a type of software (generally malware) designed to operate at the lowest OS-level of the infected machine, thus avoiding detection and providing system admin-level access to the computer, as illustrated in Figure 3.4.

In most cases, the installation of a Rootkit requires root-level access. This can be gained when working on the machine (for example, as a contractor), by cracking password protection via malware attacks, or by socially engineering the passwords from the authorised administrators – conning them, in other words. Poor staff practices, such as sharing passwords or writing them down, can also contribute to such infections.

The purpose of a Rootkit might be to execute any of the malware attacks already listed. The key point is that they are very difficult to detect and removal might require a complete re-install of the OS itself.

Rootkit attacks

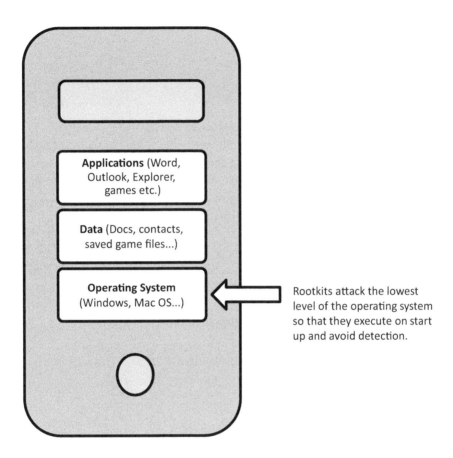

Figure 3.4   A Rootkit attack

Malware Exploits and Payloads

The preceding malware descriptions are of delivery mechanisms or models. Each delivery (or access) mechanism has an accompanying payload (or exploit) and some versions of malware carry multiple payloads. The most common forms of payload are:

• Spyware

• Crimeware

- Attackware

- Adware

- Rogueware.

SPYWARE

Spyware is a form of malware designed to sit secretly on a target machine and capture information about the users' activities without their knowledge, including not only passwords and user names but also Internet usage habits, and many types of personal data. Spyware is often delivered to and installed on computers via Internet Worms, as hidden downloads when a user navigates to a malicious site, or as Trojan malware concealed within an innocent-looking application.

In fact, Spyware frequently comes bundled (but unannounced) with other software that users download deliberately. Well-designed Spyware has little impact on system performance or user processes and is therefore difficult to detect.

Common Spyware capabilities include, but are not limited to:

- passwords and user name capture;

- visited URLs capture;

- keystrokes logging;

- credit card and bank details capture;

- other personal data capture.

Spyware has also been seen to change computer settings, for example by turning off Firewall and Anti-virus settings, or by changing default Internet homepages.

KEY LOGGERS

Spyware isn't just for hackers and fraudsters and advertisers, it is now a consumer product. You can visit sites like http://www.mspy.com/ and purchase Spyware that will run on your partner's (US) cell phone and report their activities back to you. This is not an endorsement, merely a welcome to the future, and if you get caught I am not responsible for your actions.

Key loggers are forms of Spyware that record all keystrokes made by a user in order to capture passwords, credit card numbers, bank account details and more. The Key logger software offered for sale at http://www.relytec.com/ needs to be installed directly on the target PC. This is yet another example of the commercialisation of cyber-snooping.

DISHONEST ADWARE

Dishonest Adware is software that infects user's machines and then displays advertisements without the user's consent. Adware infects computers for commercial gain by promoting products or services and much Adware is actually Spyware in the sense that it advertises offers to users based on analysis of user data and habits it has discovered surreptitiously after being installed without their knowledge. Common Adware techniques include:

- triggering unsolicited pop-up ads;

- triggering pop-ups based on monitoring of user habits;

- routing Internet HTTP requests to other sites for advertising or sales purposes.

Thus, even though Adware might not be patently malicious, and may not harm the infected machine, it is still regarded as unethical malware. Like Spyware, Adware often comes secretly bundled with other products.

SCAREWARE

Some Adware crosses the line when it promotes unneeded 'solutions', such as disk cleanups for non-existent infections. The Dogma Millions case, referred to earlier and described in more detail under Crimeware, provides a good example of dishonest Adware in action. That attack involved the sale of fake anti-virus products to consumers.

Reports vary, but it seems reasonably certain that many millions of Scareware infections occur worldwide every year. In Scareware cases the victim often pays for the program. A common example involves fake Anti-virus scanners, which pop-up a message when you visit the Scareware website, or a partner site and tell you that you need a free PC scan. If you run the 'scan', the malware will invariably claim to have found infections on your device and it will offer you the option to remove these by purchasing a removal tool. There was of course no infection and the removal tool you download may even deliver a malware payload of its own.

One prolific example of Scareware is WinAVPro. This professional looking bundle has been around for a long time and has deceived untold millions of users into downloading and installing it. The WinAVPro Scareware has gone through numerous name changes and to-date has been it has also been sold as:

- AVSystemCare

- DriveCleaner

- Ecsecure

- ErrorProtector

- ErrorSafe

- FreePCSecure

- Home Antivirus 20xx

- PCTurboPro

- Performance Optimizer

- Personal Antivirus

- PrivacyProtector

- StorageProtector

- SysProtect

- SystemDoctor

- VirusDoctor

- WinAntiSpy

- WinAntiSpyware

- WinAntiVirusPro

- Windows Police Pro

- WinReanimator

- WinSoftware

- WinspywareProtect

- XPAntivirus

- Your PC Protector.

All of these are in fact the same WinAVPro package.

Malware Attack Vectors

As you may have noticed, there are numerous routes by which malware attacks are perpetrated against systems and it's a complex, confusing and scary cyber world out there. Table 3.6 summarises some of the most important attack vectors.

Table 3.6   Malware attack vectors

Attack Vector	Examples
Drive-by Downloads	Occur when a victim visits an infected website which triggers an automatic download of malware to their device.
Web attack toolkits	Sold to would-be attackers as a 'do-it-yourself' mechanism.
Malicious peer-to-peer files	Infected content on file sharing sites.
Anti-virus bypass	Re-packing, encryption and more used to avoid anti-virus detection.
Email	Containing links to infected pages or file attachments.
File download	Files are offered to site visitors for free download.
Physical devices (USB, DVD)	USBs and DVDs are left lying around the target's office.

Let's look at some of these examples in a little more detail.

DRIVE-BY DOWNLOADS

The phrase 'Drive-by Download' has two meanings:

1.   downloads which a user has authorised but without understanding the consequences;

2.   any download that happens without a person's knowledge.

The second usage is the most common. Drive-by Downloads often involve the insertion or injection of malicious code by an infected website that exploits vulnerabilities in many browsers. This may happen when a victim visits such a website, but it can also happen when viewing an email message, or clicking on a deceptive pop-up window.

Hackers use the drive-by technique to obfuscate malicious code and anti-virus software is often unable to recognise it as the code is executed in hidden frames and can go undetected even by experienced users.

WEB ATTACK TOOLKITS

Finding holes is a non-trivial task for most attackers and web attack toolkits have been designed to make it easier for them. These toolkits can be obtained online and are often well supported by their creators who will even engage in online social spaces to provide advice on usage and troubleshooting.

Most attack toolkits are clearly built with the non-technical user in mind and as a result they feature simple interfaces with no deep technical skill being needed to launch many of the attacks. This is a good example of the Script Kiddie model in action.

Recent examples of toolkits include:

- Neosploit

- MPack

- Icepack

- Adpack.

MALICIOUS PEER-TO-PEER FILES

Peer-to-peer file sharing is a commonplace method for sharing both legal content and illicit content such as ripped video or audio content. The concept originated with the Napster service, which was server-based, offering a centralised location for downloading ripped content. This service was eventually shut down as it was clearly breaching the IPR of numerous firms and individuals.

Today's 'Bit Torrent' peer-to-peer users must first download and install a peer-to-peer software client which will search online for other users with content to offer for download. Bit Torrent creates a new connection for each session rather than using 'Super Nodes', servers or web caches to store content centrally. While the sharing of much content is not illegal, this model makes detection of copyright infringements far more challenging and reduces the risk of being caught for everyone involved.

Knowing the popularity of content shared by these means, and also the lack of security awareness on the part of most users, malware authors often bind their code into popular Apps or files and make them available for distribution via peer-to-peer file sharing. Celebrity or popular brand names are used to attract users to the infected download.

BEATING ANTI-VIRUS PROTECTION

Malware creators are engaged in a running battle with anti-virus firms and security managers and they put a great deal of effort into finding new ways to bypass or otherwise defeat anti-virus protection. In order to defeat anti-virus scanning programs developers use various obfuscation techniques. The top six are:

1. code packing and encryption;

2. code mutation;

3. stealth techniques;

4. blocking anti-virus and anti-virus updates;

5. masking;

6. quantity attacks.

Code packing and encrypting

The majority of today's Worms and Trojans are packed and encrypted. 'Black-hat' programmers design special utilities for this purpose and anti-virus programs must either add new unpacking and decoding methods, or store signatures for each sample of a malicious program.

Encrypted malware consists of a small decryption module and the encrypted body of the malware App. By using different encryption keys for each infection, each package of decryption module plus viral code is made to look unique thereby passing some anti-virus detection routines, although modern anti-virus scanners can often recognise the format of the decryption code itself. Once introduced to the host, the virus decrypts itself and becomes active.

Code mutation

Code mutation involves changes to the malware package designed to prevent it from being recognised by anti-virus applications.

- Polymorphic viruses mutate their decryptors but not their viral code. They represent a response to the process of detection based on recognition of the decryptor code. Such Polymorphic viruses will change or mutate their decryptors with each new generation. Thus an encrypted polymorphic virus contains no parts that remain constant on each subsequent infection. However, because these viruses still carry a constant virus body that remains identical once decrypted, detection is still possible based on the pattern of that decrypted code.

- Metamorphic viruses change shape by rewriting their own code. They take many forms and were created in response to the technique of decrypting and then analysing viral code. A metamorphic virus changes both its decryptor *and* its virus body on each infection. Each new generation looks different to the preceding one, whether encrypted or decrypted. Nevertheless, while metamorphic viruses change their shape they do not always change their behaviour, which leads to them being detected via behavioural analysis. In response, some metamorphic viruses contain several viruses within them, allowing them to launch different types of attack depending on the types of systems and applications they encounter, yet another example of the anti-viral arms race.

So, code mutation allows for changes in a malware App's appearance while retaining its functionality. It may also be mixed with Spam instructions that cause the mutated form of the malware to spew itself out to multiple new targets.

Stealth techniques

As demonstrated by the Dogma Millions case, malware developers have become adept at using Backdoor techniques to stealthily avoid detection and maintain persistence. The current family of Backdoor Trojans is very appropriately named the 'Backdoor' family and one of the most recent 2012 threats is the Backdoor Conpee Trojan which infects both 32-bit and 64-bit versions of Windows 7. According to Symantec, this malware again allowed attackers to elevate privileges of restricted processes without user knowledge or permission, a recurring theme in Backdoor infections.

Many Backdoor-type Trojans can intercept system functions to make the infected file invisible to the OS and to anti-virus and they may even include hidden registry entries.

Blocking anti-virus and anti-virus updates

In order to ensure that updated versions of the installed anti-virus programs cannot be downloaded and used, many Backdoor Trojans are designed to search the infected host for a list of active anti-virus applications and then attack those Apps directly by:

- deactivating each anti-virus program;

- damaging the installed anti-virus database of malware types and signatures;

- blocking updating of the anti-virus App to extend the Trojan's Zero Day window of opportunity.

Anti-virus Apps therefore have to secure their databases and hide their presence and processes from Trojans as a counter to this form of attack. The anti-virus battle is more than just cops and robbers; it plays out more like a kind of cat and mouse struggle.

Masking

'Masking' refers to the practice adopted by malware developers of masking the presence of malicious code on a website. In this case, infected websites are specially configured to spot download attempts originating from any domain associated with an anti-virus firm. If an anti-virus firm tries to download the infected file, an uninfected file is delivered by the website instead. Anti-virus firms now have to mask their own online identity in response, in order to access infected sites anonymously.

Quantity attacks

As anti-virus applications have become more sophisticated and quicker at detecting infections, some attackers have moved to the generation and distribution of large quantities of different Trojans in a small period of time to flood anti-virus firms with huge numbers of new samples that require analysis. This is effectively a form of 'volley fire' and quantity attacks can greatly increase the time and effort demanded of the anti-virus firms, once again extending Zero Day windows.

Physical Attacks

Cyber attacks often have a physical component, particularly when they are executed by an insider or a trusted third party. There is a close interplay between traditional physical security and cyber security and their separation into different organisational silos should not be allowed to prevent them from working hand-in-glove.

HARDWARE KEYLOGGERS

Hardware Keyloggers are physical devices that can be attached to your computing devices or to your network. A number of approaches have been used over many years, including:

- USB sticks that contain software which, once installed on the target device, monitors and stores all activity. The captured data is normally saved on the USB stick until it is retrieved during a second visit.

- Modified keyboards have also been seen that include the same functionality.

- Adapted serial devices (for example, the 'SerialGhost' device) can be inserted between an existing serial device and your machine. These also contain Spyware, but their use is much less common as we move to ubiquitous USB usage and the serial port slowly becomes redundant.

- WiFi-enabled network plug-ins such as the 'Pwn Plug' hacking tool are plugged into an available network socket and attached to an adjacent power socket. These then remain in situ while the attacker uses remote WiFi access to attempt network penetrations via the device. Unless trained to spot such attacks, most security and other non-technical staff will hesitate to remove any piece of equipment from a network port for fear of causing technical problems.

In the same way as software Keyloggers, the hardware versions can capture all keystrokes and transmitted files and either store these for later collection or send them to a specified address via a radio link.

EQUIPMENT ROOM INTRUSIONS

If a well-equipped attacker can gain physical access to the communications equipment room in an office building or other facility, he may be able to access the network by connecting a cable to a port. Often, this involves a social engineering scheme to fool staff into granting access to the room.

An equipment room intrusion is a one-to-one attack. Intruders often gain access by posing as engineers. Once a physical connection is made to the network, passwords may be obtained from staff, guessed or hacked and the attacker will attempt to navigate to corporate systems and data.

COLD BOOT ATTACKS

A cold boot attack takes place when an attacker with physical access to a computer uses a reboot to restart the machine and then retrieves encryption keys from the OS. The attack relies on the ability to retrieve memory contents which can remain readable in the seconds to minutes after power has been removed.

To execute the attack, the machine is 'cold-booted', meaning that power is turned off and back on without letting a computer shut down cleanly. This may also be done by pressing the 'reset' button, if the machine has one.

In one scenario, an OS belonging to the attacker is held on a USB Flash Drive and this is inserted so that it loads when the device immediately reboots. The contents of any pre-boot memory are dumped to a file which can be read by the attacker using purpose built automated tools that find sensitive data, including encryption keys.

This is a one-to-one hardware attack and any data held in memory may be vulnerable, often regardless of the software encryption techniques in use.

Social Engineering

Social engineering is the art of manipulating people:

- to perform unplanned actions;

- to refrain from planned actions.

In cyber security terms, social engineering is a human issue that exploits human failings and makes them a vehicle for crime. Most financial firms are familiar with social engineering as a tool criminals use to trick gullible people out of their savings and in fact social engineering has a rich history and is widely used by criminals, con men, advertisers, marketers, sales people, politicians, penetration testers and many others. When used by criminals, it is regularly employed to get confidential information, such as:

- personal information;

- bank account details;

- business information;

- user names and passwords.

Social engineering may also be used face-to-face to negotiate access to restricted areas. Social engineering is one of the biggest cyber security threats we face because it exploits human weaknesses or naivety in ways that mean it cannot easily be 'designed out' in the way that software flaws can. Increasingly, social engineers are turning to social media sites like Facebook and LinkedIn to identify targets and to launch social engineering attacks. As a result, social media is now emerging as one of the most important cyber security vulnerabilities.

PHISHING

Phishing refers to online social engineering attempts to obtain secret data, such as passwords or bank and credit card details, from unsuspecting users by sending fake messages that appear to come from credible sources, such as trusted websites, bank staff, system administrators, and so on.

Phishing is normally executed in one-to-many mode and intended to facilitate unauthorised access to systems or fraud via identity theft, but some malware (for example, Spyware) may also be used for Phishing purposes. It is the use of malware that places Phishing in my list of cyber crimes, for much Phishing is actually an e-Crime. Phishing has become increasingly common and user awareness and alertness is one key tool for preventing this kind of crime.

On 28 December 2012, UK newspaper *The Daily Telegraph* ran the following Phishing story.

NATWEST CUSTOMERS TARGETED BY 'PHISHING' EMAIL SCAM

Worried NatWest customers are being targeted by bogus 'phishing' emails promising them access to their accounts if they reveal their passwords.

Similar emails have been around for years and many consumers know that they should ignore them. But experts warn that the latest opportunistic campaign, cleverly designed to play on the anxiety of NatWest customers locked out of their accounts, could cause some to drop their guard.

One fake email, purporting to be from Stephen Hester, the head of RBS, apologises for the problems at RBS and says a 'security upgrade' requires them to update their information.

But if customers follow the web link in the email, they are taken to an 'incredibly realistic' copy of the NatWest website. If they do enter their account details on the fake site, the fraudsters will be able to log in to their account and steal all their money.

Alan Woodward, a professor of computing at Surrey university, said: 'This shows how on-the-ball these opportunistic criminals are. Imagine not being able to access your bank account and then getting one of these.'

'I specialise in security but I could see myself thinking, "oh, it's from NatWest" and then clicking on the link, which takes you to an incredibly realistic website. Given the number of NatWest customers and the volume of emails that the scammers send, some people are going to fall for it, especially if they are desperate.'[2]

As this story shows, while some types of attack may be considered outdated, they can still be very effective; every new generation of users and consumers has to learn certain lessons from bitter experience. Security experts who focus solely on the latest technologies and scams while dismissing older techniques as irrelevant have much to answer for.

SPEAR PHISHING AND WHALE PHISHING

As illustrated in Figure 3.5, Spear Phishing describes a Phishing attack that targets a particular organisation or individual, as opposed to being a general attack against all Internet users, while Whale Phishing is a term used to denote a Spear Phishing scam that targets a very high-profile individual. Both Spear and Whale Phishing are one-to-one attacks.

PHARMING

Pharming attacks redirect traffic away from a legitimate website towards a false site, for example one that has been set up to look like a legitimate bank's home page. This is commonly done in order to obtain secret data from unsuspecting site visitors without having to setup a Phishing scam.

Redirects of this nature are often facilitated by malware already downloaded and installed on the victim's machine and represent a one-to-many attack directed at the widest possible network of victims.

In another newspaper article on 10 December 2012, the *Korea Times National* reported this Pharming case.

---

2   http://www.telegraph.co.uk/finance/personalfinance/consumertips/banking/9354580/NatWest-customers-targeted-by-phishing-email-scam.html (accessed 25 June 2012).

Types of Phishing

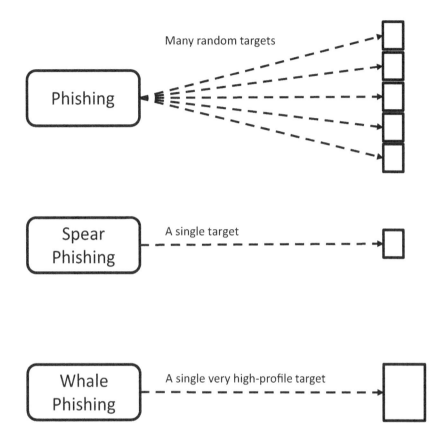

Figure 3.5   Types of Phishing attack

PHARMING ALERT!

Yoo Jong-kwan, a 30-year-old office worker in Gangneung, recently found something suspicious on the website of a local bank when he visited it to access an online banking service. As usual, he typed in its address and logged in with his ID and password. Until then, he couldn't establish that it was a fake site.

Yoo said, 'I realized that I was hooked up to the site only after finding out that an online security program installed on my computer wasn't working. I nearly fell victim to a scam.'

Like Yoo, millions of computer users are being targeted in a 'Pharming' scam, in which online banking users are redirected to a scam website.

Last month, police apprehended a 28-year-old man for withdrawing 150 million won ($139,000) from the bank accounts of two victims after acquiring their personal information through a Pharming scam.

So as you can see, it's not just us, it's Yoo too.[3]

SPOOFING

Spoofing is the act of assuming a fake identity, normally in order to trick another party (or system) into exchanging, submitting or accepting authentication or other confidential data.

URL spoofing

URL spoofing occurs when one website poses as another and refers to techniques used to edit the details of a URL displayed in an innocent user's web browser. One motive for spoofing is to conceal a Pharming attack by adopting a false URL that looks convincing.

Visitors are usually taken to the spoofed site by links on other web pages or in email messages and social media pages. In such cases, the victim may not be able to detect the fact that they have been directed away from a legitimate site simply by examining the URL.

Spoofing need not be technical. Many firms fail to buy up every version of their domain name and attackers can often purchase very similar looking domains for only a few dollars. To test this, or to audit your business, search for a domain provider (for example www.1and1.com) and see how many versions of your own corporate domain name are available for sale. Anything you find can be purchased by anyone with a credit card. A fake website, with corresponding email addresses, can then be created in a matter of minutes using today's free website authoring tools.

---

3   http://www.koreatimes.co.kr/www/news/nation/2012/12/116_126598.html (accessed March 2013).

Email spoofing

This instance of spoofing refers to the editing of the 'From' field in an email message to hide the true identity of the sender, generally as part of a Phishing attack or other fraud event, as well as during Spam attacks.

IP address spoofing

An IP address is a numerical identifier that is assigned to each device on any computer network that uses the IP protocol. It represents the address of the device on the network and it allows other devices to find it and send packets to it.

Under IPv4 (which stands for Internet Protocol version 4) this address is a 32 bit number. Although IPv4 is still in use, IPv6, now being deployed worldwide, deals with the huge increase in demand for IP addresses by increasing them to 128 bit numbers.

- IPv4 was the underlying technology that made it possible for us to connect our devices to the Web. Whenever a device accesses the Internet (whether it's a Server, PC, Mac, PDA or any other such device), it is assigned a unique, numerical IP address (such as 99.48.226.127, for example). To send data from one computer to another through the Web, a data packet must be transferred across the network containing the IP addresses of both devices, so the message is tagged as going from A to B. Without IP addresses devices would not be able to communicate and send data to each other and the Internet wouldn't work.

- Unfortunately, the Internet ran out of IPv4 addresses, meaning that the last blocks of IPv4 Internet addresses had been allocated, even if all addresses were not actually being used.

- IPv6 is a system that not only offers many more numerical addresses, but which simplifies address assignments and provides additional network security features. IPv6 is (you guessed it!) the sixth revision to the Internet Protocol. It functions similarly to IPv4 in that it provides the unique, numerical IP addresses necessary for Internet-enabled devices to communicate. However, it does have one major difference which is that it utilises 128-bit addresses as opposed to IPv4's 32 bit system.

- Because IPv6 has a 128-bit system, it can support 2^128 Internet addresses, or 340,282,366,920,938,000,000,000,000,000,000,000,000 unique addresses! IPv6 requires a hexadecimal system to display numbers of this size and there are now many more IPv6 addresses than we are likely to require in order to keep the Internet operational on a very long-term basis.

To summarise, IP addresses have two primary roles:

1. host or network interface identification;

2. location addressing.

As every data packet sent over the Internet includes the sender's IP address in the header, as well as other information about the packet, if an attacker can forge this header he can disguise its source from the recipient and make it appear to have come from a different device.

'IP spoofing' refers to such changes made by the attacker to his own IP address in order to conceal his online identity or to assume the identity of another in order to impersonate them. This may occur during DoS attacks, where the sender does not care if responses to his messages are sent back to the wrong address. IP spoofing is a non-trivial task as thousands of packet headers will need to be forged.

BLACK-HAT SEARCH ENGINE OPTIMISATION

Website owners can spend large amounts of time and money optimising their site's search results in order to rise up the search order rankings and get more visits. One approach is known as 'Black-hat SEO' (for Search Engine Optimisation) and it refers to various methods used to change the results delivered to users by search engines such as Google, Yahoo or Bing. In essence, the Black-hat route can serve as a shortcut, tricking search engines into thinking that a particular site is of high quality as an alternative to actually putting lots of useful information on the site. It doesn't involve an actual hacking attack on the search engine servers or indexes.

Black-hat SEO is often touted as being both cheaper and easier to perform than legitimate 'White-hat SEO'. Black-hat SEO attacks often divert users to short-lived, traffic-hungry sites as they constitute a malicious user search redirect and are likely to be discovered relatively quickly because search engines have their own search algorithms altered on a regular basis.

There are literally dozens of different Black-hat SEO techniques in use, but the examples included in Table 3.7 should give you a sense of what is involved.

Table 3.7   A sampling of some Black-hat SEO techniques

Black-hat SEO technique	Remarks
Hidden text	By placing hidden text on a website, possibly copied from other high-profile sites, search engines can be fooled into believing that the optimised site is of equally high quality.
Keyword stuffing	Website admins place lists of relevant keywords on their sites legitimately to increase the chances of being found. However, Black-hat SEO methods include adding popular but irrelevant keywords to increase the hit rate.
Twitter automation	The automation of Twitter accounts as 'Bots' that constantly re-Tweet messages referencing the optimised website (or to send Spam) has been a widespread problem although most search engines now filter such results out by default.

SPORGERY

In early December 2011, hundreds of cash machines (ATMs) in Latvia belonging to Swedbank, a leading Swedish financial institution, were emptied of money after rumours spread via Twitter that the bank was going out of business.

The rumours, which turned out to be unfounded and which may have been malicious, spread very rapidly online on a Sunday and thousands of customers ran to the nearest cash machine to withdraw their money as quickly as possible. This was a classic example of Sporgery, a phrase first coined by Timan Hausherr.

'Sporgery' refers to a combination of Spam and Forgery in which malicious posts or news items are sent in large volumes, attributed to another person in order to libel them.

Commonly seen as floods of false and malicious post on Usenet newsgroups, Twitter and other social media forums are also conduits for variations of this attack because of their very weak controls for validating the identity of new users.

Sporgery has the potential to cause:

- reputational harm;

- brand damage;

- market distortion;

- political, civil and social unrest or panic;

- racial tensions.

Conclusion

So far, we have been looking at the rich and varied toolset available to cyber attackers. Many of these tools are used by individuals with sometimes benign and sometimes malicious intent. Where things really get serious, however, is when the tools are put to use by organised groups of attackers. We will explore this increasingly common occurrence in the next chapter.

4

Organised Cyber Attacks

Introduction

As stated at the outset, cyber attack patterns have evolved from the one-to-one scenario, through one-to-many and into a many-to-one format. Whatever the future brings us, we should be prepared for increasing complexity and sophistication and certainly, one recent trend has been for attacks to take a more organised form. This has included organised criminal exploits conducted in order to gain financially, hacktivist attacks against firms and sectors, as well as apparently state-sponsored attacks against facilities and industries. In this chapter we will look more closely at some of these organised cyber attack scenarios, but the reader should keep in mind the fact that the lines are often very blurred and there are no hard and fast rules about where any given cyber security topic should really sit.

Crimeware

In October 2012 the following article was posted on the *Krebs on Security*[1] online Blog:

SERVICE SELLS ACCESS TO FORTUNE 500 FIRMS

An increasing number of services offered in the cybercrime underground allow miscreants to purchase access to hacked computers at specific organizations. For just a few dollars, these services offer the ability to buy your way inside of Fortune 500 company networks. The service I examined for this post currently is renting access to nearly 17,000 computers worldwide, although almost 300,000

---

1   http://krebsonsecurity.com/tag/dedicatexpress-com/ (accessed March 2013).

compromised systems have passed through this service since its inception in early 2010. All of the machines for sale have been set up by their legitimate owners to accept incoming connections via the Internet, using the Remote Desktop Protocol, a service built into Microsoft Windows machines that gives the user graphical access to the host PC's desktop. Businesses often turn on Remote Desktop Protocol for server and desktop systems that they wish to use remotely, but if they do so using a username and password that is easily guessed, those systems will soon wind up for sale on services like this one. Pitching its wares with the slogan, 'The whole world in one service', Dedicatexpress.com advertises hacked Remote Desktop Protocol servers on several cybercrime forums. Access is granted to new customers who contact the service's owner via instant message (IM) and pay a $20 registration fee via WebMoney, a virtual currency. The price of any hacked server is calculated based on several qualities, including the speed of its processor and the number of processor cores, the machine's download and upload speeds, and the length of time that the hacked Remote Desktop Protocol server has been continuously available online (its 'uptime'). Though it is not marketed this way, the service allows users to search for hacked Remote Desktop Protocol servers by entering an Internet address range, an option that comes in handy if you are looking for computers inside of specific organisations. For instance, I relied on a list of the IP address ranges assigned to the companies in the current Fortune 500 listing (special thanks to online banking security vendor Greenway Solutions for their help on this front). I made it about halfway through the list of companies in the Fortune 100 with names beginning in 'C' when I found a hit: a hacked Remote Desktop Protocol server at Internet address space assigned to networking giant Cisco Systems Inc. The machine was a Windows Server 2003 system in San Jose, Calif., being sold for $4.55. You'll never guess the credentials assigned to this box: Username: 'Cisco'; password: 'Cisco'. Small wonder that it was available for sale via this service. A contact at Cisco's security team confirmed that the hacked Remote Desktop Protocol server was inside of Cisco's network; the source said that it was a 'bad lab machine' but declined to offer more details.

The BBC and a number of other news outlets published similar articles describing the same scenario. Note also the use of an unregulated virtual currency to sell the service. It seems that hacking really has gone commercial.

THE DOGMA MILLIONS CYBER CRIME GROUP

The Dogma Millions group established a network of partners to promote their fake anti-virus software. In this case, the fake anti-virus also contained malware of its own in the form of the 'TDL Trojan/Rootkit'. Partners were offered a payment for each download triggered by their own site visitors.

The main features of the Dogma infection were a Dropper (see Figure 4.1), in the form of the fake anti-virus product, the Rootkit malware hidden inside the Trojan anti-virus, an encrypted file system to conceal the malware code from anti-virus tools and an Injector. Following a successful install of the anti-virus Trojan, the Dogma malware application then ran another instance of the Dropper which caused any Win OS to display a dialog prompt requesting an administrator password. If the user then entered the password (and here we see the importance of socially engineering the user to complete the attack), the Dropper was again re-started, this time with administrator privileges, including the LOAD_DRIVER privilege. With Admin rights activated, the malware could now load drivers for a range of malicious purposes by stealth and thus bypass many anti-virus applications.

In order to survive after reboot, the Dogma Rootkit also infected one of the system drivers, having randomly selected a driver that is loaded at boot time based on the DRIVER_SECTION list of all drivers loaded in the system. The malware would inject its own loader code and data in the first part of the selected driver and back up the overwritten driver code in a separate file so that it can restore the infected driver's original resources later. By this means, the size of the driver executable is not changed, again making detection difficult.

Some interesting additional observations clearly illustrated the orientation of the developers:

- the Dogma domain was registered in Germany;

- the Dogma IP address belonged to an ISP based in the USA;

- the malware was designed NOT to run in these countries:
  - Azerbaijan
  - Belarus
  - Kazakhstan
  - Kyrgyzstan

The Dogma Dropper

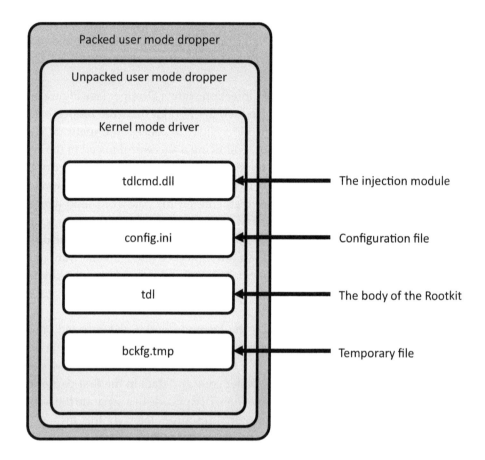

Figure 4.1   The Dogma Dropper structure

- Russia
- Uzbekistan
- Ukraine
- Czech Republic
- Poland.

The Dogma malware was also repacked every few hours to help it to avoid anti-virus detection and Dogma partners were instructed not to check whether anti-virus detection was effective on the downloaded files. As a result, the Dogma malware remained undetected by many anti-virus products.

The Dogma attack summary

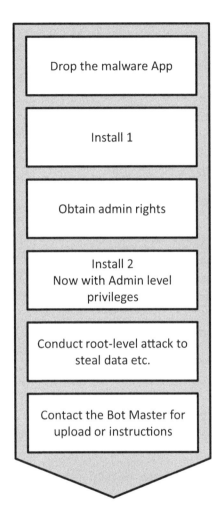

Figure 4.2   The Dogma attack summary

Once installed on each infected device, the available Dogma malware exploits included:

- download and store a file from the Dogma Command and Control (C&C);

- find a file and upload it to the Dogma C&C;

- delete a named file on the machine;

- point the machine at a URL (for example, where further drive-by infections might occur).

These capabilities were then sold in a Crimeware-as-a-Service model and the tasks listed were executed every 300 seconds on each infected machine (see Figure 4.2). In other words, Dogma reportedly used its infected network of devices to support a business model that allowed anyone to benefit from the scale and reach of the Dogma infection.

Attack Nets

Attack nets are one example of the emerging many-to-one model, although they are may not be as targeted in their activities as a pure DDoS attack, such as that launched against the banks via the LOIC can be.

There are three primary forms of attack net:

1. Botnets

2. Malnets

3. Cloud nets.

We will discuss the first two here and then look at Cloud nets later in the section on Cloud computing risks.

BOTNETS

As Figure 4.3 shows, a Botnet is a network of computers connected to the Internet and controlled by malware that has been installed by one of the means already described in Chapter 3. Individual computers in this network are called 'Bots'.

A remote controller ('Bot Master' or 'Herder') working in a C&C capacity will use the resources of this network of computers to carry out potentially

A Botnet Attack

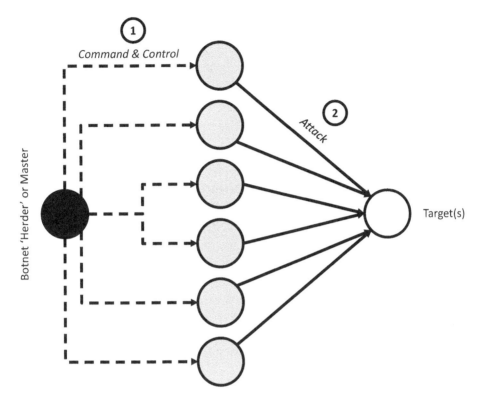

Figure 4.3   A Botnet attack

malicious activities such as DDoS attacks against another system, or to inflate traffic to other destinations in order to generate fraudulent revenue. Botnets are also widely used to generate Spam and many are rented out as a service to Spammers.

The Chameleon botnet, tracked between December 2012 and March 2013, infected an estimated 120,000 domestic personal computers in the United States and used deceptive means to simulate clicks or mouse pointer traces on or across website ads. Because advertisers pay the hosting websites for each click, this Botnet attack cost advertisers money, while potentially generating revenue for hosts.

Botnet attacks are one good example of a hybrid attack model. In the infection stage the attack targets many different devices. In the Attack Phase it may target one system in a DDoS attack or many systems via a Spam exploit.

It has been estimated that 25 per cent of PCs worldwide are connected to a Botnet without their user's knowledge.

Conficker

One of the largest known Botnets is Conficker which exploited an estimated 12 million machines. In one its most high-profile successes, Conficker forced the French Navy to take down its computer network and ground aircraft at several airbases. The UK Ministry of Defence, The Royal Navy, the German Armed Forces (Bundeswehr), the UK Parliament and Greater Manchester Police have all fallen victim to this Botnet attack.

Mariposa Botnet

Mariposa was a Spanish Botnet that infected an estimated 13 million PCs in over 190 countries. These included machines from more than 500 Fortune 1000 firms and the sole purpose of this Botnet was to gather online banking and email credentials. Mariposa was built using the 'Butterfly' Botnet Kit, another malware kit available online.

MALNETS

Malnets are effectively an evolution of the Botnet in which a combination of infected websites and seeding via Black-hat SEO techniques creates a network of infected sites that redirect users in a chain towards a malicious server. A Malnet is therefore comprised of unique domains, servers and websites *working together* to funnel users to the malware payload. The simplified visual map in Figure 4.4 shows the relationships between trusted sites, relays and the exploit servers to which users are directed.

The online magazine *The Register* explained Malnets in the following terms in an article published on 3 October 2012.

> *Malnets largely deal in mass market malware and as such are different from advanced persistent threats (APTs) associated with cyber-espionage attacks targeting large corporations and western governments.*

A Malnet Attack

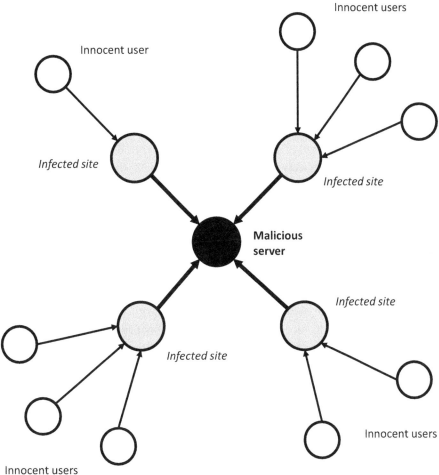

Figure 4.4   A simplified malnet map

Attacks will be updated and changed, but the underlying infrastructure used to lure in users and deliver these attacks is reused. The ease with which cyber criminals can launch attacks using malnets creates a vicious cycle, a process by which individuals are lured to malware, infected, and then used to infect others.

First the malnet drives a user to the malware. Then the user's computer is infected with a Trojan. Once the computer is compromised it can be used by the Botnet to lure new users into the malnet by using the infected machine to send Spam to email contact lists, for example. A compromised system can also be used to steal the victim's personal information or money, and, in some cases, can also function as a jumping-off point for attacks on neighboring machines.

'Their [malnet] infrastructure is comprised of several thousand unique domains, servers and websites that work together to funnel users to a malware payload,' Tim Van Der Horst, a senior malware researcher at Blue Coat, explained. 'This infrastructure of relay and exploit servers allows malnet operators to quickly launch new attacks that can be tailored to attract large groups of potential victims.'

Blue Coat expects malnets to account for more than two-thirds of all malicious cyber attacks in 2012. The firm is currently tracking more than 1,500 unique malnets, a 200 per cent (four-fold) increase from just six months ago.[2]

SPAM

'Spam' refers to unwanted or unsolicited communications, normally containing a marketing message, sent indiscriminately in large volume to people who have not consented to receive them. Spam represents another huge challenge for the Internet and for corporate networks and although most Spam is now filtered out so that users are not greatly affected, as a percentage of all traffic that the network has to be configured to carry it remains extremely high. It is in this context that Spam represents a cyber security challenge, as it always has the potential to flood a network such that normal services are interrupted.

While we normally think of Spam as email messages, there are many other forms, including IM Spam, social media (for example, Facebook) Spam and even mobile phone SMS Spam. Virtually any messaging technology comes with a Spam risk. John Naughton defines the Spam issue in these terms:

The requirements for effective Spamming are:

- Covert but effective control of lots of computers, dispersed geographically across the world, each of which can be used as a relay station for Spam.
- These computers should not be owned by, or traceable to, the Spammer. Their hapless owners should have no idea of what their computers are up to on the Net.

---

2   http://www.theregister.co.uk/2012/10/03/malnets/ (accessed March 2013).

- *Ideally, these relay stations can be switched on or off at will, so that it's difficult for the authorities to pin-point the source of the junk emissions.*
- *But when they're active, the relay station should be able to spew out a vast number of emails in a short period of time.*[3]

Denial of Service Attacks

These attacks typically involve flooding a target computer system with 'packets', such as communications requests or messages (for example, email), in order to cause it to overload and cease functioning. Any method that causes the target system to exceed its capacity can potentially be used in a DoS attack. There are many flavours of DoS attack:

- DDoS Attacks

- Permanent DoS Attacks

- Reflected DoS Attacks

- Degradation of Service Attacks

- Unintentional DoS

- Smurf attacks

- Fraggle attacks

- Ping flooding and SYN flooding.

You might be experiencing a DoS attack when computer programs run very slowly, services (for example, HTTP) fail at a high rate, large number of connection requests come from different networks, users complain about slow or zero website or network access, or servers show a very high Central Processing Unit (CPU) load. Alternatively, this might just mean that you work in a large public sector body.

---

3   John Naughton, 2012. *From Gutenberg to Zuckerberg.* London: Quercus.

A DoS Attack is designed to make a computer system or network unusable or unavailable to the intended user base by consuming and thus denying access to:

- bandwidth

- CPU

- memory.

Most targets for DoS attacks are Internet servers or websites although any type of networked system could potentially be attacked. Straightforward DoS attacks are easily detected and blocked by most modern systems and networks and so they are less frequent than they once were, as more sophisticated mechanisms are now used.

A SYN FLOODING DENIAL OF SERVICE ATTACK

In what is known as a SYN flood, a sending device is first given a forged address. The forged sender then sends a flood of requests for communication (in the form of small TCP packets called SYN packets (SYN = synchronise)) to the target system faster than the receiver can process them. Each request causes the target system to send an acknowledgment (an SYN-ACK packet) to the forged address and to allocate some capacity to handle the upcoming session.

The attacking device never responds to the SYN-ACK packet with its own final ACK packet that would establish the connection, but the half-open connections on the target system remain open for a period, consuming the capacity of the system to handle real communications requests. If performed in sufficient volume, this form of attack can block or significantly degrade all communications between the target system and other legitimate systems.

DISTRIBUTED DENIAL OF SERVICE ATTACKS

As mentioned above, a DDoS attack is an exploit involving a network of computers, possibly controlled by a Botnet Herder, to flood a target system (for example, by using SYN flooding as shown in Figure 4.5) with messages or communications requests at the same time. This approach makes the attack harder to distinguish from legitimate high traffic and helps to conceal the source of the attack.

A SYN Flood attack

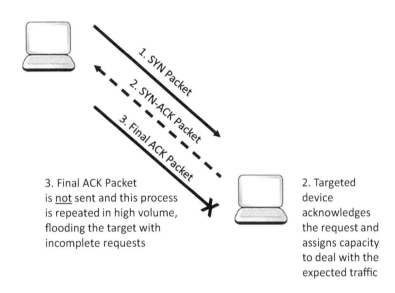

1. Attackers send incomplete communication requests

1. SYN Packet
2. SYN-ACK Packet
3. Final ACK Packet

3. Final ACK Packet is <u>not</u> sent and this process is repeated in high volume, flooding the target with incomplete requests

2. Targeted device acknowledges the request and assigns capacity to deal with the expected traffic

Figure 4.5   A SYN flood attack

The US Pentagon now regards both defences against and the ability to launch retaliatory DoS attacks in cyber space as a key part of its military strategy. Meanwhile, in September 2012, the assault on 14 leading US financial firms began, starting with JPMorgan, Citigroup and Bank of America, then moving successively to Wells Fargo, US Bancorp (USB) and PNC Financial Services Group Inc. (PNC).

The attacks denied online services to large numbers of US bank customers, although funds were safe and account information was not thought to have been exposed. Needless to say these attacks, which had been predicted weeks in advance by analysts, highlighted the potential effects of a properly organised and coordinated cyber assault on the financial services sector.

In an October 2007 article, which is still relevant today, in the online publication *Security Dark Reading* titled 'How to Trace a DDOS Attack', Kelly Jackson Higgins explained:

> At most any time of the day, there's a distributed denial-of-service (DDOS) attack underway somewhere on the Internet. Most of these attacks are being waged by Botnets – some as large as tens of thousands of Bot machines.
>
> Just like Botnets, DDOS attacks have become stealthier and tougher to trace than ever, with layers of Bot armies disguising the original source. 'Tracing a DDOS is a particularly vexing problem, with the whole notion of obfuscation and onion routing [techniques]' says Steve Bannerman, vice president of marketing and product management for Narus.
>
> And finding the origin of the attack is becoming more important than ever. Some DDOSs won't die if you don't really get to the source. 'It's critical to ID the source in some cases – not just because [you] want to know who's behind it, but [you] can't actually stop the attack' until you do,' Joffe says.
>
> But finding the source isn't as simple as identifying the IP addresses of the actual bots that sent the packets. 'In a large-scale DDOS, you don't initially ID the source, because it's often innocent,' he says. 'It tells you these 25,000 machines worldwide are the source of this attack, but it's a giant problem to track the owners of all those machines and get them to stop. Almost without exception, they are innocent owners who have no idea – and would not know how to turn [the attack] off.'
>
> There are three main stages of mitigating a DDOS attack. The key is for ISPs to stop the damage, while at the same time carefully peeling back the layers of the attack to be sure they actually get to the root of it.

There is a dependency on service providers to detect flooding attacks, for the simple reason that an attack that makes it as far as the target's local infrastructure has the potential to cause congestion before the local Firewall ever has a chance to detect it. In effect, a DDoS attack can simply overwhelm the firm's infrastructure. ISPs have much more capacity and are therefore better able to detect and block such attacks in real time.[4]

---

4   http://www.darkreading.com/security/perimeter-security/208804763/how-to-trace-a-ddos-attack.html (accessed 5 March 2012).

Advanced Persistent Threats

APTs are attacks that primarily target business and political entities. APTs require a high degree of stealth, may involve several threat actors (primary and secondary) and they can operate over a prolonged duration. Typical APT attack objectives go beyond immediate financial gain or service denial and compromised systems may continue to be of service even after they have been breached.

ADVANCED

Attackers utilise the full spectrum of intrusion technologies and techniques and although individual components may not be classed as 'advanced' (for example, malware) attackers can access or develop more advanced tools as required, often combining multiple attack methodologies and tools in a blended attack model. This is often taken as an indication that APT actors have nation state or corporate financing behind them, although that need not always be the case.

PERSISTENT

Attackers cam remain active in the target system for long periods and give priority to a specific task, rather than to opportunistic exploits and again, they often appear to be guided by external entities. Each attack is managed through on-going monitoring via a C&C channel and a 'low-and-slow' approach is often employed.

THREATS

Human involvement is central to these attacks. An APT attack does not involve a mindless and automated piece of code and APT attacks have a specific objective. The attackers are skilled, organised and often appear to be relatively well funded.

LOW AND SLOW

The low and slow approach involves attackers remaining invisible for as long as possible, while stealthily moving from one compromised host to the next without generating regular or predictable network traffic for C&C or data exfiltration purposes as they hunt for specific data or system targets. The typical anatomy of an APT malware tool is shown in Figure 4.6.

APT Malware

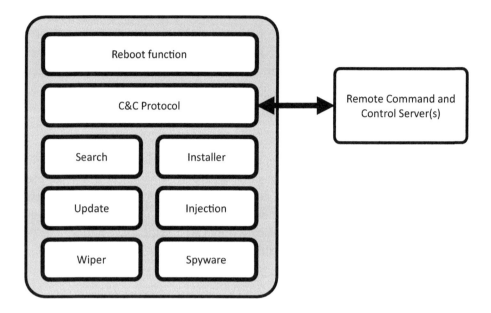

An APT operation may involve several threat actors (primary and secondary) and may be ongoing for a prolonged period of time.

Figure 4.6   Anatomy of APT malware

APT malware is commonly deployed to:

- infect digital systems;

- hide from detection systems;

- navigate networks;

- capture and extricate key data;

- set up covert channels for remote control;

- wipe or re-install itself;

- execute other payloads.

As of 2013, the current generation of APTs have an average file size of 121.85 KB, making them quite small files, although one of the best-known recent examples, Shamoon, is massive by comparison at 20 MB. Reportedly, only 24 per cent of APT cases are detected by anti-virus software, accentuating threat persistence.

COVERT REMOTE CONTROL

Remote C&C is often required to navigate to specific hosts, exploit and manipulate local systems and gain continuous access to critical information. Flame, for example, has been associated with over 80 remote C&C hosts or linked servers. If an APT cannot connect with its operators, then it cannot transmit any intelligence and this makes APTs similar to Botnets in many ways. APT malware can remain stealthy at the host level but network activity associated with remote control is more easily identified.

COMMAND AND CONTROL CHANNELS

Because APT malware is intended to target specific systems, it often requires remote C&C. Various C&C channels have been found, including Internet Relay Chat (IRC) or embedding in legitimate traffic, but most C&C is now web-based.

ADVANCED PERSISTENT THREAT DROPPER TECHNIQUES

APTs often follow the Dropper, Reporter, Wiper model. Common APT Dropper techniques, all of which have been covered earlier in the text, include:

Web-based attacks

- Drive-by Downloads (including via social media);

- Trojan malware infections;

- code injection or XSS attacks.

Spear-phishing attacks

- social engineering;

- physical media:
  – gifts (USB, CD, camera);
  – USB, DVDs, CDs left behind.

Advanced Persistent Threat Backdoors

APTs often include backdoor programs to allow re-entry following discovery and cleaning, and they support further access and hacking for lateral movement within a network. They can possess in-situ update capabilities so that the APT code itself can be patched or Wiped.

ADVANCED PERSISTENT THREAT DATA EXFILTRATION

APTs may steal credentials such as root passwords, Outlook passwords and other stored passwords. They can also steal and upload files by name or file type or by keywords and other parameters.

Custom storage and upload protocols are sometimes used to store the stolen data on the infected device itself, possibly in a back end SQL database that forms a part of the infection. This is done to allow for future retrieval or upload of the stolen data on command.

ADVANCED PERSISTENT THREAT STAGING AND DROP SITES

Many APTs use a combination of C&C, staging and drop site servers. The Flame attack involved over 80 such devices. As Figure 4.7 shows, this allows the attacker to mask his identity and most of the dropper or staging servers will themselves be infected sites whose owners are unaware of the part their device is playing in the attack.

KEY ADVANCED PERSISTENT THREAT STATISTICS 2012

- 100 per cent of APT backdoors made only outbound connections;

- 83 per cent used TCP Port 80 or 443;

APT Drop and Staging Sites

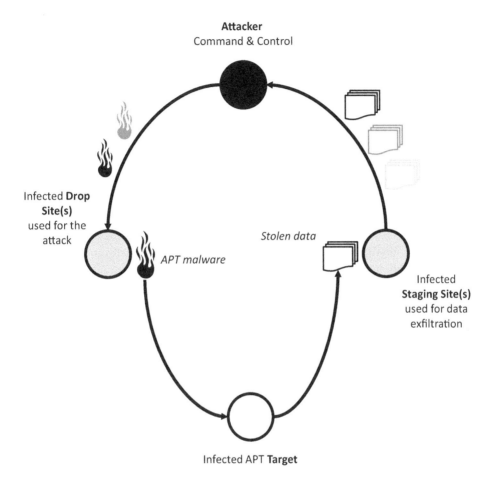

Figure 4.7   APT staging and drop sites

- 71 per cent used encrypted communication;

- 60 per cent were persistent on the machine.

ADVANCED PERSISTENT THREAT EXAMPLES

I have already referred briefly to three very prominent examples of APT attacks:

1.   Stuxnet

2.   Flame

3.   Shamoon.

Stuxnet

During the Second World War, when modern cryptography began to come of age, Germany's communications security rested on an encryption machine called Enigma, as well as on a subsequent series of increasingly advanced machines. In order to read enemy signals and gain the upper hand militarily, British and American intelligence had to build on work already done by Poland and France to crack the Enigma codes. This they proceeded to do and one of the most important intelligence coups in history was partly facilitated by the habit of one lonely German signaller who always used his girlfriend's name as his start of day test message. This meant that the Allied code breakers knew in this case, regardless of which Enigma settings were being used, exactly what the message was that they were decoding. In the simplest of operational user errors the greatest of strategic vulnerabilities may reside.

Stuxnet is an advanced computer Worm specifically designed to target systems running Siemens supervisory control and data acquisition (SCADA) systems, which normally run on industrial platforms. As it so happens, the Iranian nuclear programme runs SCADA systems on its secretly procured Siemens platforms and Stuxnet was used to attack these platforms in 2010, causing what is believed to have been significant physical damage.

Exactly how Stuxnet was introduced to the Iranian's SCADA systems is a matter of speculation, but it has been suggested that likely scenarios might include an employee picking up a discarded USB stick, or returning from home with an infected laptop. If so, this is little different from the type of error that undermined Enigma and lost Germany the last World War. It is also believed that Stuxnet used rogue certificates to evade detection during the attacks.

We don't know with certainty who created Stuxnet, although we can make a pretty good guess, because security firm Symantec has reported that almost 60 per cent of all known Stuxnet infections have occurred in Iran, suggesting that either there is a state or multi-state backer for the malware, or that there are some very angry anti-Iranian freelance hackers out there somewhere.

Flame

In June 2012, *The Washington Post* published a report[5] on the Flame virus, a form of Spyware Worm, which that paper suggested was jointly developed by the US National Security Agency, the CIA and Israel's military from as early as 2007 in order to gather intelligence in preparation for a sabotage campaign aimed at harming Iran's nuclear programme. So it appears to be the case that Flame gathered some of the data subsequently exploited by Stuxnet to launch the eventual attack, although this is merely conjecture.

It also appears that Flame primarily attacks computers running the Microsoft Windows OS and that the malware is being used for cyber espionage against a number of countries, most of which are in the Middle East. Like Stuxnet, Flame is used to target specific systems or network components and Flame can even evade most security software by adopting the Rootkit approach, attacking the OS at its root and thus bypassing system security. Flame may have been used during a cyber attack on Iran's main oil terminal at Kharg Island which resulted in the terminal being disconnected from the Internet in April 2012. Various versions of this tale abound and, as with most cyber security stories, the full facts may never be known.

CrySiS Lab of the Budapest University of Technology and Economics stated in its report on Flame that it 'is certainly the most sophisticated malware we encountered during our practice; arguably, it is the most complex malware ever found'. The report also speculated that the malware may have been operating in the wild for over four years before being discovered. How much secret data Flame discovered during that period can only be guessed, but the message for any major enterprise with less than national security grade security must surely be that all of your data is potentially at risk of exposure via attacks of this kind.

It is also worth noting that Flame is not designed to be industry specific; it can be used to attack any cyber espionage target and if history is a guide, we can expect either Flame, or at the very least the principles it uses, to find its way into the hands of private sector hackers and organised crime in due course.

Like several other Spyware Worms, Flame can spread to other systems over a local network or via USB sticks and DVD drives. It is said to record audio, to capture screenshots in a process known as 'screen scraping', and

---

5   www.washingtonpost.com/world/national-security (accessed 19 June 2012).

to log keyboard activity and network traffic. It is claimed that Flame can eavesdrop on Skype conversations, and also cause infected computers to track for Bluetooth signals in order to download contact information from nearby devices that have Bluetooth switched on. Any data collected by these means is delivered electronically to Flame's C&C servers scattered around the world. Remote commands can also be sent from these servers to the infected network to instruct Flame as to what to do next. Finally, Flame can be sent a 'kill' command which causes the malware to delete itself from the computer, hiding its tracks.

Describing Flame as being '20 times' more complicated than Stuxnet, Kaspersky Lab, another leading security firm, has commented that a full analysis of this cyber weapon could take ten years to complete. Of course, ten years in cyber security terms is a lifetime and by then we will no doubt have passed into an era of even greater complexity.

Shamoon

On 17 August 2012, the online publication *TechRadar*[6] carried a report on the Shamoon virus, which is believed to have been used in an attack on the computer systems of Saudi Aramco, one of the world's largest petro-chemical firms. Shamoon was described as a new, 'swipe-and-wipe' form of malware that is under investigation by security experts worldwide as they 'try to determine its source and how to keep it from infecting any more PCs'.

The virus works by infiltrating a system connected to the Internet and then spreading to other PCs within that network, including ones without a web connection. According to *TechRadar*, Aramco was the first major organisation known to have been attacked and an astounding total of 30,000 Aramco PCs had to be taken off the network and destroyed.

Meanwhile, security firm Symantec[7] described Shamoon as 'a new threat that is being used in specific targeted attacks against at least one organisation in the energy sector,' in a Blog post. 'It is a destructive malware that corrupts files on a compromised computer.. in an effort to render the computer unusable.'

---

6   http://www.techradar.com/news/world-of-tech/shamoon-malware-virus-swipes-and-wipes-pcs-1092677 (accessed 18 August 2012).
7   http://www.symantec.com/connect/blogs/shamoon-attacks (accessed 18 August 2012).

Shamoon is also known as 'Disttrack' and it steals data from PC folders like Documents and Settings and System32/Config, as do many other forms of malware. What is different about Shamoon is that it is 'able to overwrite the master boot record of the machines it infiltrates, crippling them completely'.[8] In the case of Aramco at least, stolen data was reportedly replaced by JPEG images, thus preventing any future recovery of the lost files.

Analysts think that Shamoon is a copycat virus, taking its main cues from the Flame 'Wiper' virus that swept through Iran, although it is thought by some that there is no connection between the two at a development level, given the differences observed in the way the programs have been designed. It is now also known that these attack tools are much older than was originally thought, with estimated creation dates going back as far as 2007 or 2005 being offered. This suggests that the infections might have been operating in the wild for several years before being detected. In fact, *TechRadar* reported that some experts think Shamoon is likely to be the work of 'Script Kiddies' inspired by the Stuxnet and Flame stories, implying that anyone might be next in line for this form of attack.[9]

Shamoon actually launches a three-pronged attack. Symantec say that they broke down the malware's components into these parts; a Dropper, a Reporter and a Wiper (see Table 4.1).

Table 4.1   The functions of Shamoon's main components

Shamoon's Components	Functions
The Dropper	Implants the malware on the system and supports its spread across the infected network of machines.
The Reporter	Collects data from the infected device and relays it back to the malware source, often replacing the stolen data with an image so that the data is both stolen and destroyed in one go.
The Wiper	Removes all evidence of the malware from the device in order to cover the tracks of the attacker.

Through each step Shamoon gathers, destroys and retrieves information from the target network for the attacker. Some think the virus's name may be taken from the Shamoon College of Engineering in Israel. Another theory has it named after one of the virus's authors – Shamoon being an Arabic version of

8   http://www.techradar.com/news/world-of-tech/shamoon-malware-virus-swipes-and-wipes-pcs-1092677 (accessed 18 August 2012).
9   Ibid.

the name 'Simon'. However, my own enquiries indicate that Shamoon might simply have been the work of a disgruntled Aramco employee, a less exciting scenario than state-level attacks, but a common one nonetheless.

Both the naming and the apparent copy cat nature of this virus should remind us of the fragmented, asymmetric and complex nature of risk in cyber space. All that is required to launch what might easily be mistaken for a state-sponsored high-grade attack is a single malware creation genius and a virtual gang of Script Kiddies. Trying to determine whether a state, a group of non-state actors, or a lone individual is responsible for any given attack is likely to be challenging and in many cases a definitive answer might never be found.

Much has also been made, mainly by anti-virus firms, of Shamoon's relatively massive file size, weighing in as it does at around 20 MB. Some anti-virus presenters have pointed to this as a mark of Shamoon's sophistication, although to my simple mind big isn't sophisticated, it's merely clunky.

The Blackhole Exploit Kit

The Blackhole Exploit Kit is currently the most prevalent web threat (as at Q3 2012) accounting for 28 per cent of all web threats detected by Sophos. Blackhole delivers various malicious payloads to a victim's computer and the suspected creators are a pair of Russian hackers nicknamed 'HodLuM' and 'Paunch'. Another example of this form of kit is the Phoenix Exploit Kit.

Blackhole and Pheonix work by allowing a would-be attacker to buy the kit and specify the desired attack options. The victim is tricked into loading a compromised web page or clicking on a malicious link in a spammed email and the malformed web page or email sends the user to a Blackhole landing page. This landing page contains obfuscated JavaScript that determines what OS is running on the victim's computer and then selects all of the exploits to which it is vulnerable. These exploits are then delivered via a Trojan.

Blackhole targets vulnerabilities in old versions of browsers as well as many popular plug-ins, so making sure that browsers, plug-ins and OS are up to date, running a security utility with good anti-virus and good host-based intrusion prevention system are all key defences.

In case you want to learn more about this threat type, the following domains[10] provide a great deal of information about current APT threats:

- malwaredomainlist.com

- abuse.ch

- spamcop.net

- team-cymru.org

- shadowserver.org

- mandiant.com

- hbgary.com.

Insider Threats

Although my previous title, *Demsytifying Communications Risk* (2012), addressed the insider threat in some detail, in a chapter written by Nick Mann, it would be remiss of me not to briefly mention the issue again because insiders and their trusted connections account for such a significant proportion of cyber security breaches. Table 4.2 summarises the insider threat as it relates to cyber security.

Table 4.2   The nature of the insider and trusted connection threat

Category	Remarks
Rogue employees	These are employees who either wish to hurt the organisation or who have decided to profit illegally from their position.
Malicious sub-contractors	Sub-contractors, particularly when they are single individuals, can be 'bought' or subverted by attackers or competitors and then used as an attack channel.
Social engineering	Employees may be vulnerable to this and social media, which may include promises of romance, has an increasingly important role.
Funded placement	In this scenario, an attacker is placed in the organisation via, for example, a work placement programme that is actually funded by a hostile organisation.
Walk in	Simply walking into a building, for example by using social engineering on security personnel, can provide sufficient access to allow for systems to be attacked.

---

10 All accessed during December 2012.

Category	Remarks
Trusted connections	Friends, associates, contractor's staff, regular visitors, delivery personnel and many others can often gain access or extract data with relative ease.
Shared credentials	Employees frequently share passwords or other authentication methods and these may be exposed or used by an ex-employee.
Partner system breaches	Those employed by partner businesses often have more access to our systems than we would consider wise, if we knew the details.
External hosting breaches	Data hosted or processed externally is potentially at greater risk that that held in-house and we often have very limited awareness of who the external users are.
Grey market equipment	Equipment can come with Spyware APTs pre-installed. The risk is increased for kit purchased second hand or at grey market rates.

Conclusion

Many of today's advanced attacks actually involve the use of a combination of attack techniques, for example:

- intrusion and takeover;

- followed by data theft;

- followed by DDoS attack directed at another system.

As the following chapter explains, The Cloud adds even more facets to the already complex picture that confronts us as cyber criminals pick from a growing cyber attack lexicon to construct innovative new blended attack techniques, and The Cloud represents yet another layer of complexity added to the cyber security landscape.

5

Cloud Risks

Introduction

What is a 'virtual machine'? Simply put, a virtual machine is a piece of software installed on another machine that looks feels and performs as if it was a separate device. For example, if I install the Windows OS and applications in a separate space on a Mac computer running the Apple OS, I can then choose to either run my Mac software or alternatively to run my 'virtual PC' on the same piece of kit. My PC-on-the-Mac is a 'virtual machine'.

This is a concept known as 'virtualisation'. Using variations of the virtual machine technique, it is possible to establish virtual machines or virtual applications ('VM-ware') on remote platforms anywhere that one can access and use across a network, typically the Internet, as shown in Figure 5.1. This approach is commonly referred to as 'Cloud' computing and it is normally intended to reduce the costs of hardware, software and support. This is all good, as long as my device keeps running, the power keeps flowing, my network connection keeps working, the Internet itself stays up and the remote Cloud service stays online. As you can see, the list of dependencies gets longer the more virtual things become and because any chain of dependencies is only as strong as its weakest dependency, virtualisation in the Cloud has attendant risks as well as rewards.

The Cloud

Virtualisation has created global computing resources that greatly exceed global computing needs and this provided an opportunity to sell that spare capacity cheaply. 'The Cloud' is a marketing term for the provision of these virtualised computing resources (normally via the Internet)

Virtualisation

1. The 'traditional' computing model

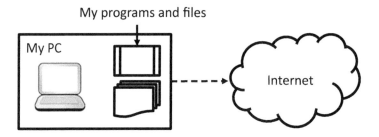

2. The 'virtualised' computing model

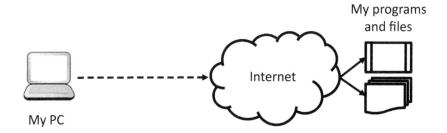

Figure 5.1   The road to virtualisation

and it consists of:

- infrastructure, services and platforms;

- provided remotely online;

- scale-able upwards or downwards;

- with no requirement for ownership;

- paid for on a usage basis.

The supply of low-cost capacity drives the process so that Cloud users can now access remote servers from anywhere and those servers may host VM-ware to provide any manner of user capabilities. A billing or customer relationship management system, for example, can be hosted in the Cloud, giving users exactly the same experience they would have had when the system sat on a main frame or server in their own building.

As noted, the main drivers for virtualisation are economic. There are clear economies of scale to be achieved by placing systems and processes in a Cloud setting, not least because of the immediate savings to be made in terms of hardware footprint and support. In addition, it is conceptually much easier to support growth and expansion if your systems are virtually located on a large platform than if they or physically close but sitting on a relatively small platform.

CLOUD CHARACTERISTICS

In *Cloud Computing for Dummies*, Judith Hurwitz, Robin Bloor, Marcia Kaufman, and Fern Halper state that:[1]

> *Cloud computing is the next stage in the Internet's evolution, providing the means through which everything from computing power to computing infrastructure, applications, business processes to personal collaboration can be delivered to you as a service wherever and whenever you need.*
>
> *The 'Cloud' in Cloud computing can be defined as the set of hardware, networks, storage, services, and interfaces that combine to deliver aspects of computing as a service. Cloud services include the delivery of software, infrastructure, and storage over the Internet (either as separate components or a complete platform) based on user demand.*
>
> *Cloud computing has four essential characteristics: elasticity and the ability to scale up and down, self-service provisioning and automatic de-provisioning, application programming interfaces (APIs), billing and metering of service usage in a pay-as-you-go model. This flexibility is what is attracting individuals and businesses to move to the Cloud.*
>
> *The world of the Cloud has lots of participants:*

---

1   http://www.ingrammicro.com/visitor/servicesdivision/cloudcomputingfordummies.pdf (accessed November 2012).

- *the end user who doesn't have to know anything about the underlying technology;*
- *business management who need to take responsibility for the governance of data or services living in a Cloud. Cloud service providers must provide a predictable and guaranteed service level and security to all their constituents;*
- *the Cloud service provider who is responsible for IT assets and maintenance.*

Cloud computing is offered in different forms: public Clouds, private Clouds, and hybrid Clouds, which combine both public and private.

Cloud computing can completely change the way companies use technology to service customers, partners and suppliers. Some businesses, such as Google and Amazon, already have most of their IT resources in the Cloud. They have found that it can eliminate many of the complex constraints from the traditional computing environment, including space, time, power and cost.

THE CLOUD IS NOW THE MACHINE

So, 'Cloud computing' is Internet-based computing, (the Internet *is* the Cloud and the Cloud is now the machine) where shared IT platforms, typically remote, provide resources, software and data storage services to local computers and other devices on demand. Take note that these Cloud servers are often large industrial facilities, some the size of several football fields, that look like something dreamed up by a science fiction movie director, so the reality is as far removed from a lightweight fuzzy 'Cloud' as it could be.

Some vendors of security and analytics software solutions have moved towards providing services in the Cloud. What this generally means is that your data will be transported to a remote point for processing and you will be given access to the results online. Whether or not this is appropriate for your business depends on how you balance risks against cost savings. Nevertheless, Cloud computing has been designed to lower the cost of ownership of IT infrastructure by eliminating excess capacity and leveraging the purchasing power of larger infrastructure owners, but Cloud computing also introduces major new challenges for IT Security, Fraud Control and IT Audit teams because sensitive data might now be stored and processed outside the secured perimeter.

THE SOFTWARE/PLATFORM/INFRASTRUCTURE MODEL

Cloud computing presents organisations with a rich set of options and the Software/Platform/Infrastructure Cloud deployment model demands informed decisions around what to deploy, how and where. These decisions must be based on both a cost/benefits analysis and a risk assessment; what is the value of the data or the criticality of the processes and systems you propose to deploy in the Cloud, and what is the impact of exposure, loss of data or loss of access to services over various time periods?

The three service options in the conventional Software/Platform/ Infrastructure model and their attendant features from a risk management perspective are:

- Infrastructure as a Service (IaaS) – the user does not manage the underlying Cloud infrastructure, but does have control over OS, storage, deployed applications and Firewalls, and so on.

- Platform as a Service (PaaS) – in this model the user does not manage the Cloud infrastructure (network, servers, OS or storage) but controls some or all of the deployed applications.

- Software as a Service (SaaS) – in this model the software, platform and infrastructure are all managed for the user by the Cloud service provider. This represents the ultimate evolutionary phase for Cloud services.

Increasing use of the Cloud has triggered a number of risk and security challenges, but most cyber security risks in the Cloud are essentially no different than those risks found anywhere else in the Internet and computing fields, although the structure of the Cloud does force us to think about the topography of risk in slightly different ways.

Conventional cyber security thinking focuses on 'securing the perimeter' as a key first step, because most risks manifest themselves as either intrusions, inbound across the perimeter, or as exfiltrations, outbound across the perimeter. With virtualisation and the Cloud this model makes less sense as it is hard, if not impossible, for the data owner to even define where the perimeter lies, much less control it.

A slight revision of the chain of thought results in the following list of Cloud security priorities in ascending order. There is nothing new on the list, but the order maps onto the structure of the new Cloud technology and service mix.

- **User level** – users of Cloud services need to be viewed in the traditional context as individuals capable of introducing infections or disclosing data and therefore subject to security controls and needing to be educated. But they also need to be thought of in terms of the joint tenant model – your users might be logging onto the same Cloud platform as the users of another firm. What is the scope for those other users to access your data, attack your services or simply cause a failure through infection of the shared platform?

- **Device level** – device security requirements don't change merely because your devices are connecting to the Cloud, but the likelihood that device types will proliferate as virtualisation becomes the norm does increase. This marriage of BYOD culture and Cloud technology means that firms now have to manage security issues related to a very extensive range of user devices, or that they need to introduce tight controls on what devices can be used and for what purposes.

- **Network infrastructure level** – as the key characteristic of most Cloud services is remote access across the Internet or a wide area corporate network, the model increases dependency on the network to the point where a loss of Internet access can equate to an inability not only to share data but to do any work at all. Dependency on connectivity has always been there, but the Cloud accentuates this dependency and makes it absolute for many Cloud users and their employers.

- **Cloud services platform level** – a similar dependency on remote platforms availability and security implies that running proper due diligence on Cloud service providers is essential. Who are they, where are they and are they actually providing the redundancy and hot backup they have promised? These are not questions you want to be asking in the middle of a crisis, so ask them before you sign on the dotted line.

- **Cloud services application level** – if your Cloud service provider is providing the applications you use, are those applications secure in terms of the confidentiality, integrity and availability of your data? Has the Cloud services provider patched every application to address known vulnerabilities? Is your data adequately protected from unauthorised access by the service provider's own staff, contractors or other Cloud service clients?

Any estimate of the risks associated with exposure of data placed in the Cloud should take into account the type of service being used and the relevance of the risks that are associated with most IT outsourcing projects and there are some additional questions any organisation needs to ask with respect to Cloud risks:

- Can you really outsource your accountability?

- What can you safely put in the Cloud?

- What data do you need to keep in-house?

- Who are you sharing your Cloud platforms with?

Table 5.1 summarises some of the main categories of Cloud risk.

Table 5.1   Main categories of Cloud risk

Risk	Short Description or Comments
Reputational	In the information age, customers and citizens hold service providers accountable for the security of their personal data. Cloud-based incidents will have huge potential impacts on brands and trust.
Litigation	Moving data, processes or applications to the Cloud is a business decision and liability for unexpected outcomes may well sit with the decision makers.
Regulatory	Regulations, such as those addressing data protection and billing accuracy, must still be complied with in a Cloud context. Organisations must assess the ability of third parties to comply.
Espionage	The theft of secret or commercially sensitive data is a growing trend. When data is placed in the Cloud, the number of points of access is multiplied.
National security	Government departments and defence contractors are particularly important targets for data theft and the Cloud will increase their exposure. Another consideration for non-US firms is the possibility that the provisions of the US Patriot Act might allow US authorities to access Cloud data situated within the US, even in cases where such access would contravene the data protection and privacy laws of the data controller. EU firms, in particular, should actively investigate this question before moving any regulated data to the Cloud.

Risk	Short Description or Comments
Data integrity	The completeness and accuracy of corporate and government data are directly proportional to service quality levels. Cloud computing puts even greater demands on us to validate data integrity.
Communications	By definition, the efficacy of the Cloud hinges on the performance and availability of the data networks. Security and redundancy, combined with realistic disaster planning, are therefore essential.
Systems	The migration of business processes, particularly real-time transaction processes, to the Cloud implies that organisations may no longer have full visibility of and control over mission critical functions.
Revenue	Revenue assurance, cost assurance, margin assurance, credit control and counter-fraud management must all work to ensure that a move to the Cloud does not increase levels of revenue leakage.
Third parties	Fraud and other risks related to third-party activities are increased by the Cloud as the dependence on a matrix of outsourced sub-contractors increases.
Cyber security	Similarly, exposure to cyber security attacks and cascading failures might potentially be exacerbated by Cloud technologies, particularly where infrastructure is shared with other organisations.

CYBER SECURITY RISKS IN THE CLOUD

Cyber security risks in the Cloud can be further divided by type:

- **Cloud malware** – software, which operates automatically without the presence of a user during the execution of the scenario.

- **Cloud attacks** – malicious attacks, which don't operate automatically and require the actions of an attacker during execution, either locally or remotely.

- **Co-location risks** – risk related to those you share the Cloud service with, as described in the example that follows.

CLOUD SERVICES 'SIDE CHANNEL ATTACKS'

Many Cloud adherents tend to dismiss security concerns by saying that security is built-in by design. However, an article appearing in *Technology Review* on 8 November 2012 referenced a report by security firm RSA regarding the potential for side channel attacks (attacks that sniff out encryption keys by exploiting physical access to a device, as depicted in Figure 5.2) on shared Cloud platforms:[2]

---

2   http://www.technologyreview.com/news/506976/how-to-steal-data-from-your-neighbor-in-the-cloud/ (accessed 10 November 2012).

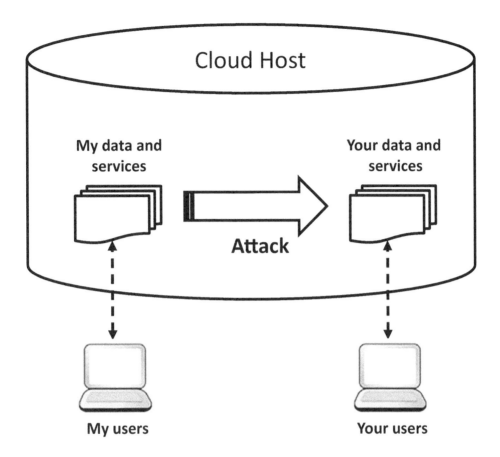

Figure 5.2   A conceptual Cloud 'side channel attack'

The (RSA) researchers have shown it is possible for software hosted by a Cloud-computing provider to steal secrets from software hosted on the same Cloud. In their experiment, they ran malicious software on hardware designed to mimic the equipment used by Cloud companies such as Amazon. They were able to steal an encryption key used to secure emails from the software belonging to another user.

The attack demonstrated is so complex that it is unlikely to be a danger to customers of any Cloud platform today, but the experiment answers a longstanding question about whether such attacks are even possible. The proof suggests that some very valuable data should not be entrusted to the Cloud at all, says Ari Juels, chief scientist at RSA and director of the company's research labs. 'The basic lesson is that if you've got a highly sensitive workload, you shouldn't run it alongside some unknown and potentially untrustworthy neighbour,' says Juels.

*Michael Bailey, a computer security researcher at the University
of Michigan, notes that the software attacked (an email encryption
program called GNUPrivacy guard) is known to leak information,
and that the experiment wasn't carried out inside a real commercial
Cloud environment. However, he says, the result is significant and will
inspire other researchers – and perhaps real attackers – to prove that
such attacks can be carried out.*

*'The reason I'm excited is that someone's finally given an example
of a side-channel attack,' says Bailey. 'It's a proof of concept that raises
the possibility that this can be done – it will motivate people to look for
more serious versions.'*

*A particularly concerning demonstration would be to use the
method to steal the encryption keys used to secure websites offering
services such as email, shopping and banking, says Bailey, although
that would be much more challenging. Juels says he's working on
exploring how far he can push his new style of attack.*

From this research we can draw a few important lesson about shared resources
in the Cloud. We need to identify them, investigate their vulnerabilities and
also determine who our joint tenants might be, or at least include contractual
clauses to exclude lists of specific tenants or types of tenant from our shared
platform or resource.

DROPBOX-LIKE SERVICE RISK

As with any online storage system, files secured in Dropbox, GoogleDrive or
iCloud-type services are only as secure as you (and the Cloud service provider)
make them. Many of the risks we see are the same ones that afflict any other
IT storage platform. The most common vulnerabilities are non-technical and
include:

- simple, easily guessed passwords;

- password reuse across multiple sites and accounts;

- storing of sensitive documents in the Cloud – a failure of data
  classification;

- storing of unencrypted data in the Cloud.

While none of these vulnerabilities is new, the added factors of transmission during upload, download and synchronisation, plus the dependency on an often unvetted Cloud service provider's security processes and staff simply increases the risks. Once your data is in the Cloud you no longer have control over it, so be thoughtful about what you put there and what you keep on your own systems.

Employee behaviour and awareness

Our own employee's behaviour is another factor. My firm was recently invited to share a Dropbox folder with a client company that wished to give us access to a report. Instead of just sharing the folder containing the report, the Admin at the client shared her firm's entire Dropbox archive with us – every single report covering hundreds of unrelated matters, most of them highly sensitive. The best password in the world won't prevent that kind of error and who knows how many times the same person had made the same blunder in the past?

Top tips for Dropbox-type security

Simply saying 'We don't use Dropbox' might not be a sustainable position given the direction of travel most users and firms are taking. Think about all those corporate leaders who said, twenty years ago, we won't use email. So, once again, you need to develop and promulgate some guidelines:

1. Make employees aware of the risks.

2. Define and communicate a sensible data classification strategy; what can and what must not go into Cloud sharing and storage?

3. Evaluate the security provided by various Cloud service providers and specify the ones that staff can use.

4. Purchase corporate licences and give staff user rights, rather than allowing them to make use of personal accounts.

5. Ensure that your Dropbox-type contract includes a provision for full data backup and restore.

6. Encourage the use of strong passwords.

7.   Discourage repeat password use.

8.   When a password breach does occur, require ALL users to reset their passwords, not merely the ones you believe to have been compromised; often, you won't really know the true extent of the compromise, merely the passwords that attackers have exploited *so far*.

9.   Always assume the worst and regard all unencrypted Dropbox or iCloud files as public data, then use the services with that mindset.

10.   Consider using optional services that support centralised administration of user data in the Cloud to prevent disgruntled staff from denying you access to their work files. Note however that this can be a costly proposition.

The bottom line is that ignoring the Cloud and its associated services is like ignoring the wind. You can try not to think about it, but it's going to push you around anyway. Dropbox-like services are genuine business enablers that can give users real competitive advantage in the marketplace.

The responsibility for designing and delivering a secure Cloud service really lies with Cloud service providers, but many of their offerings still fail to live up to even the most rudimentary corporate security standards. Until they redress that failure, we probably need to strike a balance between allowing staff to use effective tools and keeping data secure.

CLOUD ATTACK NETS

There's a lot of talk about cyber criminals using the Cloud as a platform for their attacks, but it is still unclear as to whether or not so-called 'Cloud nets' will become a dominant means of attack. From a pure anonymity perspective, it is always going to be better to takeover other devices than to rent them and leave a possible audit trail and there is the added advantage that a takeover carries zero investment risk, whereas setting up in the Cloud, while cheap, is not free.

On the other hand, it will probably be harder to detect a Cloud-based attack that does not involve the infection of 'Bot' machines because the Cloud devices will not have an owner running anti-virus and other system checks or logging system statistics. This reduced chance of being detected technically is complemented by the fact that it may be faster and easier to develop an effective DDoS framework in the Cloud, so we should not completely discount the threat of Cloud-based attacks.

Conclusion

As there is a financial limit to what we can construct in terms of technological defences, it is awareness of how cyber attacks are constructed that must take precedence and, as the following chapter explains, the emergence of Web 2.0 technologies means that user awareness is more important than ever before.

6

Web 2.0 Risks

Introduction

While the Internet is a global network-of-networks running TCP/IP, the World Wide Web ('www' or 'The Web') is something different. 'The Web' refers to a system by which billions of web pages are linked to each other to be accessed *via* the Internet, but the Web is not the Net, although the two terms are so close that this can be confusing. These are two separate technologies and the Internet supports several other applications, including email and FTP. When people talk about the combined beast that is the Internet *plus* the World Wide Web (plus everything else 'online' as well) they sometimes refer to it as the 'InterWeb'.

INTERWEB 1.0, 2.0 AND 3.0

You will no doubt come across references to the evolving Web/InterWeb from time to time and definitions abound, some being more comprehensible than others. I tend to use the following mental map to capture the fundamental characteristics of each stage in the evolutionary process:

- **InterWeb 1.0** – we used the Internet to browse hyperlinked web pages that are stored on remote servers. Only a tiny minority of people actually created that hyperlinked content and most were merely consumers. Visiting Web 1.0 was akin to going to a digital library. This is where we are coming from.

- **InterWeb 2.0** – users are both creators and consumers of content. Social media sites like Facebook, Blogs, Wikis and countless other tools put the power to publish into the hands of consumers. However, most content is still produced by humans for human consumption and it is not written in a way that machines can understand it. This is essentially where we are now.

- **InterWeb 3.0** – in the next Web generation, machine-readable content starts to take over from purely user readable content in response to the huge volumes of data held online and the limited capacity of traditional search engines to crawl through it. Computers are able to do more than just return a list of query results – they can compile a result for a human user that has the appearance of an article or web page. Online content effectively becomes infinite as its structure and presentation are no longer predefined but depend instead on the parameters of each user query, and the profile, preferences and history of the user. This is where we might be heading.

HYPERLINKED

The system used for creating linked web documents is called 'hypertext'. These documents (or web pages) are viewed in a 'web browser' such as Internet Explorer, Firefox or Chrome. The links between hypertext pages are called hyperlinks. Web users can navigate from web page to web page and read text, view movies or images or download files, all via this common set of protocols.

When you navigate to a web page, you will generally see a URL (the address of a network resource) that starts with either HTTP or HTTPS, followed by a domain name beginning with either 'www' or some other prefix. While most web servers still use the 'www' prefix, this is not mandatory.

'HTTP' refers to the Hypertext Transfer Protocol, thus telling your browser which protocol is in use. 'HTTPS' is a reference to the HTTP *secure* protocol which has an additional layer of encryption. Wherever you see 'ht' as a part of some online acronym, you can be pretty sure that it means 'hypertext' and that you are dealing with the same basic set of protocols.

Web 2.0 Risks

Social media is increasingly diverse and differentiated. What started as 'social networking', with a focus on linking friends together online or allowing strangers to become friends, has now mushroomed into a plethora of sites providing everything from commentary to games. This list of current social media functions will provide some idea of its diversity of purposes:

- publishing of content for restricted viewing or use (for example, YouTube);

- sharing of content (for example, Flikr);

- discussions and micro-blogging (for example, Tumblr);

- personal networking (for example, Facebook);

- business networking (for example, LinkedIn);

- life streaming (for example, Twitter);

- life casting (for example, Blogtv);

- virtual worlds (for example, Second Life);

- social games (for example, Farmville).

The common thread that connects them all is still the networking feature, but many of those networks have now grown in size so that the average user has access to a much wider range of services.

SOCIAL MEDIA EXPLAINED USING FOOD

This is my take on a delightful image found online that explains social media using doughnuts. In Table 6.1 I have changed the food type and added some social media sites to the list.

Table 6.1   Social media explained with chips

Social Media Site	Message or Purpose
Twitter	I'm eating chips now!
Facebook	I 'Like' chips
LinkedIn	My skills include chip eating
Foursquare	I normally eat chips here
Tripit	Next week I'll eat them here

Social Media Site	Message or Purpose
Flickr	A picture of my chips
Pinterest	Other people's great chip pics
YouTube	Watch my chip eating demo
Google	Find places for chips
Wikipedia	Explore the history of chips
Wikileaks	Learn why chips secretly rule the world

THE SOCIAL MEDIA GENERATION GAP

When it comes to social media take-up and awareness, there is a clear generation gap of sorts that affects our collective ability to understand the medium, exploit its benefits or manage its inherent risks. Commentators have broken the population down into groups, in terms of their relationship with the InterWeb, for example:

- **'Netizens' or digital natives** – primarily members of Generations Y and Z who were born after the Internet revolution and who see technology as just one more natural facet of their lives.

- **Digital immigrants** – those of us who are long-time users of social media and other Internet technologies and tools, but who remember a time when the printed word was king and even the Fax machine was shrouded in mystery.

- **Digital emigrants** – a small minority who are abandoning sites like Facebook in favour of the old ways.

- **Digital aliens** – primarily older people who have not yet engaged with the technology, whether out of fear, lack of time, poor access or lack of perceived need.

Many business and political leaders fall into this last group, with the result that their ability to engage effectively with the Netizens is very limited. When they do attempt to engage online, it generally comes across as forced and unnatural and is often painful to watch. Given society's increasing dependence on social media and related tools, this disconnect has serious implications for communication and understanding.

THE TENSION BETWEEN SOCIAL MEDIA AND SECURITY

In order to fully grasp why social media is so ubiquitous and so powerful we first need to understand the concept of 'Identity Capital'. Identity capital is the main business driver behind most social media sites and it also lies behind many of the social media risks you will encounter. The basic idea is actually very simple. In a globalised market where consumers hold power over brands, through their ability to exercise choice, gaining superior knowledge about a consumer's likes and dislikes, personal profile (age, sex, location and so on) and the extent of their social network can position a corporate player to market its offering more cost-effectively.

The ultimate goal of mass marketers is to achieve what they call 'a customer segment of ONE'. Think of it as their version of heaven. In the theoretical customer segment of ONE universe, a marketer would know *everything* about *every* individual in the market place and would thus be able to pitch his products or services in exactly the right way to each person with totally focused and customised advertising, labelling and pricing. If you have seen the film *Minority Report* you may have some idea of what this idea encompasses.

Social media is the first technology that gives corporate marketers a glimpse of this perfect future and the information that social media sites hold about their users therefore represents their real value – their Identity Capital.

A second development is the rise of the social media 'Brand Ambassador', a person who promotes a brand via their social media network, sometimes for free, even unwittingly, but potentially on contract from the manufacturer. This is viewed as being particularly effective because others are more likely to trust the messenger and because the ambassador's own social network is potentially like-minded and interested in the same things.

ADVA Games (online games offered for free, but heavily branded by firms) are another major growth area. You may have seen some of them. Again, these are viewed as excellent marketing engines because each game is tailored to appeal to a different demographic, allowing the advertising to be focused on the target market. The ad or product placement may also be more subtle, such that the game might give you a branded car to drive as part of a game mission, rather than just flashing up an annoying car advert on your screen. The days of 'click here to skip the ads' are probably numbered.

Each of these evolutionary developments increases the potential of many social media sites to act as very powerful marketing engines, although each faces its own challenges.

Social Media Vulnerabilities

Cyber attacks are, in the main, conceptually simple:

- gain entry;

- execute the attack payload;

- wipe evidence and/or exit the system.

Our collective technical defences are now relatively advanced and most large organisations already have these defences in place, yet the attacks continue. One common point of entry is via users and social engineering via social media is believed to have become a preferred technique for learning passwords or exposing other confidential and personal data.

This represents a widespread challenge for organisations and the BYOD culture makes control even more difficult because of the blurring of the traditional boundary between corporate device use and personal device use. Services like LinkedIn complicate the picture even further since they have a clear business benefit while also serving as a social networking tool.

As social networking sites become the default way of keeping in touch and sharing photos, interests and experiences with associates, friends and family, companies need to come to grips with the fraud risks that this technology can introduce. Many corporate firms have also started to use social networking sites such as LinkedIn, Pipl, Spoke and Naymz to network their employees or to search for expertise. In addition, many are using Facebook and Twitter to market their brands and reach out to customers and employees.

Social engineering via social media

While anyone can clearly see the benefits of social networking, and while it is important that corporate users also experience them, we must also accept that there are potentially serious downsides arising from poor social media practices and companies need to make sure that employees and consumers use these sites responsibly to avoid putting themselves, or their businesses at risk.

It is no coincidence that 'social media' and 'social engineering' both start with the same word. Social media businesses often use very clever social engineering ploys to persuade users to post personal data on their site. Facebook, for example, uses the implied promise of new friendships to get singletons (and sometimes, not so singletons!) to put their relationship status, photos, contact details and much else online.

In 2012, UK insurers Legal and General (L&G) published the results of a study they had commissioned into Facebook user's habits.[1] They were concerned that burglaries affecting their policy holders were regularly facilitated through social engineering attacks via Facebook. Burglars were reported to be setting up fake profiles, normally using attractive female identities, and then 'friending' strangers in order to search for potential victims. They would try to ascertain through online dialogue when their 'friends' might be away on holiday, where they lived and their financial status.

The survey produced some very interesting results which security and risk managers should consider. While 46 per cent of women surveyed admitted that they had made friends via Facebook with at least one person based purely on them having an attractive photo on their profile page, 52 per cent of men made the same admission. No surprises there, one might say. The implications, however, are very serious. Even if one has never 'friended' a stranger on that basis, how many of your online friends have? We are now connected, one step removed, to those strangers and our friends may innocently share information about us without our knowledge or consent.

A SIMPLE SOCIAL MEDIA EXPERIMENT

In support of the L&G survey my own company ran a simple social media experiment. This involved temporarily setting up two fake Facebook profiles, purely for test purposes. The first was for an unattractive male; a Neanderthal image and name were used to remove any subjectivity. The second was for a very appealing female; subjectivity in this case was largely removed by asking male members of the team to pick from a set of 100 images.

---

1   http://www.legalandgeneral.com/_resources/pdfs/insurance/digital-criminal-2012-report.pdf (accessed November 2012).

The results of this test reinforced the findings of L&G. After three days, the Neanderthal had 12 Facebook friends while the attractive female had 110. A month later the male's tally had risen to 35 while the female had 136. Approximately 30 per cent of the female's friends had actually asked to be added to her network without being approached, often because they had a friend in common. The scope for social engineering using this ploy is clearly immense.

TRIADIC CLOSURE

A concept in social network theory suggested by German sociologist Georg Simmel, Triadic Closure (see Figure 6.1) is the property among three nodes A, B, and C, such that:

- if a strong tie exists between A–B and A–C;

- there is a weak or strong tie between B–C.

In social media terms, this implies that I am more likely to 'friend' with you if you are already a friend of a friend.

In 2011 the University of British Colombia (UBC) decided to test this concept and a team of researchers created 100 automated Facebook 'Bots' that generated 5,000 random friend requests. The team claimed that 976 (19 per cent) of these first tier requests were accepted.

The researchers then generated a set of second round requests, this time targeted at friends of their 976 new 'friends'. A total of 2,079 (59 per cent) of these second round requests were reportedly accepted, demonstrating the effect on acceptance levels of the invitee seeing that the person approaching them already has one friend in common.

It should be noted that Facebook disputes these test results claiming that UBC exploited its trusted IP address and even that it may have distorted its figures. However, our results at TRMG clearly suggest that UBC's research is on the right track and we can draw a set of conclusions related to social engineering via social media:

- looks are more important than Triadic Closure as a determining factor in friend request acceptance;

Triadic Closure applied to social media

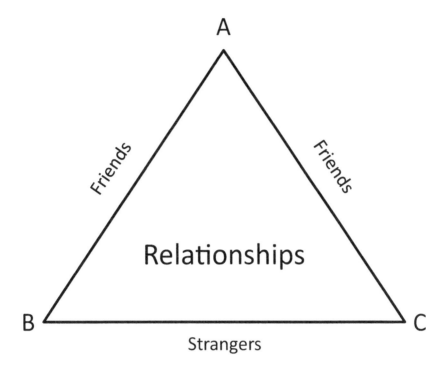

C is markedly more likely to accept a friend request from a stranger (B) if:
1. C and A are already friends and;
2. C believes that A and B are also friends.

Figure 6.1   Triadic Closure

- Triadic Closure is nevertheless important;

- Triadic Closure can override natural caution even when a profile is clearly faked;

- apparent good looks combined with Triadic Closure represent a 'killer app' for social engineering.

The underlying risk is the ease with which fake social media profiles can be created. Additional social media engineering ploys include using images of babies to trigger positive associations in the viewer's medial orbitofrontal cortex, using images taken from a height, which have again been shown to trigger positive responses, selecting images that relate to particular target groups and ensuring that images and text conform to known width-to-height ratios.

Top Social Media Risks

Many risks arise from these social media vulnerabilities and I will describe the main ones here, but you can no doubt come up with a few of your own.

PEOPLE RISKS

The key risks in social media are the people risks. These are the risks that affect each of us, our colleagues or our families directly, although they may also have an impact upon the business.

Harassment of employees via social media sites by persons with a grudge against the business, for example by single issue extremists who rightly or wrongly associate the business with an objectionable or unethical practice, has become a major problem in many sectors. In our complex and interconnected world we can't always predict when such grudges might arise and we may merely be providing a service or product for another firm that is engaging in alleged unethical practices without our knowledge. This distance won't always protect us.

Identity theft leading to fraud affecting employees or customers can be perpetrated, in part, via social media. Questions about age, birth dates, address information and family details, as well as images posted online, can provide the bulk of the material that an identity thief requires. Our awareness of this potential risk is essential if we are to protect ourselves and our families from what is an increasingly common form of crime.

Personal security risks include cases where employees give out personal details online, such as those reportedly given out to burglars. One should also bear in mind that the information we post about others might be equally sensitive.

Child exploitation is a growing problem, for example in relation to images of and information about children, their schools, addresses, names and ages, likes and dislikes. Children may be a target of criminals if they use social media, because children will often give out sensitive information about their parents innocently, particularly if they have been engineered into believing that they are communicating with another child.

INFORMATION SECURITY RISKS

Loss or disclosure of information via social media sites is a huge risk and incidents are regularly reported in the press. Examples of how this can happen include:

- Data theft facilitated by technical exploits that can use social media as a vector. In one major case, reportedly targeting senior executives in a leading online firm, hackers hijacked the Facebook accounts of the executive's children. They then sent messages via Facebook to the executives from their children's accounts saying, 'Click this link, it's cool.' When the executives clicked the links, believing the messages actually came from their kids, they unknowingly downloaded malware (malicious software) onto their hard drives. This malware then extracted secret corporate data and sent it to the hackers own servers in a foreign country.

- Disclosure of sensitive information by employees via social media sites where employees innocently post share sensitive information. Examples are disclosures about pending profit warnings, job losses, missed sales targets or faulty products. Any of these disclosures can seriously damage a firm's share price, putting jobs at risk, and when they are made via social media sites they may go viral, spreading around the Internet in minutes. Retrieving the message or correcting the damage done is usually impossible.

- Social engineering of employees by persons using false identities online in order to extract confidential information from them. Corporate espionage is a growth sector and corporate spies use social media to target the employees of competing firms. A brand name or company name search of LinkedIn can produce a list of hundreds or thousands of potential targets for such a spy who will then proceed to send messages using faked identities, possibly talking about job opportunities or even posing as a member of the same firm in a distant location. Once the online relationship has been built up, the spy will start to ask more sensitive questions and a small but significant minority of people may be inclined to provide answers.

TECHNOLOGY RISKS

There are forms of malware that can be introduced onto a corporate PC or laptop as a result of following a link or opening a file attachment in a social media message. One example is the Koobface malware App which was specifically designed to be spread via Facebook.

BRAND AND REPUTATION RISKS

Naturally, a concern for any firm is the protection of its brand and reputation. This affects share value and profitability and therefore the job security of everyone employed. The scope for business harm via misguided or malicious use of social media sites by employees or outsiders is truly immense.

Brand damage may occur through the fabrication of fake branded sites that send out negative messages purporting to come from the company itself. Examples of this form of malicious attack have already been seen on Twitter and the effort required to deal with them can be enormous. Setting up a fake Facebook account or a Twitter feed is a trivial task. No identity verification is needed and no checks are conducted to ensure that, if a corporate name and logo are used, this is being done with the knowledge and consent of the owners of the brand, yet another failure of corporate responsibility on the part of the social media industry.

Damage to shareholder value through disclosures of socially engineered insider trading data is another important risk. A clever online social engineer or corporate spy may set up a network of contacts within the business by way of social media. Again, the only way to avoid risks of this kind is for employees to be aware and to ask themselves why an online friend might be asking particular questions.

Interception of sensitive communications may occur if social media is used as the medium. The barriers between email, SMS, IM and social media are becoming increasingly blurred. It is so easy just to stick that little piece of information into a Facebook post rather than to email it. However, what employees enter into any social media site has the potential to go global – it is even worse than accidently sending an email to the whole company; it may go to millions of users outside the business.

TWITTER STORMS

In June 2012, online activists organised a 'Twitter Storm'[2] to protest against governmental fossil fuel subsidies offered to industry. The effort was so successful that it achieved top trending status in the USA and was in second place globally. The blitz was supported by actors Stephen Fry, Robert Redford and Mark Ruffalo, as well as numerous politicians and environmentalists and used the hash tag #endfossilfuelsubsidies. The potential impact of social media of brands and reputations has rarely been better demonstrated.

FACT CHECKS

Other interesting social media effects include fact checking and collective intelligence. Fact check feeds allow the collective voice of the global community to challenge virtually any public statement. This is having an important effect on what political and business leaders can say, constraining their remarks and, hopefully, keeping them honest. (Well, if not actually honest then a lot more careful than some have been in the past).

Conclusion

Social media is merely the most prominent market in which Identity Capital (that is, personal data and usage profiles that are captured and stored as a business asset) is paramount. This trend is clearly in conflict with some of the principles of data protection that many westernised societies adhere to. How this conflict plays out and whether social media will need to adapt to meet data protection requirements, or whether the opposite will happen, is one of the most interesting topics in cyber security, but for the time being many threat actors view Web 2.0 data sets and users as prime targets. In the next chapter we will take a closer look at who these threat actors are and what motivates them.

---

2   http://www.guardian.co.uk/environment/2012/jun/18/twitter-storm-fossil-fuel-subsidies (accessed 28 June 2012).

7

Cyber Security Threat Actors

Introduction

To again paraphrase John Naughton, by looking at web technology as a system, taking into account its inter-relationships and dependencies (rather than simply examining it node by node through a purely technical lens), we come to understand that change within the whole is systemic; when one component changes, the effects ripple through the entire system. In like fashion, risk can also be systemic; its effects can ripple through a system in a cascade, having many unforeseen impacts at a distance in both physical space and in time. This is chaos theory in action and the more complex the InterWeb and cyber security technologies become, the more chaotic the risk picture.

Before we can even hope to interpret these complex and interwoven events, we need to develop models for assessing the motivations of those behind them. This will always be a moving target, but we can make a start. There are at least four main classes of cyber threat source and they have very particular characteristics:

- disasters:
  - natural disasters;
  - man-made disasters;

- failures:
  - beyond control of organization;
  - of controlled resources and technical or mechanical processes;

- human errors:
  - of omission;
  - of commission;

- attacks:
  - cyber attacks;
  - physical attacks;
  - social engineering attacks;
  - attacks on brand or reputation.

When considering cyber crime and security, we focus on attacks and on the threat actors behind them, of which there are again several types.

Access techniques are shared, which is to say that any attacker may select any access technique, according to the situation and their own levels of skill. However, exploitation methods are many and varied. They are determined not only by skill but also by motivation. Different types of attacker can have very different motivations and this will affect how an organisation needs to deal with the effects of an attack and its exploit mechanisms.

A well-constructed cyber security plan must address the prevention of access and the management of various forms of exploitation as distinct issues. In addition to protecting the perimeter, the plan must address scenarios in which the attack is persistent and in which the attacker is still active within the system(s) even after he has been detected, as we saw in the APT examples.

Attacker Profiles

There are many possible motives behind any cybercrime attack and before we talk about controls, we need to develop a sound understanding of what the most common of motivations might be. Although there is inevitably a lot of grey in the picture, I like to place attackers into one of the following groups:

- cyber warriors and spies;

- techno-criminals;

- technology-enabled criminals;

- opportunists.

CYBER WARRIORS AND SPIES

We are living in the age of cyber conflict and cyber espionage. This shouldn't come as a surprise because our key infrastructures have always been the primary target for enemies and competitors.

Cyber warriors and spies fall into three main categories:

1.   state-sponsored;

2.   corporate;

3.   terrorists.

State sponsors

State sponsors tend to be less driven by short-term business cases and are more interested in developing and refining their cyber warfare capabilities over the long term, although we are now entering an era in which execution may eclipse planning and reconnaissance as the primary goal.

- **Cyber warfare capacity** – many state sponsors appear to be still testing and refining their cyber warfare capabilities and a minority are clearly very far advanced in this arena. Much of what happens today on the Internet, in terms of state-sponsored attacks, is probably part of that testing process.

- **Mapping of targets** – intelligence in war has always been a leading requirement for victory and this was never truer than in the cyber warfare sphere. The Internet is more complex to map than physical geography, and it also shifts and evolves constantly, with dramatic growth expected to continue for some years until the bulk of the world's population is online. Therefore, the task of locating, accessing and assessing targets for cyber attacks is a mammoth one, and once mapped every target will need to be constantly reassessed for changes in technology or security mechanisms.

- **Secret data** – states want secret data of several types, including military, economic, political, commercial and personal. This data is needed in order for them to assess the intentions and capabilities of potential opponents, identify their strengths and weaknesses, advance the business goals of their own national corporations and target key individuals.

- **Deniability** – finally, states require deniability in peacetime, for diplomatic and political reasons. Therefore, we will continue to see fledgling cyber attacks and penetrations being carried out by non-state actors, some of whom will doubtless be acting as proxies.

Corporate sponsors

Corporate espionage on the Internet and within cyber systems in general has become increasingly serious over the past decade. In 2009, the German Government accused state-owned Chinese companies of conducting espionage activities against German firms that cost them several billion dollars.[1] Some of the main motives for this form of attack include:

- **Competitive advantage** – by accessing data on pricing, the status of bids and similar matters, a company can position itself to undercut the competition in bidding situations.

- **Design theft** – theft of secret R&D work and product designs can cut the thief's R&D budget and product development time lines dramatically.

- **Client data theft** – access to a competitor's client databases will allow a company to make targeted approaches to key prospects and thus subvert the sales and account management processes of the competitor.

Cyber terrorists

There is an ongoing debate as to whether there is in fact such a thing as cyber terrorism. On the one hand, leading thinkers on the topic like Louise Richardson, a Harvard University scholar and author of the seminal work, *What Terrorists Want*,[2] argues that terrorism by definition requires acts of *physical violence* against non-military targets and that the concept of cyber terrorism is therefore hype.

---

1   http://www.guardian.co.UK/world/2009/jul/22/germany-china-industrial-espionage (accessed 14 August 2012).
2   *What Terrorists Want* by Louise Richardson. 2007. London: John Murray.

However, a hypothetical group with political motivations, hacking into air traffic control systems with the intent of causing terror and creating the potential for fatal air accidents is clearly a cyber terrorist group, in my view, whether or not any fatalities actually result. By extrapolation, individuals or groups who carry out data theft deliberately in order to obtain information that will facilitate a conceptual future physical attack are also acting as cyber terrorists.

Ultimately, the goal of any terrorist is to inspire terror for political ends. This may not require any civilian deaths, merely the threat of death or injury, or the threat of damage to key infrastructures sufficient to terrorise a large part of the population, thus exerting political pressure on a nation's leadership. So, if a criminal act on the Internet meets these criteria, it is cyber terrorism and if it doesn't, then it is merely cyber crime. Whether cyber terrorism is actually a 'manifest risk', with a measurable frequency and impact, remains an unanswered question.

One of several things that Louise Richardson does very effectively in her book is to categorise the key things that terrorists want. I have paraphrased her findings and applied them to cyber terrorists:

- **Revenge** – the cyber terrorist seeks revenge for perceived wrongs inflicted by the state or by powerful entities aligned to the state. These wrongs may not necessarily have been suffered by the terrorist personally, but he or she will feel a sense of mission in righting or redressing wrongs believed to have been suffered by others.

- **Renown** – the cyber terrorist seeks renown, both within his or her movement, or in the public eye, for the skill and audacity exhibited during a cyber attack. This should not be confused with the secrecy a terrorist craves during the preparatory phases of an attack, and many actions of the cyber terrorist will be concealed. When the ultimate attack occurs, however, the politically motivated terrorist generally seeks the widest possible publicity.

- **Reaction** – the cyber terrorist wants the state to react to any attack in a disproportionate way. The best outcomes for the terrorist are state reactions that adversely affect innocent people, or which limit the rights or reduce the quality of life of the state's own citizens.

The terrorist's expectation is that such reactions will have the dual effect of underscoring the success of the terrorist act, while also causing more people to seek revenge against the state, thus perpetuating the 'struggle'.

TECHNO-CRIMINALS

Techno-criminals are technically clever individuals who have decided to use their skills for criminal gain. They include:

- hackers and 'Hacktivists';

- malware creators.

Hackers

Loosely speaking, there are five key main classes of 'hacker':

- traditional hackers who like to tinker with the technology;

- ethical hackers who test systems on behalf of the systems' owners;

- Hacktivists who are pursuing a political or social cause;

- criminal hackers who hack for financial gain or similar motives;

- agents of the state, otherwise known as 'spies'.

Criminal hackers are more correctly termed 'crackers', but the media generally fails to make this distinction. However, technical people will sometimes state that a 'hacker' is simply a particularly skilled computer expert. Hackers/crackers may be acting independently or they may have been recruited by one of the other groups listed above. Individual hackers are commonly thought to be motivated by several factors:

- **Challenges** – most hackers are proud of their technical skills and derive immense satisfaction merely from defeating the efforts of teams of corporate or government programmers to create secure systems.

- **Status within the hacking community** – while some hackers shun the limelight, many want to be recognised within the hacking community for their skill and this creates a competitive environment with individuals vying for status.

- **Freedom of information or software** – a large proportion of hackers have their ideological roots in the free software movement and hold a sincere belief in the principle of freedom of information, while abhorring the sale of software for profit. They strongly resent corporate and state efforts to secure data and limit access to information that they feel should be in the public domain.

Malware creators

Malware creators may also be acting independently or they may have been recruited by another party or organisation. There are three common motives for those who create and disseminate computer malware:

- **Demonstrating vulnerabilities** – highlighting vulnerabilities in computing systems and networks, or in the training of users and administrators, for the sole purpose of encouraging administrators to up their game.

- **Accessing information** – using malware attacks to access key data, possibly in order to sell it.

- **Generating revenue** – by fraudulently directing traffic to a commercial site that receives payments based on traffic volumes, thus inflating said revenue in a fraudulent manner, or providing DoS attack capabilities for money.

TECHNOLOGY-ENABLED CRIMINALS

Technology-enabled criminals are less technically sophisticated people who rely on technology developed by others for their own criminal exploits. These include:

- Spammers;

- organised crime;

- financial fraudsters.

Spammers

Regardless of the channel used, Spammers are generally motivated by a desire to market goods or services. Some of these offers are actually valid, even if the marketing technique is misguided, while others are fraudulent or relate to products that it would be unlawful to sell over the counter in the target country.

Organised crime

The UK's SOCA believes that organised crime is now turning to the Internet as a domain in which a great deal of crime activity can and is being perpetrated. Today's cyber security attacks are therefore not solely the purview of governments and hackers. Organised crime uses the same techniques to address their own particular requirements:

- **Criminal gain** – theft of data for resale, to facilitate identity fraud, or to provide access to credit card or bank account details are just a few of the ways in which organised criminals exploit the Internet.

- **Leverage and intelligence** – cyber attacks can provide a criminal with a wealth of information on a target individual or location. Web browsing habits, personal details, email content, social networking contacts and messages can all be used to blackmail a person in a key position or as intelligence during the planning stage of a criminal act.

- **Concealment** – spoofing and other such techniques can be used by criminals to avoid surveillance during the planning phase, and who make police investigations difficult post-event. Concealment may also involve the concealment of sources of funds or facilitation of the laundering of the proceeds of crime.

Financial fraudsters

As the name implies, financial fraudsters are thieves who commit fraud. In cyber security terms, examples would include people to hack into a bank's systems in order to divert funds to their own accounts, or someone who steals data by using another person's logon details and then sells that data to a competitor.

You can probably come up with many more fraud examples of your own, as there seems to be no end to the ways in which people commit fraud online or via ICT systems. Tax avoiders and those making corrupt payments may also fall into this category, if cyber systems play a part in their schemes.

OPPORTUNISTS

Opportunists are otherwise honest people who, when confronted with an opportunity to profit from crime, choose to do so. Depending on our personal circumstances, values, the nature of the opportunity itself and the risks of being caught, many of us are potential opportunists.

Examples of cybercrime opportunists seen in the wild include:

- employees;

- mules and cashiers;

- Virtual Wizards.

Employees

Employees may be motivated to commit opportunistic cybercrimes, or to facilitate their commission by third parties for any number of reasons. Criminal greed and corruption are oft cited, although the role of twenty-first century social aspirations should not be discounted and nor should the 'Robin Hood' mentality; the sense that it's OK to steal from large corporations or from the Government because both owe us anyway.

The concealment of trading or accounting errors is a common driver for many forms of fraud and this may extend to the commission of some forms of cybercrime. Also, we have briefly looked at the role of revenge as a driver, but misguided personal values are also an important factor.

Mules and cashiers

Mules and cashiers are individuals who are persuaded to take part in a chain of criminal financial transactions, sometimes innocently, by receiving and then forwarding funds in exchange for a commission. This is done in order to keep criminal's transaction levels below those that trigger alarms in the financial services sector. By spreading the flow of transactions across a number of mule accounts, online criminals can transfer and launder funds.

Virtual Wizards

Virtual Wizards specialise in the use of virtual currencies and other assets as a mechanism for transferring the proceeds of crime on behalf of third parties. This virtual money laundering can be carried out via web-based unregulated money services such as WebMoney Transfer and BitCoin, or potentially by using the currencies created by online gaming firms such as World of Warcraft, Second Life or Eve Online.

Conclusion

This very wide range of motivations and attacker profiles demands an equally wide-ranging and sophisticated set of responses, but before we look at what those entail, we should wrap up Part I by summarising the vulnerabilities that many organisations exhibit and which allow these problems to manifest themselves in the first place.

8

Common Vulnerabilities

Introduction

Many of the critical infrastructures and commercial targets for cyber security attacks were once targets of the Allied strategic bombing campaign during the Second World War. They were recognised at that time to be critical to the cohesion and economic survival of a nation. Now, they are all connected to a shared global communications network which can be accessed by friends and potential enemies alike.

Cyber security is therefore also a national security issue that should be of equal concern to both the public and private sectors. In our complex, interconnected world, no private company of significance can consider itself completely immune or isolated from the risk of cyber attack by either state or non-state actors.

Web-facing Applications

The Open Web Application Security Project (OWASP) is an open source project set up to produce freely available guidelines and other documentation of current cyber security vulnerabilities. It works across government, educational, private sector and individual boundaries. OWASP is also starting to emerge as a possible standards body.[1]

The top ten application risks currently defined by OWASP are summarised in Table 8.1. Several of these are too complex for our purposes and a couple are repeats of explanations provided earlier, but you should read through them to get a flavour of the kind of weakness that cyber criminals look to exploit,

---

1   You can read more about OWASP on their website at: https://www.owasp.org/index.php/Main_Page.

if only to better appreciate the ever-present gap between normal management thinking and technical cyber security realities.

Table 8.1   The OWASP Top Ten, 2013

Name	Description
A1 – Injection	Injection flaws, such as SQL, OS and LDAP injection, occur when untrusted data is sent to an interpreter as part of a command or query. The attacker's hostile data can trick the interpreter into executing unintended commands or accessing unauthorised data.
A2 – Broken authentication and session management	Application functions related to authentication and session management are often not implemented correctly, allowing attackers to compromise passwords, keys, session tokens or exploit other implementation flaws to assume other users' identities.
A3 – Cross-site scripting (XXS)	XSS flaws occur whenever an application takes untrusted data and sends it to a web browser without proper validation and escaping. XSS allows attackers to execute scripts in the victim's browser which can hijack user sessions, deface websites or redirect the user to malicious sites.
A4 – Insecure direct object references	A direct object reference occurs when a developer exposes a reference to an internal implementation object, such as a file, directory or database key. Without an access control check or other protection, attackers can manipulate these references to access unauthorised data.
A5 – Security misconfiguration	Good security requires having a secure configuration defined and deployed for the application, frameworks, application server, web server, database server, and platform. All these settings should be defined, implemented, and maintained as many are not shipped with secure defaults. This includes keeping all software up to date, including all code libraries used by the application.
A6 – Sensitive Data Exposure	Many web applications do not properly protect sensitive data, such as credit cards, tax ids, and authentication credentials. Attackers may steal or modify such weakly protected data to conduct identity theft, credit card fraud, or other crimes. Sensitive data deserves extra protection such as encryption at rest or in transit, as well as special precautions when exchanged with the browser.
A7 – Missing Function Level Access Control	Virtually all web applications verify function level access rights before making that functionality visible in the UI. However, applications need to perform the same access control checks on the server when each function is accessed. If requests are not verified, attackers will be able to forge requests in order to access unauthorized functionality.
A8 - Cross-site request forgery	A cross-site request forgery attack forces a logged-on victim's browser to send a forged HTTP request, including the victim's session cookie and any other automatically included authentication information, to a vulnerable web application. This allows the attacker to force the victim's browser to generate requests the vulnerable application thinks are legitimate requests from the victim.
A9 – Using Components with Known Vulnerabilities	Vulnerable components, such as libraries, frameworks, and other software modules almost always run with full privilege. So, if exploited, they can cause serious data loss or server takeover. Applications using these vulnerable components may undermine their defenses and enable a range of possible attacks and impacts.
A10 - Unvalidated redirects and forwards	Web applications frequently redirect and forward users to other pages and websites, and use untrusted data to determine the destination pages. Without proper validation, attackers can redirect victims to Phishing or malware sites, or use forwards to access unauthorised pages.

Database Vulnerabilities

We commonly call an automated data storage and retrieval system that links several types of data table together a Database Management System, normally shortened to 'database' or 'DB'. Although the data and the system are really supposed to be thought of as separate items, a Database Management System has these key characteristics:

- easy addition, editing or retrieval of pieces of data;

- data is stored in tables with specific fields being assigned for each type of data;

- contains complete sets of fields organised as discrete records;

- collections of records are organised as discrete files;

- fields or files are linked to each other in some kind of planned architecture to support one or more computational processes.

Some types of database also use hypertext to link any database object to any other object.

Databases have come to dominate our working lives and are now used in almost every business with many technologies depending on either database access or an embedded database in order to function.

COMMON DATABASE VULNERABILITIES

Weak access control and poorly managed user rights represent the biggest threats to database security. We have already looked at the issue of password sharing, but even where passwords are kept confidential their vulnerability to dictionary attacks is often exacerbated by the weak nature of the passwords themselves.

Weak authentication

Many organisations and most personal users still employ simple user name and password logins to sensitive systems and databases. Here is a short list of typical password errors, based in part on a Blog on general password security by Internet security commentator Hayley Kaplan:

- Reusing passwords across many applications or systems. (Who, me? Never!)

- Simple passwords – a failure to use combinations of uppercase and lower case letters, numbers, punctuation and special characters. According to Kaplan, 'Password1' is one of the most commonly used passwords.

- Short passwords – shorter passwords (fewer than nine characters) are easier for hacking software to crack.

- Repeated digits – repeated digits can make cracking easier.

- Use of real words, names or dates – these are all easy for software to 'guess'.

- Using usernames as the password or within the password (as in Username = Mark, Password = Mark1). This may look dumb but it is commonly used because people really do struggle to remember passwords.

- Storing password lists in unencrypted computer documents – these lists can be accessed if computers are hacked and they can often be found online via a search engine.

- Writing passwords down and keeping them near the device – taped to the bottom of the keyboard for example. (I can see you peeling the tape off now).

- Storing passwords in mobile phones or other contact databases – this is often made worse by a failure to use a password on the phone itself.

- Entering a password for another site in a third-party App.

- Allowing browsers to store passwords.

User rights

Some of the errors committed even by very large organisations filled with highly educated experts are simply mind boggling. A lot of this has to do with the fact that one of the most critical business assets (data) is stored in systems that only a tiny minority understand. This makes it difficult for managers to ask the right questions and they also make assumptions about the care being taken by administrators to protect their systems and data.

This is not to say that most system administrators and database administrators are careless – they certainly are not. But it only takes are few individuals and incidents to cause massive harm.

I was recently engaged by a major client to examine and comment on the value of a large set of computer evidence in an important court case. I was excited about this project, not least because the client had a large budget and the work looked likely to run over many months. Writing books earns very little by way of spending money! Unfortunately, within a matter of days I had established that the data in question had been stored in an unencrypted file system for over two years and that it had actually been lost for much of that time, with the client being unable to locate it. When recovered, the data had then been read and edited (to make it easier to comprehend) but no copy of the original unedited data had been created and so it was impossible to validate that the edited version did not contain deletions, errors or additions. The bottom line was that I had to advise my client that the evidence was worthless and my project came to an immediate halt.

This one example captures many of the vulnerabilities that apply to databases in terms of user rights and data integrity:

- Who can read the data?

- Who can edit the data?

- Who can delete records?

- Who can insert records?

- Is the data encrypted while stored?

- Is it stored in a secure place?

- What remote access is possible?

- Has it been backed up?

If you can provide proper answers to all of the above, you are a long way down the road towards having a secure data storage system.

A Lack of Risk Awareness

Neira Jones holds a Masters in Applied Computer Science from the French Institut Superieur de Gestion and is one the cyber security industry's most prominent practitioners, thought leaders and Bloggers. Jones is also the Senior VP Cybercrime at the Centre for Strategic Cyberspace and Security Science. In this capacity Jones is involved in helping to guide government policy and thinking on the topic of cyber security and is therefore extremely well placed to understand the nature of the threat, its evolution and the kinds of thinking leaders in both the public and private sphere are engaged in.

I asked her whether the risks are increasing or merely evolving:

> In one sense what we see is just a changing risk landscape. Recall the process of email introduction all those years ago. Email was seen as a risk rather than as a key business enabler: 'Don't give it to everyone' we were told. Today some large organisations are telling the world that email is passé, and they are using instant messaging instead. So the while the new risks are superficially different, the principles are the same; to protect the perimeter, implement acceptable usage policies, and distinguish clearly between the physical and the virtual world.

Jones continued:

> On the other hand, DATALOSSdb[2] has published statistics for data breaches today and already the number of breaches in 2012 is 35.8 per cent higher than for the same period last year. Either more breaches are being reported or we haven't learned the lessons of the past and I tend

---

2   http://datalossdb.org/ (accessed 8 March 2013) is a research project aimed at documenting known and reported data loss incidents world-wide.

towards the second view. Take for example the SQL injection form of attack, such as that seen in the Sony Online Entertainment case in 2011. This is still a very prominent form of attack even though we have known about the problem, which is easily solved, for the last 15 years. To put it bluntly, we are not implementing even the most basic security controls. Before worrying about complex threats such as Malnets and so forth, we need to address those basics. Today's attacker has an estimated six months to navigate through the average organisation's systems and data before he or she is detected. We need better security and we need to develop much better incident responses.

Jones is also a firm believer in the notion that cyber security is a risk management-and-people challenge and not a technical one at heart. She explains this by pointing out that in her banking sector roles she has dealt with a range of business-to-business clients (B2B), from very large retailers to the owners of corner shops. What she has come to realise is that while the cyber security breaches reported in the news are not very sophisticated there is still a great need for better education and awareness. Few decision makers have even the most rudimentary grasp of the topic, she reports, although their businesses are entirely dependent on cyber technology.

In Jones's opinion, there are two problems:

1. Corporations have the resources and potential to understand cyber security in general. Their challenge is in understanding where to focus their resources and many of them turn to costly technology as a tool to fix all issues without really examining root causes.

2. Small businesses are already struggling in a tight economy and they simply don't know where they should be focusing or what they should be doing about cyber security. They are working in the dark with no capacity to spend money on the problem and no awareness of the simple and low-cost security steps they could be taking.

The solution is to prioritise awareness training alongside a risk-based approach to security, says Jones. 'Cyber security is still seen by most as a technology issue. There is insufficient focus on people and process. There is a lot of hype in the news about Malnets, Stuxnet and so forth but in the UK the big fraud cases still involve relatively low-tech identify theft and mass marketing techniques.

The pressing issues are good passwords and user awareness, not technology. Firms also need to make cost/benefit judgments about risk; whether to correct, mitigate or accept – this is the range of decisions needed rather than just a knee-jerk response that involves buying more tools.

Jones adds:

> Awareness at board level is also a big factor and many senior decision makers remain unconvinced that there are real risks that could hit their own business. The risk message is not filtering down because behavioural change needs to start from the top. To a large extent, this is a consequence of CISOs[3] still being focused purely on the technical side of the equation; they appear unable to demystify and articulate risk to board level in straight forward operational and financial terms. In fact, the consulting firm Ernst and Young has just published a survey[4] of chief executive perceptions of information security in their organisations and one of the main findings is that CISOs are still seen as hindrance to progress. This is very damning and it must be addressed because the risks are very real.

Jones also argues that organisational structures, and the resulting process of competing for and allocating budgets, are a part of the problem. While a few forward-thinking firms have already taken the step of consolidating all of their risk functions under a single umbrella, as depicted in Figure 8.1, the vast majority of businesses still maintain separate 'silos' for fraud, risk, IT Security and so forth. In many cases she reports that there is almost no dialogue between these groups. There are, in fact, real opportunities to achieve wins by exchanging ideas and information internally about risks, in Jones's experience, but these are generally missed. Instead, each operational silo spends money trying to solve the problems it has decided to focus on, in isolation from the rest.

Data Disclosures

While the lack of awareness remains a vulnerability, the inadvertent disclosure of confidential data or information remains one of the main risks faced by cyber security managers, whether it relates to losing devices, leaving data CDs

---

3   Chief Information Security Officers.
4   http://www.ey.com/GL/en/Services/Advisory/2011-Global-Information-Security-Survey---Into-the-cloud--out-of-the-fog (accessed April 2012).

A coordinated response

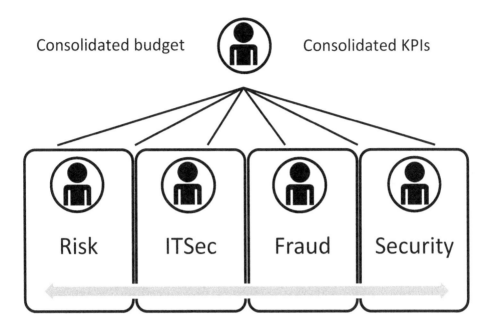

Consolidated budget   Consolidated KPIs

Risk   ITSec   Fraud   Security

We need to move away from the model in which we have different organisational silos addressing many of the same issues towards a model in which we have a single budget, allocated on the basis of perceived and manifest risk, a single set of consolidated KPIs and a coordinated approach to awareness and control.

Figure 8.1   Consolidating the risk silos

on buses, transmitting unencrypted sensitive data, sharing user names and passwords or saying too much to strangers online via social networking sites. Awareness training is essential but, as we shall see, penetration testing is also an important tool for assessing the extent of this kind of risk.

Un-vetted Contract Staff

Contract staff, ranging from office cleaners and security guards, through to consultants and IT experts, can be as big a threat to an organisation's information security as anything else. Unless contractors are managed very tightly, their staff may not be vetted, trained or motivated to the required level.

Their loyalty may be to their own employer, rather than to your business, and their backgrounds, personalities and lifestyle (all things that help us to assess risks) can be completely hidden from you. My own sense of things is that there are probably large numbers of unsuitable people working in sensitive locations as a result of the outsourcing model.

Key Personnel

On the other end of the spectrum, there will often be a small handful of key staff within your business that has access to and control over the bulk of your most sensitive information assets and your critical infrastructure. It only requires one of these people to become disenchanted, or to develop a criminal plan, for a major incident to result.

Inadequate Anti-virus Controls

An anti-virus (or anti-malware) application is designed to prevent viruses, Trojans, Worms, Adware or Spyware from affecting computer systems. Anti-virus programs generally achieve this in three ways:

- they prevent malware from being installed in the first place by detecting the malicious code as it being introduced (for example, as a file attachment or executable file);

- they detect malware when it is operating on the protected device or systems;

- they respond by removing malware from infected systems, or rendering it harmless and they alert users, security teams or system administrators to the presence of the infected or infectious code.

However, thousands of new malware programs emerge every month and as anti-virus techniques have matured, malware developers have deliberately aimed for shorter malware life cycles, to lower the profile of their code and make detection harder. Modern malware is often capable of evolving by itself, changing its form and attack technique so as to circumvent new controls.

Consequently, a simple failure to regularly update anti-virus applications can render them useless against current threats. Many users regard these automatic updates as an annoyance and they disable them, also failing to run them manually. Once again, it is the human user who lies at the centre of so many risk scenarios.

Poor Distributed Denial of Service Resilience

A number of techniques are available for providing resilience to DDoS attacks, including scheduling, anomaly detection, server load analysis and distributed web architectures. In the absence of such controls to enhance resilience DDoS will remain a key threat.

Other Network Vulnerabilities

Keeping external parties and malware off your network by using Firewalls, anti-virus and other tools is only half the struggle. The other half involves those threats that manifest themselves within the network itself, as summarised in this Top Ten list:

- **Laptops and other portable devices** – there are two main facets to laptop vulnerability. Firstly, laptops can operate both on and off the network, so any infections they pick up while they are in travel mode may be introduced to the network once they log back in. Secondly, the laptop itself may hold sensitive data and if the laptop is lost, stolen or merely accessed temporarily, that data may be at risk.

- **USB drives** – small, low-cost and easily hidden, these simple devices can be quickly inserted or carelessly interchanged between machines. The Stuxnet Worm is believed to have been spread partly via USB and many other forms of malware can be automatically executed whenever a USB is inserted.

- **Other USB devices** – we often forget that a camera, MP3 device, iPod or 3G dongle, each of which can connect to my PC or laptop via USB, can also be used to store other data or programs, including malware. For example, I know a colleague who stores confidential encrypted client files on his digital camera's internal storage while travelling, in place of photos, on the basis that a data thief will probably target the laptop and a camera thief will probably ignore any data files he finds.

- **CD and DVD writers** – as with USB drives, PCs or laptops equipped with CD drives capable of writing data to a blank CD provide an easily exploited loophole for anyone intent on stealing data or programs, as well as being a potential route for the introduction of malware. The US military analyst who was arrested for his part in the 2010 Wikileaks case is alleged to have burned the stolen files onto blank CDs he brought into the building with music labels stuck to them.

- **Children** – today's mobile communications devices are actually handheld personal computers that can, by the way, also make telephone calls. Many networks will allow access directly from such devices using a wireless connection, yet a majority of these devices still have no anti-virus or other security software installed. To make matters worse, most of us will allow our children to use these devices extensively, for example while we are on a long journey, and child users may access malicious sites and even download malware without our knowledge.

- **Wireless network signal leakage** – the very nature of wireless networks is such that they may extend beyond the physical limits of the building, thus giving outsiders a route in that does not exist for wired networks. I have worked at client sites where former employees, whose accounts had not been deactivated, were still parking on the road outside the office and logging onto the corporate network.

- **Printing** – some of the confidential data stolen from networks and databases since computers were first introduced to the workplace has come from printers, often because the person printing the item failed to go and pick it up, or because they assume that there was a printer error and simply print again when they discover that their printout is missing. Printers also store data in memory and repair technicians, whether genuine or fake, may be able to access those files.

- **Human memory** – in the long course of human history, espionage has always been an important area of endeavour and for most of our history our only storage device has been our brain. This remains a popular tool with some. Never lose sight of the fact that an intruder only needs to read and remember what he has read in order to cause harm. Once read, a data breach has occurred, even if no printed or electronic version of the data ever leaves the network, database or building.

Cybercrime Impacts

At the end of Chapter 1, I proposed a simple 'Harm Matrix' to summarise some of the types of impact that cybercrime can have on organisations and people. Now that we have a more complete understanding of the threats, risks and vulnerabilities, we can think about the impact of cybercrime in a more granular way:

- impact at the device and user level;

- impact at the network level;

- impact at the organisational level;

- impact at the national and transnational level.

IMPACT AT USER AND DEVICE LEVEL

It is at the device or user level that the largest number of discrete significant impacts can be enumerated, as Table 8.2 shows, and for most people this is where the pain is felt most keenly.

Table 8.2   **The impact of cyber crime at the user and device level**

Class of Attack	Types or Area of Impact
Web server exploits in which a user's device is hijacked	Device is used to run a Phishing site
	Device used as a malware download server
	Device used as a Piracy server for the downloading of ripped content
	Device used as a child pornography server

Class of Attack	Types or Area of Impact
Email server exploits	Device used to send Spam
	Device used to send 'stranded abroad' 419-type email messages
	Harvesting of email contacts
Botnet exploits that use the device as a…	Botnet client
	DDoS zombie
	Click fraud zombie
	Anonymous proxy machine
Theft of virtual goods from the device itself	Game characters or digital game assets
	Game currency
	Software licence keys
Theft of sensitive user credentials, such as…	eBay accounts
	PayPal accounts
	Bank accounts
	Credit card details
	FTP credentials
	Skype and IM accounts
	Passwords
	Encryption certificates
	Other personal data
Reputational harm to the user	Takeover of email or social media accounts.
	Reading message content.
	Posting of fake online messages using the user's credentials.
	Exposing the user's search history, Blog posts, and so on
Loss of…	Funds through fraud
	Data through deletion or corruption
	Service through infection or hijacking

IMPACT AT NETWORK LEVEL

The impact of cybercrime and security breaches at network level is predominantly felt in terms of:

- loss of service;

- data corruption;

- quality and reliability.

In accounting or financial audit circles, these effects would be said to lead to challenges in terms of the completeness, accuracy and timeliness of data, and this terminology seems relevant to cyber security as well.

IMPACT AT THE ORGANISATIONAL LEVEL

At the operational or business level, cyber security events can have a wide range of effects, including but not limited to:

- brand and reputational harm;

- shareholder value;

- regulatory fines or legal liability;

- supplier status (to public sector);

- design theft and intellectual property rights (IPR) issues;

- loss of critical system access;

- direct financial harm in terms of costs, revenues and opportunities.

Few of these effects are technical and it is generally the case that issues with a direct impact on the brand and reputation of a business are the most serious concerns.

IMPACT AT THE NATIONAL AND TRANSNATIONAL LEVEL

We have already looked at some key sectors at risk during a major cyber crises and it seems clear that at the national or transnational level the primary risks relate to loss of service with potentially serious knock-on effects on:

- energy security;

- food security;

- water security;

- defence;

- health.

Cyber communications crises affecting one or more of these sectors at national/ transnational level could also have very serious cascading effects for many other sectors and this is what makes cyber security resilience a matter of strategic importance. Given the way in which we are globally interconnected, we are all now players on the international security stage.

Conclusion

There is a need for businesses in strategic sectors to adopt cyber security protocols and standards that live up to a national cyber security resilience benchmark. This requires us to start asking questions along the lines of, 'What are the implications of our Cloud services strategy in a time of international crisis?' or 'What are the cascading effects of a loss of access to our services likely to be nationally and how do we mitigate them?' In Part II we take a look at the framework for thinking about cyber security controls and at the range of controls available to address the risks and challenges I have enumerated.

PART II

The Cyber Security Response

Preamble

In Part I we looked in some detail at cyber security threats and threat actors. These, however, only represent half of the equation and in Part II we will discuss the, the regulatory, legal and governance frameworks that apply, some considerations for the classification of information assets, the performance of cyber security risk assessments, as well as many of the available operational and technical choices open to organisations and individuals in terms of cyber security controls.

The purpose of Part II is therefore to equip you to consider appropriate, proportionate and cost-effective responses to validated cyber security risks, either by removing vulnerabilities, or by adding defensive structures and raising awareness. It is not my intent to scare monger in order to encourage the uninformed to allocate budget to address conceptual issues. Instead, the goal is to arm the reader with the tools needed to ask the right questions and to make rational judgements. The chapters that follow should be read with that goal in mind.

Towards the end of Part II, I will also introduce one of the main opportunities arising from the evolving cyber model, that of digital intelligence. I will provide some guidance on how you can exploit the vulnerabilities of the social media and web models to your advantage, while simultaneously underscoring the risk that others may be doing the same to you.

Finally, we will take a brief look at what the future might hold in cyber security terms as we discuss the implications of 4th Generation mobile communications, cybernetics and cyber conflict. I hope that by the end of the final chapter you will have developed your own models for thinking about the technological universe and for reasoned decision making on cyber security matters.

9

Cyber Security Control Frameworks

Introduction

In December 2010 a major data breach via a Spear Phishing attack[1] occurred at Silverpop Systems Inc., a US eMarketing firm that sent out email marketing messages on behalf of international clients. The Office of the Data Protection Commissioner probed one of the UK clients affected by the data breach. In its findings, the Office of the Data Protection Commissioner stated that it would have expected to see a robust data-processing contract between the UK client and the US marketing agency that had experienced the security breach, and that this contract should have addressed data protection issues in a manner that is consistent with UK regulations.

This statement has profound consequences for anyone doing business with an overseas supplier. Not only must we abide by our own rules here and by their rules over there, but we must also ensure that our rules are adhered to abroad. In many cases, the opposite may also apply. What we are seeing is one symptom of a globalised market that lacks globalised rule sets and benchmarks for challenges like cyber security.

Governance

'Governance' refers to a requirement for consistency in the management and execution of information security processes, and to the need for clearly defined ownership and accountability for the supervision of these processes at senior levels within the organisation. Most modern regulatory guidelines stipulate

---

1   http://www.zdnet.com/play-com-admits-data-breach-3040092221/ (accessed 10 December 2012).

a need for good governance and the demonstration of due diligence, and a failure to comply is often the first red flag that a regulator will look for when reviewing a business or investigating a data breach.

Organisation of Information Security

'Organisation' refers to the management structures in place to implement and maintain the information security framework within any organisation. This may extend from the top level through intermediate levels such as IT Security teams, system administrators or penetration testers.

The organisation of information security describes the roles and responsibilities of all staff who engage in ICT security at an operational level. Many organisations already have an Information Security Officer (ISO), more commonly called a Chief Information Security Officer or CISO. However, the authority and reporting responsibilities of CISOs can vary between firms and regions, but some useful models are available and one generic listing of core CISO responsibilities includes the following:

- risk management of information assets;

- definition of the technical, organisational and legal measures required to control risks;

- ensuring implementation and monitoring of risk controls;

- improving measures in place to address existing risks.

The growing importance of the information security management role in today's world is to be welcomed.

Security Policies

A security policy defines what it means to be secure for a given organisation. As a policy, it is expected to be written down, shared *and understood* by everyone affected. The fact that this is the case should also be well documented.

An ICT or cyber security policy describes the controls or constraints that must be implemented to:

- manage the actions and capabilities of authorised users within the organisation;

- manage the actions and capabilities of authorised external visitors or users, including customers, sub-contractors, visitors (to facilities as well as online), auditors, and so on;

- constrain the actions and capabilities of attackers or intruders so as to protect the organisation's assets, particularly its brand and information assets, and;

- assure compliance with data protection regulations.

Any organisation that uses information technologies in any form should have a properly crafted ICT or cyber security policy in place and enforced. The key characteristics of any policy are that it should:

- be consistent with other policies;

- provide a basis for objective setting;

- be justified by a risk assessment;

- clearly state objectives;

- provide a mandate for audit and improvement processes;

- commit to comply with regulation and law;

- be visibly endorsed by top management;

- be documented and implemented;

- be available and accessible.

People Risk Management

People are both our greatest asset and our greatest risk. In many sectors, staff involvement in fraud or theft of stock is estimated to account for anywhere between 25 per cent and 75 per cent of all incidents. There are two primary models for considering people risks:

- **Risks related to employment roles** – which roles within the business put people in a position where access or authority levels imply that temptation may become an issue?

- **Risks related to personal profiles** – what personal profiles might indicate added levels of risk and what lawful measures, compliant with both industrial relations and other regulation, as well as with organisational policies, can be employed to assess these risks, especially during pre-employment screening?

Physical Security

The goal of physical security is to make it too expensive to an attacker to warrant him making an attempt to access or steal an asset. Physical security should also prevent accidental access to or damage of assets. Applied to ICT/cyber security, this includes physical controls such as walls, floors, ceilings, doors, locks, cages, CCTV, alarms and so forth, plus controls that lock down hardware to prevent tampering and removal.

There are two broad categories of physical security to consider:

- **Passive defences** – designed to deter intrusions or delay intruders if they do attempt access.

- **Active defences** – designed to detect intrusions and respond to them.

Some systems may provide a combination of passive or active defence.

Logical Security

The goal of logical security is to ensure that only authorised users can access and use systems or the data they hold and that all usage is in accordance with defined policies. The main components of a logical security model are:

- user authentication and access control;

- defined user rights and privileges, as well as defined access levels;

- defined access points or methods;

- logging and reporting of access events, if required;

- logging and reporting of other events, such as execution of queries, database changes, printing, messaging and web browsing.

Environmental Security

Environmental security is a broad topic that looks at:

- how environmental trends or events affect people;

- how the activities of people (and their organisations) affect the environment.

In cyber security terms, environmental security is perhaps most tightly linked to the manner in which computer equipment is disposed of when it is no longer to be used. Disposal raises two further primary areas for thought. The first is the security of any data held on the systems being discarded. Even when a computer's hard drive has been erased or overwritten, techniques still exist for recovering the sensitive data previously stored there. Disposal of all cyber security systems should be performed by a qualified expert in this area.

The second consideration is the potential impact on the environment of the physical components within those systems. Computer systems contain various amounts of lead and other heavy metals that can contaminate water supplies. Improper recycling methods such as 'roasting' of circuit boards over open flames to melt the solder can also release significant quantities of toxic materials to the atmosphere, including numerous organic chemicals, heavy metals, flame retardants and persistent organic pollutants (or POPs).

Examples of Current Regulation and Guidance

As discussed at the start of this chapter, globalisation and the Internet force us to consider not only the local rules under which we operate, but those applied in every country with which we do business. It might be heavy going, but it never hurts to at least skim through the brief examples of current regulation and guidance in Table 9.1, if for no other reason than to get a sense of the direction of travel.

Table 9.1   An overview of selected international cyber crime and security regulations and guidelines

Regulation or Guideline	Commentary
ISO/IEC 27002	Provides best practice guidelines for anyone responsible for information security. Published jointly by the International Organisation for Standardisation (www.iso.org) and the formidably named International Electrotechnical Commission (www.iec.ch), the ISO standards cannot be reprinted here and your organisation is required to pay for copies. Many firms can be expected to hold a copy and you may be able to access one by speaking to your CISO or head of information security.
US Communications Assistance for Law Enforcement Act (CALEA)	Enacted by Congress on 25 October 1994, and intended to preserve the ability of law enforcement agencies to conduct electronic surveillance by requiring that telecommunications carriers and manufacturers of telecommunications equipment modify and design their equipment, facilities, and services to ensure that they have the necessary surveillance capabilities.
US Computer Software Privacy and Control Act	Designed to prevent deceptive software transmission practices in order to safeguard computer privacy, maintain computer control and protect Internet commerce.
US Digital Millennium Copyright Act (DMCA)	Enacted in 1998, the basic purpose of the DMCA is to amend Title 17 of the United States Code and to implement the World Intellectual Property Organization (WIPO) Copyright Treaty and Performances and Phonograms Treaty, which were designed to update world copyright laws to deal with the new technology.
US Economic Espionage Act (EEA)	Passed in 1996 and intended to put a stop to trade secret misappropriation.
US Electronic Communications Privacy Act	Passed in 1986 as an amendment to the federal wiretap law, the Act made it illegal to intercept stored or transmitted electronic communication without authorisation.
Section 1030(a)(1) of the US Atomic Energy Act	Makes it illegal to access a computer without authorisation or in excess of one's authorisation and obtain information about national defence, foreign relations or restricted data as defined in the Act, which covers all data concerning design, manufacture or utilisation of atomic weapons

	and production of nuclear material. It is worth noting that section 1030(a)(1) requires proof that the individual knowingly accessed the computer without authority or in excess of authorisation for the purpose of obtaining classified or protected information. Section 1030(a)(1) criminalises the use of a computer to gain access to the information, not the unauthorised possession of it or its transmission.
US Fraudulent Online Identity Sanctions Act (FOISA)	Attempts to tackle the problem of criminals registering online domains under false identification, it includes a provision that would increase jail times for people who provide false contact information to a domain name registrar and then use that domain to commit copyright and trademark infringement crimes.
US Internet Freedom Preservation Act of 2008	Establishes broadband policy and directs the Federal Communications Commission to conduct a proceeding and public broadband summits to assess competition, consumer protection, and consumer choice issues relating to broadband Internet access services, and for other purposes.
US National Information Infrastructure Protection Act (NIIA)	Passed in 1996 to encompass unauthorised access to a protected computer in excess of the parties' authorisation.
US Computer Fraud and Abuse Act	First enacted in 1984 and revised in 1994, makes certain activities designed to access a 'federal interest computer' illegal. These activities may range from knowingly accessing a computer without authorisation or exceeding authorised access to the transmission of a harmful component of a program, information, code or command. A federal interest computer includes a computer used by a financial institution, used by the US Government, or one or two or more computers used in committing the offence, not all of which are located in the same State. The Legal Institute provides Title 18 of the US Code, which encompasses the Computer Fraud and Abuse Act.
US Cyber Security Act	Failed in the Senate 2 August 2012 due to privacy concerns,[2] highlighting the continuing tension between security and privacy that has exercised practitioners and legislators worldwide.
UK Computer Misuse Act 1990	Became law in the UK in August 1990 and was amended by the Police and Justice Act 2006 which introduced an offence that also penalises the making, supplying or obtaining of articles for use in offences.
UK The Data Protection Act 1998 (DPA)	Came into effect in 2000 and applies to personal data held in all formats, whether electronic, paper, audio, visual or digital records. Processing, under the terms of the DPA, covers all conceivable manipulations of personal data including collection, use, storage, disclosure and amendment. Under the Act, mere possession of such data amounts to processing. Personal data is 'any recorded information about a living individual that can be identified from that data and other information, which is in the possession of the Data Controller'.
EU Data Protection Directive	The right to privacy is a highly developed area of law in Europe, but until the introduction of new regulations EU guidelines were non-binding and each member was free to develop its own interpretation of the stated principles. Eventually, the European Commission (Europe's central government) realised that diverging data protection legislation amongst EU member states impeded the free flow of data within the EU and accordingly proposed the Data Protection Directive.

---

2 http://www.washingtonpost.com/world/national-security/cybersecurity-bill-fails-in-senate/ 2012/08/02/gJQADNOOSX_story.html (accessed 25 October 2012).

THE MAIN PROVISIONS OF THE (UK) COMPUTER MISUSE ACT 1990

The terms of the UK Computer Misuse Act are clearly phrased and supported by good examples and the Act therefore provides a worthy model for many jurisdictions, although the reader is also strongly advised to find and read the terms of his or her own national legislation.

Under the UK Act, hacking and the introduction of viruses are criminal offences. The Act identifies three specific offences:

1.   Unauthorised access to computer material (that is, a program or data).

2.   Unauthorised access to a computer system with intent to commit or facilitate the commission of a serious crime.

3.   Unauthorised modification of computer material.

The Act defines (1) (the basic offence) as a summary offence punishable on conviction with a maximum prison sentence of six months or a maximum fine of £2,000 or both. The Act goes on to describe offences (2) and (3) as triable either summarily or on indictment, and punishable with imprisonment for a term not exceeding five years or a fine or both. These sentences clearly reflect the perceived gravity of the offence.

Example 1 – unauthorised access to computer material

This could include:

- using another person's logon details (user name and password) without proper permission or authority, or hacking into a computer system in order to view data or use a program, or to alter, delete, copy or move any program(s) or data, or simply to output data (for example, by printing), computer source code or any other stored material;

- installing or causing the installation of Spyware, for example, to obtain a password;

- reading confidential information.

In each case above, the offender must know that what they are doing is unauthorised. Depending on the particular circumstances, a person lending their logon details to another in order to facilitate unauthorised access and/or use would similarly be guilty of an offence.

Example 2 – unauthorised access to a computer system with intent to commit or facilitate the commission of a serious crime

This would include gaining access without authorisation to any data or systems, but with intent to use such access and/or data or programs in order to carry out further offences. Intent would have to be proved in such cases.

For example, a person obtains another user's logon details through subterfuge or hacks in, in order to access the computer systems of a business to obtain confidential data that would then be used to facilitate fraudulent trading in stocks and shares. In such a case the logon and data theft would constitute an offence/offences under the Computer Misuse Act, while the subsequent fraudulent activities would be covered by the Fraud Act 2006.

Example 3 – unauthorised modification of computer material

This could include unauthorised activities, such as stealing another person's logon details or hacking into a computer system and then:

- deleting files;

- modifying system files;

- introducing a computer virus;

- changing data.

Useful guidance on and full details of the UK Computer Misuse Act 1990 can be viewed at http://www.cps.gov.uk/legal/a_to_c/computer_misuse_act_1990/.[3]

EUROPEAN UNION DATA PROTECTION AND PRIVACY

The three principles of EU data protection law are:

---

3   Accessed 6 November 2012.

1. **Transparency** – the data subject has the right to be informed when his personal data is being processed. The controller must provide his name and address, the purpose of processing, the recipients of the data and all other information required to ensure the processing is fair.

2. **Legitimacy** – personal data can only be processed for specified explicit and legitimate purposes and may not be processed further in a way incompatible with those purposes.

3. **Proportionality** – personal data may be processed only insofar as it is adequate, relevant and not excessive in relation to the purposes for which they are collected and/or further processed. The data must be accurate and, where necessary, kept up to date; every reasonable step must be taken to ensure that data which are inaccurate or incomplete, having regard to the purposes for which they were collected or for which they are further processed, are erased or rectified. The data shouldn't be kept in a form which permits identification of data subjects for longer than is necessary for the purposes for which the data were collected or for which they are further processed.

There is a great deal of fear and misunderstanding in business circles about the requirements of EU data protection law, to the extent that many businesses hesitate to implement basic controls in the areas of fraud prevention or debt management because business leadership is wary about keeping or processing any personalised data. Much of this fear is misguided and the law does in fact permit reasonable and proportional storage and analysis of data.

Risk Control

An effective information security risk control programme allows you to validate your risk mitigation strategies and alternatives on an ongoing basis. Such a programme also allows an organisation to take corrective actions quickly when actual events occur and to assess the impact of all actions taken in terms of financial costs and benefits, time and resources.

Risk control also allows a business to identify any new risks that result from risk mitigation actions themselves. To achieve this, you need to ensure that the Risk Control Plan is regularly updated and that change control processes are in place to address risks associated with any proposed change to business processes, infrastructure of geographic deployments. These ongoing tasks include:

- revising the risk assessment process to capture the results of mitigation actions;

- revising the risk control and response plans regularly;

- communicating and educating staff and customers to raise awareness.

RISK MANAGEMENT

The term 'risk management' describes the steps taken to protect assets, based on levels of risk acceptance, in terms of:

- identification of manifest or potential risks;

- assessment of the impact of each risk on identified business assets;

- reduction of each risk through the design and implementation of controls;

- response and recovery in the event that a risk event occurs.

Information security risk management applies these same principles in order to assure the integrity, availability and confidentiality of information assets by identifying and quantifying cyber security and information security threats, vulnerabilities and risks, quantifying the possible impact on the organisation of each risk, designing and implementing controls and developing response plans to cyber security incidents.

RISK ASSESSMENTS

An information security risk assessment is a very effective way to prioritise and communicate the activities of information security risk management any organisation. A basic risk assessment need not be overly complex and the core components are:

- the threat assessment;

- the asset register;

- the controls assessment;

- the risk register.

An iterative approach may be required to the assessment of risk and the design of controls in any organisation as each control has the potential to reduce one set of risks while triggering new risks or an increase in risk in other areas.

Before launching any risk assessment it is always a good idea to determine the lay of the land in terms of the responsibilities of key players within the organisation, their authorities and accountabilities. This allows you to anticipate potential sensitivities and to ensure that that you obtain buy-in from all concerned parties.

As part of the planning process you should consider plotting the following graphically to provide reference points for your team:

- the organisational structure;

- technical architectures;

- business process flows and the service mix;

- third parties involved in delivery or support, for example Cloud service providers.

Finally, you should document your terms of reference and any assessment boundaries, and ensure that you obtain sign-off from the appropriate senior management for your project.

THE THREAT ASSESSMENT

As a precursor to an effective risk assessment, you need to conduct a threat assessment. Risks are after all a function of how threats exploit vulnerabilities in order to impact assets. The basic questions to be answered by a simple threat assessment are:

- Who is targeting you?

- What do they want?

- Have they already succeeded?

- Are they still active?

- What have you already lost?

- How can you respond?

Don't forget to consider the magical list of three; People, Processes and Technology.

THE ASSET REGISTER

Having determined what your threat situation looks like, you should now create a register of your assets. For cyber security or information security risk assessment the assets you are concerned about are key ICT assets, which can include both physical and information assets, that have a measurable value, that are vulnerable to threats and which require protection.

If assets are any items of value to an organisation, effective asset management in information security terms encompasses physical inventory, BYOD asset management, Cloud resources, network infrastructure, data classification and criticality, software applications and licenses. While the focus is on information assets and systems, other assets such as brand, reputation, trust and even financial assets can be directly affected by cyber security breaches, so they should be given consideration as well. A summary list includes:

- **Inventory** – what relevant information security assets do you hold? A checklist of infrastructure assets can prove useful:
    - Servers of various types;
    - Internet points of presence;
    - VPN concentrators;
    - all Windows domains.

- **Data** – what data is held, where and in what formats?

- **Valuation** – what is the value of both physical assets and data to the organisation? Value can be determined by considering the following:
    - financial value (cost of replacement and recovery or loss of revenue);
    - operational value (for example, dependency for business process purposes);
    - reputational value (for example, the impact of publicity around a cyber security breach, loss of sales or investment, marketing and PR costs).

- **Regulatory and legal costs** – for example, the effects on the organisation of a regulatory breach such as loss or exposure of protected customer data).

- **Responsibility and/or ownership** – who is accountable for the control and integrity of each asset? Are there instances where nobody is accountable for a critical information security asset?

Producing a network diagram of the core ICT infrastructure can assist you in ensuring that you have conducted a comprehensive assessment.

Don't forget to include those assets, such as customer data or payment card information, that require protection due to regulatory requirements. The value of an asset can also be expressed as the cost of the regulatory fine or brand damage resulting from its loss or exposure.

Listing your assets by type, value or criticality and location allows you to map each threat in relation to each asset. Bear in mind that you might see one-to-many, one-to-one or many-to-many relationships between threats and assets. Figure 9.1, below, depicts the threat-to-asset relationship.

THE CONTROLS ASSESSMENT

You have defined your threats and listed your assets by value and location. Now you need to list and score your controls; what protections (people, process and technology) are in place to secure each asset from each identified risk? In some cases, the controls you have in place will offset the threats to a given asset. In other cases, you will identify a gap or a weak control; this represents a 'vulnerability'.

Risk simplified

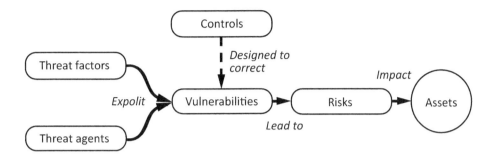

Figure 9.1   The threat-to-asset relationship

RULES AND LOGS

Collecting information on information security rule sets and logging is an important part of the Controls Assessment:

- compile the rule set of the core Firewall(s);

- compile rules for logging failed and successful logons on Windows workstations and servers;

- compile information related to any centralised logging currently in place.

If it does not already form a part of your information security practices, the integration of important log files into a centralised logging utility might be considered. This supports both the detection of incidents in progress and the investigation of incidents after the fact.

Robust logging is a critical component of a good information security operation. At a minimum, you should be storing key logs in a controlled central location. You should implement logging on all DNS and DHCP, VPN, Firewalls and Intrusion Detection Systems (IDS). Other steps include:

- ensuring that Windows application, system, and security event logs are appropriately sized and logged locally;

- ensuring that both success and failure audits are being logged for all systems;

- increasing the storage capacity of key logs (such as VPN, Firewall, DNS) to ensure they are not overwritten;

- configuring anti-virus and/or host-based intrusion prevention to write logs to your centralised logging utility;

- implementing logging on all internal web proxy servers to log date/time, hostname and IP address pairing, and URL browsing data to the centralised logging utility;

- implementing logging of all traffic on all Firewalls to the centralised logging utility. (Note that packet *contents* are not required);

- implementing disaster recovery backups for all logs.

THE RISK REGISTER

By identifying threats, assets, controls and gaps or vulnerabilities, you are now in a position to produce your Risk Register, the king of all risk documents. Where the threat is high, the value of the asset is high and the control is weak or absent, a higher level of risks exists. These higher-scoring risks are the ones you should consider prioritising for remedial action.

THE ACTION PLAN

There's not much point in having a register of risks if you don't follow it up with an Action Plan. The Action Plan should take your risks, sort them by score or priority and then describe the planned remedy, due date and/or phases of implementation and the owner responsible for each action.

Writing and agreeing an Action Plan allows you to track progress. It also feeds back into any audit or risk assessment work that follows on, because a Risk Register should be a living document, frequently revised to account for fixes, new threats and new vulnerabilities, not to mention new business processes, assets and regulations.

THE RESPONSE PLAN

The Response Plan draws on the Risk Register and scopes the organisation's high-level response to any of the risk events described. A good Response Plan will:

- select best response(s) based on a cost/benefit analysis;

- describe the actions to be taken to mitigate the risk;

- describe the actions to be taken when the risk event occurs (contingency plans);

- assign responsibilities and timing for each response;

- provide the details of key people and agencies to be contacted during or immediately following the risk event.

I have included a sample Response Plan in the Appendix. As you can see from the Appendix, the plan also stipulates the mitigation dates and actions, the actions taken when risk events occur and also any subsequent actions taken or planned.

Conclusion

Taken together, your threat assessment, asset register, controls assessment, risk register and response plan should provide a very sound basis for prioritising fixes, for training staff, for defining audit and penetration testing tasks and for reporting on risk to senior management. In the next chapter we will discuss some of the cyber security controls you might choose to apply in practice.

10

Cyber Security

Introduction

The management of cyber and information security does not come prepackaged and 'off the shelf'; it must be tailored to fit each and every organisation. As explained in previous chapters, there is a relationship between assets, vulnerabilities and threats that needs to be fully understood before effective and proportionate controls can be designed and implemented. This is likely to be an cyclical process and it is complicated by the fact that the environment is constantly changing. The process needs to be repeated regularly to account for new assets, vulnerabilities and threats, the effects of new controls and the potential for technical or business process failures.

In this chapter I will describe some of the most important cyber security controls. Whether these will be relevant to you and your organisation depends on the results of your own organisational risk assessment.

Data Classification

Data classification refers to a process or tool for ensuring that an organisation knows collectively the answers to several questions, such as the sensitivity, access levels and protections in place for each type of data at each location where data are stored and that it is compliant with all relevant regulations and corporate standards.

There are several types of classification that can be assigned:

- **Geographical** – according to location.

- **Chronological** – according to creation date.

- **Qualitative** – according to value.

- **Magnitude** – according to size.

- **Sensitivity** – according to confidentiality.

In any large organisation, the data classification task and its maintenance are likely to be major undertakings. Corporate firms tend to employ a variety of data classification approaches, but the system developed by the British Government over a period of many decades (see Table 10.1) is a useful guide as to how data might be classified.

Table 10.1   Examples of government security classifications

Classification	Meaning
Top Secret	Normally the highest level of classification – the public disclosure of this material could cause severe damage to security. (During World War Two, the Allies used at least one higher classification, 'Ultra', for data obtained through the breaking of enemy codes).
Secret	Exposure of this data could cause serious damage to security.
Confidential	Exposure of this data could be prejudicial to security.
Restricted	The exposure of such material would cause 'undesirable effects'.
Unclassified	This is not a classification level but it is used for government documents that do not have a classification.

Authentication

As the number of threats increases, from password guessing and hacking to WiFi man-in-the-middle attacks, the need for more advanced authentication will also increase. A password is only one of the three common methods of authenticating someone's identity and truly effective authentication often requires a combination of at least two, often three, of the available means, or authentication 'factors'.

THREE AND FIVE FACTOR AUTHENTICATION

The three most common authentication factors are:

1. **Something one knows** – for example, a secret password.

2. **Something one possesses** – a discrete 'token' which strongly resists counterfeiting, such as a credit card or security token, or a password dongle.

3.   **Something one is** – a biometric measurement such as a fingerprint, signature, voiceprint, picture, retinal pattern, DNA sample, and so on.

So, 'two factor authentication' refers to the use of two of the above (for example, a password plus a dongle) while 'three factor authentication' involves all three at once.

Some consultants are now talking about five factor authentication which adds 'somewhere you are', or are not, and 'something you trust' such as a particular technology or communications mechanism. Whether this will take hold or not remains to be seen particularly in light of the privacy implications of disclosing your location.

BIOMETRICS

The term biometrics refers to the science of understanding the distributions of biometric traits within given populations. Biometric security systems attempt to map those traits against people, principally in order to validate their identity. However, according to the US National Research Council, the scientific basis of biometrics and the understanding of just how effectively humans interact with biometric systems needs 'strengthening'.

New technologies are often plagued by problems and the area of biometrics has been no exception. Famously in the UK, the IRIS retinal recognition project that was in place at all major airports for immigration screening was terminated at two sites in early 2012 and all registrations of new users were halted nationwide after a long series of performance issues made the system ineffective.

While fingerprints remain the most common biometric signature, iris and retinal scans, voiceprints, hand geometry and even palm prints, where the vein structure of the palm is analysed via infra-red light, are all used. The most popular applications for biometrics are:

- access control:
    - to ensure that we only let this exact person in;
    - to verify other authentication methods;
    - to weed out impersonators;

- identification checks such as those employed during payment processes;

- to catch wanted criminals as they pass through control points.

Biometric results can be hit and miss and their 'Big Brother' image makes them controversial and often unwelcome. Their use should be carefully considered and applied only where the risk assessment warrants it and where they will genuinely add value in terms of increasing security or reducing costs.

Perhaps the most important question to be asked before taking the biometric route is, how do we validate the person from whom we are going to collect the biometric data at the outset? In other words, if you are about to collect Mark Johnson's very first biometric record, how will you confirm that I am actually Mark Johnson. In many situations, for example in a corporate setting, you may be reasonably (if not 100 per cent) confident that everyone on the payroll is legitimate. In some overseas managed service facilities, on the other hand, it can be virtually impossible to do more than trust each individual to tell you their true name. In such settings, investments in biometrics might not pay off.

RADIO FREQUENCY IDENTIFICATION

The term 'Radio Frequency Identification' refers to wireless systems that employ electromagnetic fields to transfer data between a Radio Frequency Identification tag and a Radio Frequency Identification reader. The normal uses of this technology are access control based on automatic identification and object tracking for supply chain and inventory management. The tag contains a profile of the object such as name, serial number and type and it can potentially be read from a distance of several yards, without necessarily being in direct line of sight of the reader.

Criticisms of Radio Frequency Identification as an authentication mechanism often include the following points:

- it is a universally available technology and anyone can get their hands on it;

- because of its supply chain derivation, Radio Frequency Identification has been made as cheap as possible, with minimal security being in-built;

- Radio Frequency Identification applications that envision implanting the tag within the body, for example in a military or penal setting, may violate privacy and other personal or human rights.

Radio Frequency Identification manufacturers dispute these claims and maintain that the access control versions of their products are built to the highest standard and have a proven track record. When looking at Radio Frequency Identification or any other technology, you should go armed with the right questions and then make your own assessment of the answers you are given.

DEVICE PROFILING

Device profiling based on IP session data, which can include large amounts of 'meta-data' regarding the connecting device, is a hot topic in both authentication and fraud detection. Essentially, the visited network or website collects meta-data and looks for:

- devices associated with earlier incidents; or

- devices with a particular profile.

The kinds of profile information used include the device type and manufacturer, the OS installed, the applications in use (for example, the browser type), users' language preferences and the device clock setting. Some devices, digital cameras being one example, may leave additional data about the user and this can sometimes include any email, name and address or phone number data input by the user when they first set the device up.

Device profiling allows automated systems and analysts to build rich data sets about good and bad users. This will be personal data in some cases, so before taking this approach you should seek advice.

WEBSITE VISIT PROFILING

Website visit profiling is another hot topic on the eCommerce customer authentication or fraud detection front. Online sellers know from painful experience that fraudsters and intruders often take very different routes through their websites than regular customers. While the regular customer might generally be expected to visit product pages, then look at pricing options before going to the checkout and printing or emailing the payment confirmation, all taking several minutes or more, a fraudster will often go very rapidly from product to checkout and will rarely print or email the receipt.

This type of knowledge, developed over decades, has allowed retailers and their security services suppliers to construct additional layers of profiling for online transactions. With the rising use of mobile devices, the seam of data to be mined in this regard is growing larger and this promises to be a very useful and interesting field of activity.

Encryption

Encryption is the act of encoding information, such as a message, so that adversaries or casual eavesdroppers cannot read it but the intended recipients can, after decrypting it. The science of encryption is known as cryptography and today it involves a combination of mathematics, computer science and electronics. It is widely used by governments, the military and increasingly by private companies, including your mobile phone provider.

KEY CONCEPTS IN ENCRYPTION

Table 10.2 briefly explains the items depicted in Figure 10.1, below.

Table 10.2   Encryption concepts

Concept	Short Explanation
Plaintext	The original message in a readable format.
Encryption key	A secret key that is used by the mathematical encryption algorithm to encrypt the plaintext message.
Encryption algorithm	The mathematical process or formula by which the plaintext is converted to an encrypted format.
Ciphertext	The encrypted text.
Decryption key	A second secret key that is used by a mathematical decryption algorithm to decrypt the ciphertext message. This may be the same as the encryption key or different (see below).
Key generation algorithm	A mathematical process for producing random secret encryption keys.

The plaintext message or data is first encrypted using the encryption key and the encryption algorithm. This converts it into ciphertext which cannot

Encryption and Decryption

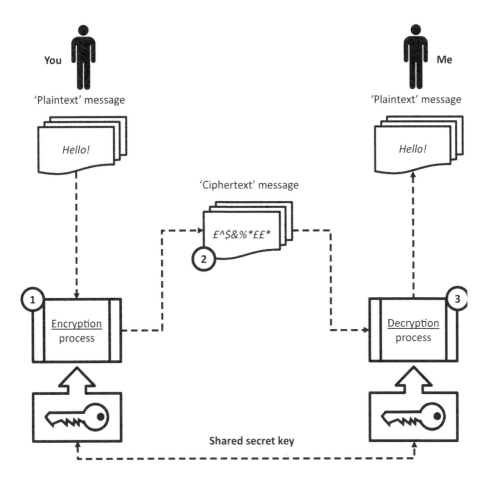

Figure 10.1   Encryption and decryption

be read without the decryption key. The ciphertext can now be sent to the receiving party.

On receipt, the receiving party decodes the ciphertext using the secret decryption key and algorithm. The message is restored to plaintext and can now be read by anyone.

There are two common categories of encryption scheme:

1. **Private-key encryption** – the sender and recipient share the same encryption key and endeavour to keep it secret, or 'private'. This is the traditional method.

2. **Public-key encryption** – the encryption key is public – anyone can encrypt messages with it. However, the decryption key is private and only the recipient can decrypt the message. This is a modern construct.

Encryption is used both to protect data that is being transmitted across a network, as with the example of the message cited above, and also to protect data 'at rest' in storage devices. You can, for example, encrypt your entire hard drive, encrypt only selected files on the drive, or encrypt just the messages you transmit from your device. Encryption however is only as good as the procedures for managing keys and protecting secrecy, and history is therefore full of examples of very clever encryption mechanisms being cracked and exploited.

ENCRYPTION ON THE INTERNET

The Transport Layer Security (TLS) protocol and its predecessor the Secure Sockets Layer (SSL) are cryptographic protocols that provide communication security over the Internet. Both protocols encrypt the network connection using:

- asymmetric cryptography for key exchange;

- symmetric encryption for confidentiality;

- message authentication codes for message integrity.

Versions of these protocols are in widespread use in web browsing, email, IM and voice-over-IP (VoIP) applications and certificate-authenticated (see below) SSL is considered mandatory by all security guidelines whenever a website hosts confidential information or performs eCommerce-type or financial services transactions.

The use of encryption is not limited to companies and the public sector and malware developers use advanced encryption very extensively to hide their malicious code from anti-virus applications, Firewalls and IDS.

CERTIFICATES

In a public key infrastructure (PKI) scheme, a public key certificate is an electronic document that uses a 'digital signature' to bind a public key with an identity, including information such as the name of a person or an organisation and their address. The certificate can be used to verify that a public key belongs to an individual and the digital signature will belong to a recognised Certificate or Certification Authority. There are a limited number of Certification Authorities around the world.

In layman's terms, the Certification Authority is making a statement to the effect that the owner of this domain is Mark Johnson and that you can assume that to be true when you communicate with him at that address. The most common use of certificates is for websites using the HTTPS (HTTP-Secure) protocol. The web browser examines the certificate served up by the visited domain and which validates that:

- the web server is authentic;

- the communications link is secure.

One way to subvert this process would be to obtain fraudulent certificates that identify you as another trusted party. Although relatively rare, a few notable case of Certification Authority subversion like this have occurred.

- In 2001 the certificate authority VeriSign issued two certificates to a person claiming to represent Microsoft. The certificates bore the name 'Microsoft Corporation', and could potentially have been used to trick users into installing malware disguised as Microsoft updates. The fraud was detected quickly and Microsoft and VeriSign jointly took steps to limit its impact.

- In 2011 fraudulent certificates were allegedly obtained from Comodo and DigiNotar, both Certification Authorities, supposedly by Iranian hackers. The fraudulent DigiNotar certificates may have been used in Iran, but this has not been confirmed.

- Stuxnet, Flame and other APT malware may also have used rogue certificates during their attacks.

All web browsers come with an extensive built-in list of trusted root certificates, although most of these refer to organisations that are unfamiliar to the vast majority of users and so users are not really in a position to assess their risk. There is total dependence on the developers of browser applications to maintain accurate and up-to-date certificate lists and on Certification Authorities to operate securely and efficiently. Incidents, however, are rare and this is not the most exposed facet of Internet security by a long shot.

IPSec

IPSec is an IPv6 (Internet Protocol version 6) framework that provides communication security at the network layer. It is a mandatory component for all IPv6 networks but it can be used with both IPv4 and IPv6. However, IPSec needs to be retrofitted to IPv4 'stacks' as it did not form part of the IPv4 protocol. There are three IPSec implementation options:

1.   **Integrated** – as a part of the IP stack in any IPv6 network.

2.   **Bump-in-the-stack (BITS)** – added to IPv4 router software.

3.   **Bump-in-the-wire (BITW)** – installed on a separate hardware node between the IPv4 routers and the external network.

Fail-open vs. Fail-closed

Imagine that you have installed a security system at home to protect your valuables and that this system has the ability to lock all of your doors and windows in the event of an alarm. What would you like the system to do if it experiences a technical failure?

•   **Fail-open** – leave your doors and windows unlocked so that you can still get in and out of the house?

•   **Fail-closed** – so that the house is locked down tight and nobody can get in or out?

Your choice will probably be determined by your risk assessment. What value do you put on your possessions, how does that stack up against the inconvenience and cost of having to stay at a hotel or with relatives until you can get the system fixed, and how often do you expect failures like this to occur – how reliable is the system?

Now, applying the same thought process to your corporate data, do you want your IT security systems to fail-open or fail-closed? Do you want different types of response for different systems? What is the trade-off between the possible impact of a data breach and the cost of lost business resulting from a security system fail-closed situation? There is no correct answer that covers all scenarios, but the fail-open vs. fail-closed question is one you need to address to any supplier of ICT security systems.

Firewalls

A Firewall is an application, device or group of devices designed to prevent unauthorised network or systems access by applying various rules to network traffic in an attempt to detect and block improper access attempts. Firewalls are active parts of the network that inspect incoming data packets and attempt to filter out any that have suspicious characteristics before they can enter the secure zone.

Firewalls incorporate both gateways and filters (they allow some traffic to pass through and they filter out other traffic) that sit on the boundary between the trusted network or system and the external or un-trusted network in what is commonly referred to as the Demilitarised Zone or DMZ. They are generally 'fail-closed' systems; if the Firewall fails, network access is not possible.

Firewalls have evolved over the years and they fall into three evolutionary categories:

1.   **Packet filters** – these first generation Firewalls inspected each data packet as it arrived and applied sets of rules (some very advanced) to each packet. Any packet that met one or more criteria would be blocked or diverted.

2.   **Stateful filters** – second generation Firewalls built on the packet filter approach by adding a new layer of analysis that looked at the circuit or communications layer. So, in addition to looking at the packet itself, Stateful filters apply rules to the state of the

connection, for example, based on whether it is a new connection or an existing session.

3. **Application layer filters** – third generation Firewalls add a set of filters based on rules applied to the 'application layer', which is the top layer in the Open Systems Interconnection model for network architectures. These Firewalls employ a technique known as 'deep packet inspection' to inspect the header and data part of each packet as it arrives at the Firewall. Packet contents are checked for their compliance with protocols and evidence of malicious code. Deep packet inspection is controversial as it is also often used to collect information of user activities and to facilitate censorship.

Intrusion Detection Systems

IDS are built based on an assumption that even the best defences can be defeated or circumvented. IDS provide an additional layer of defence and are generally passive in nature and 'fail-open'; if the IDS should fail normal network operations are not affected. An IDS monitors system and network events but does not form part of the actual process flow in the way that a Firewall does.

IDS functionality is dependent on two important assumptions:

1. the relevant system or network activities can be observed by the IDS;

2. there are distinctive attributes to normal and intrusive events.

IDS systems therefore require two logical components, one to capture event or other records from available sources and a second to apply models to that data in order to identify suspicious events. In terms of their technical architecture, this breaks down into the following modules:

• data collection and processing;

• filtering to eliminate unneeded information;

• a knowledge base – this represents the 'hard coding' of expert knowledge about past or potential security incidents;

- a decision engine which may be designed to learn based on system experience and user decisions about alerts;

- an alert generation and management engine;

- countermeasures (normally automated) designed to prevent an action from being executed or to restore the system to its secure state.

There are two primary classes of IDS:

1. **Host-based IDS** – these use OS auditing mechanisms to log all events, monitor user activities and the execution of programs.

2. **Network-based IDS** – these deploy sensors at strategic locations in a network to sniff packets, detect protocol violations and unusual patterns, and to inspect packet content for malicious code.

Key decisions to be made when selecting or implementing an IDS include the detection methods to be used and the character of the analysis engine, the behaviour to be exhibited on detection of a possible attack, which can range from passive reporting to blocking execution, the kinds of data the IDS will receive (that is, the audit source) and the usage frequency – will the IDS run in real-time or in offline mode. There are several obvious interdependencies here.

DEFEATING INTRUSION DETECTION SYSTEMS

Ironically, network-based IDS are often defeated by encryption, this time employed by the attackers, or by the insertion of code to obfuscate the attack. Both of these techniques are explained under anti-virus, below.

IDS can also be defeated via DoS attacks, in which CPU resources, memory or network bandwidth are deliberately exhausted. Reactive forms of IDS can be subjected to flooding with fabricated 'error' packets designed to trigger large volumes of false alerts (false positives) in order to persuade operators to either ignore the alerts, amend the rules, or even to take the IDS offline.

Distributed Denial of Service Resistance

Enhanced resistance to DDoS attacks using both Firewalls and IDS can be gained through the following means:

- **Scheduling** – when session requests are made to a server, a piece of software called a Scheduler determines which sessions will be processed and when. Historically, these decisions have been based on fairly simple rules such as 'first come, first served'. More advanced scheduling factors in the risk score assigned to a packet in order to ensure that the server is not flooded with high-risk session requests.

- **Anomaly detection** – in simple terms, traffic patterns can be examined in a number of ways to detect anomalies that may be suspect.

- **Volumetric analysis** – this involves looking for evidence of lots of requests in a short time period.

- **Header characteristics** – this includes searching for high-risk IP addresses or Ports in incoming packets.

- **Traffic flow pattern analysis** – to identify changes or fluctuations in patterns of traffic flow that match known or suspected attack scenarios.

- **Server load analysis** – during a DoS or DDoS attack, the target server's load counter will show a high amount of time delays to attend processes and a much larger than normal number of processes. Depending on the variety of the attack, access log and error log files may also grow abnormally. Each of these characteristics can be detected and reported to administrators in the form of alarms.

Anti-virus Software

Anti-virus software is used to prevent, detect and remove malware of all descriptions. Regularly updated anti-virus software is essential on every user device that is connected to the InterWeb. As mobility becomes the norm, anti-virus software on mobile devices is becoming increasingly important, yet very few mobile device owners have such software installed and this constitutes a major vulnerability for many networks at present.

FORENSIC MARKERS

Malware developers normally leave unintentional forensic markers behind. These markers may help to identify the developer or to link one payload with another, as is the case with Stuxnet and Flame which reportedly have several common markers. Analysis of this kind requires extensive technical expertise and deep knowledge of the malware sector and, even then, not every threat actor leaves a marker.

Some of the markers that analysts look for include the native language of the software, its syntax and any clues about what kind of keyboard or device language setting might have been used. Spelling errors in comments that accompany the code can also provide a clue.

Any indications as to whether the target or user is expected to speak a certain language can help to identify the attack vector or the nationality of the target (and hence that of the attacker) and the structure of the malware itself may provide indications about the type of intended target. Again, it has been reported that Stuxnet, for example, was specifically designed to target the kind of computer systems used in nuclear facilities, pointing to both victim and attacker.

It is important to keep in mind the fact that the malware developer is often not the same person as the threat actor or actors. Any of the 34,000 potential threat actors who downloaded the LOIC App in the UK are the potentially people guilty of a crime, but not necessarily the person who developed the LOIC itself.

ATTACK GROUP MARKERS

Attack groups also display variations in technique that might allow them to be identified and profiled. The types of malware used, their access methods, the method of privilege escalation and the types of exploitation observed, be they data exfiltration, lateral movement or file deletion and editing, can each help to paint a picture of who the threat actors might be, what their motivations are and how much inside knowledge they possess about your systems and security. All of these deductions help in the development of countermeasures and damage limitation strategies.

SIGNATURE-BASED DETECTION

Signature-based detection takes the form of searching for known patterns of data within executable code itself in order to find commonalities. There will always be infections active in the wild for which no signature is yet known; these are Zero Day threats, as we have already learned.

For Zero Day threats heuristics may be used, looking for seemingly malicious code or for slight variations of code previously seen. Anti-virus tools can also predict what a given file will do by running it in a 'sandbox' and observing its behaviour.

POTENTIAL DRAWBACKS OF ANTIVIRUS

Some anti-virus applications can unintentionally degrade device performance and users often opt to uninstall and replace anti-virus products in an attempt to optimise their systems. Less aware users uninstall and never reinstall, leaving their machines totally exposed.

Users may not understand anti-virus prompts and choices and many will make incorrect decisions that may lead to security breaches. If the anti-virus employs heuristic detection, success depends on achieving a balance between false positives and false negatives and false positives can be as destructive as false negatives, particularly when users become frustrated and again uninstall or deactivate their anti-virus security.

Cloud Security Assessments and Controls

Cloud security risk assessments should map the pathways through Cloud infrastructure and applications and establish clearly the routes by which key data travels or operational processes are executed, in order to assess the potential technical or business (operational, commercial or legal) impact of intrusions, fraud, data loss or process failures on the organisation, stakeholders, customers and brand. The impact of loss of service, governance failures and regulatory breaches should also be assessed.

Cloud security risk assessments require organisations to go beyond the standard analysis of business needs, assets and controls to cover the corresponding needs, assets, controls, responsibilities and capabilities of *every*

Cloud provider *and each of their sub-contractors*. As the Cloud Side Channel scenario described earlier illustrates, Cloud users might also want to get a better understanding of exactly who is sharing their remote hardware and restrictions in this regard might need to become a feature of Cloud service agreements.

In a Cloud context, risks and the responsibilities associated with the control of risks and the protection of key assets, cascade down from the subscribing organisation though every tier of the outsourced service provider model. The scope of risk management does not end, therefore, with the prime sub-contractor; risk control in the Cloud is an end-to-end function in the full meaning of the term.

A CLOUD APPROACH TO SECURITY

As Figure 10.2 illustrates, a layered approach to Cloud security is required, striped across the remote users and devices, the Cloud infrastructure itself, and the particular applications and data residing on that infrastructure.

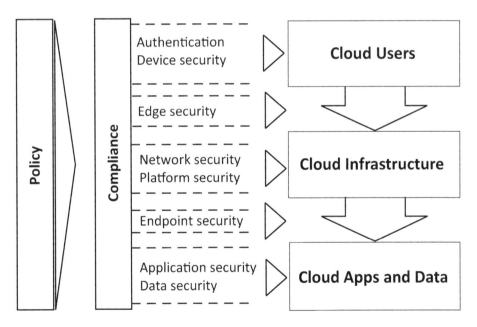

Figure 10.2   Cloud security considerations

The Cloud security model must support a virtualised multi-tenant environment with secure and isolated virtual tenancy, as well as a protected virtual network infrastructure. Tenant anonymity is essential, to limit informed attacks.

Data protection and integrity in the Cloud is also paramount, as is full support for all client types at the user end of the equation:

- **Thick clients** – primarily standard PCs running applications.

- **Thin clients** – devices using web-based or Cloud hosted applications and data storage.

- **Mobile clients** – thin or thick clients operating across a mobile data network, normally provided by a third party.

The Cloud is important and it's here to stay but there are risks and there have been Cloud security incidents. Cyber security continues to be a challenge for Cloud service providers and users and simple dependency on connectivity is a huge issue in and of itself.

Social Media Risk Policy and Practices

If you are involved in determining or managing an organisation's social media policies or usage, here is a basic list of activities you should consider undertaking:

- **Conduct a needs assessment** – what are the business drivers for the adoption or continued use of social media by employees and what roles or employees levels have a genuine need for work-related social media access? How important is personal social media access while on the job, for example, to support networking or to attract new employees?

- **Conduct a risk assessment** – what are the key risks to the organisation arising from, or exacerbated by social media use? Examples might include reputational harm, data disclosure and data protection issues, social engineering of employees, facilitation of insider trading, introduction of malware or loss of productivity.

- **Update your policies** – this should be based on the *balance* between risks and needs, and must set out in straightforward terms the organisation's policy on corporate and personal social media use.

- **Define a set of usage standards** – define the manner in which approved use of social media should occur, the language, branding and approval processes for public statements, and the references to the organisation and its employees that employees may or may not make via their personal social media pages. These standards can either be added to existing security guidance or adopted as separate guidelines.

- **Develop work-from-home and mobility standards** – set standards for employees' home WiFi usage and security, including password length and structure, as well as for the control, use and configuration of corporate mobile devices that might be used as a private social media portal by employees when away from the office.

- **Develop BYOD guidance** – provide guidance to employees on the minimum standards expected of them with respect to social media use and security on their personal devices (mobile phones, PDAs, tablets, laptops, and so on).

- **Organise awareness raising** – provide clear guidance to all employees and joiners on the terms of the organisation's social media policy and standards and explain the risk landscape that justifies those policies and standards.

- **Run best practice audits** – review actual social media practices, both via branded corporate pages and also via personal accounts where references to the brand are publicly made.

- **Conduct reputational risk monitoring** – monitor more general brand references or references to key employees and business events or issues (alleged corruption, mergers, acquisitions, share value, pricing, product launches, social responsibility, environmental issues, alleged design flaws, and so forth).

Cyber Security Tips for Travellers

Many of us travel for business on a frequent basis and even when we go on holiday we often take our work devices with us. Given the potential for these devices to be lost, stolen or examined by security personnel while abroad, I have come up with my personal list of cyber safe travel tips.

- always backup your important files before you go and leave the backup in a safe place;

- use data encryption for your portable devices and for your backups or sensitive Cloud documents based on some form of data classification;

- make sure that you use strong passwords for all of your devices;

- consider having a separate 'travel laptop' holding only the data you need for the trip;

- be wary of free WiFi zones as some of them might allow your data to be intercepted;

- assume that everything you do online while overseas is being monitored by local security officials;

- avoid using your credit card online or logging on to online banking while abroad;

- delete all files and recover all printouts if you use a hotel business centre;

- avoid leaving your devices in your hotel room and plan for this when you pack by including a small bag for your laptop or tablet;

- think twice before accepting USB sticks or DVDs/CDs from anyone.

Penetration Testing

The main threats to cyber security systems today are social engineering, intrusions of various types, application exploits, DoS attacks and malware.

Penetration testing is designed to identify and correct vulnerabilities in systems to these increasingly sophisticated attacks. Penetration testing can support your risk assessment and validation processes and it is one of the main tools used to combat cyber security and cyber crime risks. So what does it involve?

A good penetration test will convincingly simulate a credible attacker in order to identify genuine vulnerabilities. This form of testing is not effective if it is too tightly constrained by guidelines on what is and what is not acceptable, although testers must work by the medical standard of 'first, do no harm'. Tests must evaluate realistic exploits and describe plausible impacts. This allows testers and those tested to propose practical solutions to proven vulnerabilities. Tightly restricting testers to managers' preconceived (and often outdated) notions of what is possible tends to undermine the value of the test and testers should be given relatively free reign to experiment with various techniques. After all, actual attackers have free reign by default.

There are several types of penetration test and each requires a different set of skills, tools and techniques:

- physical site penetrations may require burglary or related skills;

- network penetrations require hacking skills;

- WiFi network penetrations require password cracking and lower-level hacking skills;

- social media penetrations or data extraction via online forums call for solid Web 2.0 skills;

- social engineering tests demand good role play or acting skills and a con man's gift of the gab.

Each of these types of test can be combined during the course of any particular Pen Test project.

INFORMED VS. UNINFORMED TESTS

Pen Tests may be either informed or uninformed. An informed test involves the testers being given details of the client's security arrangements in order that these may be stress tested. In an uninformed test, the testers have to approach the target blind and must find their own way around the systems and controls. Informed tests are useful when known risks or recently added controls need to be validated. Uninformed tests serve to highlight new risks or potential avenues of attack.

The goal of both types of penetration test is to ensure that the selected physical facilities, web-facing applications, networks or platforms are secure in terms of both technology and staff awareness in relation to unauthorised network access, including detection of and access to hidden WiFi networks and on-site physical network attacks. Typically, evidence in the form of screen captures and packet capture is required in the event of a successful penetration.

STANDARD PENETRATION TESTING METHODOLOGY

A majority of penetration tests adhere to the following four step methodology:

1. **Scoping** – defines the scope and approach of the test and sets markers for abort, test limits, authorisation and liability exceptions.

2. **Reconnaissance and scanning** – determines the systems and applications in use and identifies any potential vulnerabilities or access points.

3. **Execution and verification** – attempts actual penetrations and, if successful, verifies these by using the access gained to navigate to internal systems or execute other predetermined tasks.

4. **Reporting** – gathers evidence such as screen shots and packet captures and produces a written description of the test and its results. This often includes a short storyline of the test process.

This systematic process ensures that appropriate tests have been applied. The process is iterative and may involve re-testing as vulnerabilities are uncovered.

WIFI PENETRATION TESTING

Many WiFi networks are inherently insecure, with the man-in-the-middle attack being one form of attack. Other issues include weak passwords, published passwords (for example, for public WiFi) and leakage of private network coverage beyond the property boundary.

WiFi Pen Tests take two common forms:

1.   **Social engineering tests** – to see whether employees or contractors can be easily tricked into disclosing a password.

2.   **Technical penetration tests** – using purpose-built hardware and software designed to pickup network signals and intercept or crack the passwords.

There are two common WiFi security standards, WEP and WPA2. While it is possible to crack the passwords for both, network access via WPA2 networks is certificate-based and this means that exploitation of the cracked passwords is much more challenging.

The focus of some WiFi tests includes measuring WiFi signal leakage beyond the intended perimeter, testing the strength of WiFi passwords, attempting to launch man-in-the-middle WiFi attacks in order to capture packets and socially engineering WiFi passwords from staff.

SOCIAL MEDIA PENETRATION TESTING

Social media penetration testing is increasingly used to assess the risk of data leakage and reputational harm via social media friend networks, public posts and network analysis. Testing commonly involves exploits of the woefully inadequate identity verification systems employed by social media providers to set up fake profiles and attempts to con employees into disclosing business, customer or personal data.

SOCIAL ENGINEERING

Bernhard Maier, founder of BM-Investigations, Austria is one of the most impressive social engineering experts I have had the pleasure to meet. He uses these skills extensively as a private investigator and he has developed some very useful principles covering both the use and the ethics of social engineering. On the topic of social engineering as an art, Maier has this to say:

> *Role play during social engineering exploits is essential and requires a certain skill that can only really be perfected with long practice. Special knowledge of the relevant topic is also very useful. For example, if you are going to role play a medical doctor, then some knowledge*

of medicine and hospital procedures is certainly going to help! Props can also serve to convince the target. These might be as simple as a clip board or as sophisticated as a particular type of motor vehicle, for example, a delivery truck. Credibility is another essential aspect of this – you must look the part, both in terms of your physical appearance and in terms of how you dress. You must also act the part, so sincerity is high on my list as well. And finally there is empathy – people help those whom they like, so you need to bond with them by finding common ground before you launch your attack.

TESTING LIMITATIONS AND CAVEATS

The abort conditions for any test should be agreed with the sponsor in advance. This is often defined as the point at which it is certain that staff or systems are in the process of invoking security protocols or otherwise denying access 'in a firm and certain manner'.

As a general rule, testers must not delete files or data during testing, nor deface web pages or edit and delete user accounts. New accounts might be added where needed (when possible) but any additions must be documented to allow the test subjects to remove them on completion of the test. Unless agreed in advance, testers should not use any form of DoS attack on the target network or systems. You also need to be aware that during testing it is possible for any given network device or record (for example, routers or files such as log files) to be affected and you should alert those requesting the test of this potential hazard.

Convention dictates that there are 'Six Rs' to acceptable and ethical penetration testing. Tests must be:

1. **Risk-based** – aligned with client's risk appetite and their perceptions of risk.

2. **Realistic** – they must model credible attack scenarios.

3. **Reliable** – they must be executed by expert testers.

4. **Respectful** – of people, particularly users and security staff who might be embarrassed by the test result.

5.   **Responsible** – towards systems, data, the brand, and so on.

6.   **Reportable** – via screen captures, packet captures and data exfiltration, as appropriate.

To stay safe while testing, it is a good idea to assess every step of your test plan and execution against each of these criteria as you go along.

THE ETHICS OF DECEPTION

Maier also notes that during testing you may need to deceive people – in fact, you almost certainly will. There is another simple set of guidelines you can follow to ensure that each instance of deception is ethical in its own right:

- the test that depends on the deception delivers real value;

- the deception is necessary for the test to succeed;

- the harm caused by the deception is minimal;

- prior approval from client is given for the specific deception, or at the very least for the use of deception as a tool during the test and in the context within which the deception will be used.

Disaster Recovery and Business Continuity Management

Disaster recovery and business continuity are closely related but separate planning processes designed to ensure that any organisation can deal with and recover from any disruptive or damaging event. The type of event can range from severe weather or an earthquake to a major outbreak of civil unrest.

DISASTER RECOVERY

Disaster recovery covers the immediate response to such a major event. It ensures that:

- people are made or kept safe;

- property is secured, with the most sensitive or highest value assets receiving the earliest attention;

- coordination with the emergency services and local government is effectively established and maintained;

- customers are assisted in an appropriate and timely fashion.

BUSINESS CONTINUITY PLANNING (BCP)

BCP addresses business continuity through events on all parts of the scale, from the very small to the very big and ensures that the organisation can keep on providing services and will remain profitable and efficient. BCP will address power outages, data loss, communications loss (including phone and Internet), illness, loss of key personnel and so on.

Disaster recovery/business continuity plans include directions on who decides when a crisis is underway and how employees and customers are informed. The planning process should involve managers from all parts of the organisation and regular rehearsals to test key parts of the plan are very important, in a similar way to fire drills.

Conclusion

Also, as we will see in Chapter 11, the opportunities for investigators of all types to penetrate systems or to use online means to collect information about people and organisations has never been greater and this is due in large part to an absolute lack of user awareness at all levels. This digital intelligence gathering represents both the greatest cyber security threat and the greatest opportunity for practitioners in the current era.

11

Digital Intelligence

Introduction

Search online and you will find a plethora of definitions for the term 'digital intelligence'. Those who stake a claim of ownership variously describe it as a topic addressing online marketing, analysis of social media feeds or even the ability of humans to process digital information. There is no right answer, but I use the term to refer to the application of crime, state, military or other similar forms of intelligence analysis to the digital environment, primarily the Internet and World Wide Web in all its forms, along with all the supporting platforms and connected devices.

What is Intelligence?

'Intelligence' is the *product* of an analytical process called the 'intelligence cycle'. This process is executed by people with various intelligence functions, from data collection through data processing (possibly including decryption) to analysis. Even within this narrow definition, intelligence takes many forms and Table 11.1 provides some examples.

Table 11.1   Various forms of intelligence

Intelligence Type	Explanation
Crime intelligence	Used by police, corporate security and other such functions to develop a clearer picture of what kinds of crime are occurring, or are likely to occur, where, when, using what methods, committed by whom and with what motives. This intelligence can be used to catch those responsible or, preferably, for crime prevention and reduction.
Business intelligence	Used by business decision makers to understand their consumers, their business, pricing, trending and products.
Market intelligence	Also used by businesses to understand the competitive landscape, market drivers and size, future product requirements, as well as brand and reputational issues.

Intelligence Type	Explanation
Financial intelligence	Most commonly, this refers to the work of Financial Intelligence Units whose primary role is to detect, report and prevent financial crimes such as money laundering.
Military intelligence	Once described as 'a contradiction in terms', military intelligence is now an advanced art that focuses on the capabilities, vulnerabilities, intentions, dispositions and actions of an enemy and the operational environment, including political, social, cultural, economic and geographic factors.
Signals intelligence	Technically a sub-type, signals intelligence deserves a mention because of its significance. It addresses the interception or collection of a wide range of signals data including radio transmissions, phone calls, emails, social media posts and other online activities.
National intelligence	This refers to the product of the various national intelligence agencies which is used by political, military and industrial leadership for top-level strategic decision making. Its focus is geo-political.

The intelligence product in all its many forms is therefore used by a wide range of decision makers, including military and political leaders, business leaders, financial and market analysts or other actors, investigators, security heads, marketers, product managers and many others.

DIGITAL INTELLIGENCE

Digital intelligence refers to intelligence activities that are directed towards digital data sources, primarily in an online and telecommunications context. It now represents a subset of each of the types of intelligence listed in the above table, as in 'digital crime intelligence' or 'digital market intelligence'. Digital intelligence stripes across all forms of intelligence and is used, with varying degrees of sophistication and success, by all modern intelligence teams.

Digital intelligence, as employed in cyber and communications security, is benefiting from the merging of traditional law enforcement intelligence models and processes with commercial data analytics processes as it requires the employment of statistical techniques to give structure to data taken from the highly complex and vast digital ecosystem, characterised by Big Data,[1] where guesswork and intuition often fail.

Digital intelligence differs from Computer Forensics in that the latter focuses on recovering data from devices seized during the course of an investigation, such as laptops, PCs and mobile phones, while the former focuses on live data

---

1   Big Data is data that stretches or exceeds the processing capacity of conventional database systems.

in transmission, data held in active memory, or data held in storage on devices that are still being used as intended by their owners. Most forensics, therefore, could be described as taking place in a controlled environment, post-event, while most digital intelligence work is carried out in the wild, pre-event or during and in the immediate aftermath of an incident.

Digital intelligence source data can be broken down into at least three classes:

1.   Data sourced from a storage system, such as transactional databases, system logs or message inboxes.

2.   Data held in memory but not saved or deliberately transmitted between two parties, including keystrokes, Cookies and web page visit information.

3.   Intelligence data gathered from live communications across a network such as call intercepts or packet captures.

Digital intelligence data may be gathered from storage in a number of ways. It may be located in a database on a remote system, requiring remote access, or it may be held as a post on the public pages of a subject's social media service, such as Twitter. Data held in memory is often gathered by using monitoring techniques such as Spyware Key Loggers. Data may be captured during transmission by way of intercepts of telecoms traffic (including voice, messaging and data), radio traffic, email messages, and deep packet inspection or other interception techniques.

Within each class we can think about a couple of major categories of digital intelligence data:

•   **Open source data** – public online posts, web pages, online news feeds and Blogs, broadcasts and podcasts, public speeches, and so on where there is no realistic expectation of privacy.

•   **Private data** – corporate or government systems, private online posts and messages, emails, phone calls or other digital messaging technologies such as short message service (SMS) and multi-media service.

Considerable care and thought must be given to each data source. For example, unsent draft emails are sometimes used to communicate through the sharing of account information between two distant parties (that is, I draft a message but do not send it, saving it in my Drafts folder instead. You then logon from somewhere else with the same username and password, read the draft, type a reply, and save that as a draft for me to read later). These emails are not 'transmitted' and thus fall into the data in storage bucket, as they can only be read by accessing the storage area of the relevant email account.

The digital intelligence challenges faced by any security, compliance, audit or other forms of enforcement organisation, whether governmental or commercial, are numerous and many of them relate to how and when such intelligence can and should be used. However, before even that complex question can be faced, organisations need to jump several hurdles.

The Digital Intelligence Cycle

The digital intelligence cycle depicted in Figure 11.1 describes the process by which *relevant data* is processed and converted to *usable intelligence* and distributed to whose with a *need to know*. It normally includes the following steps:

1. **Direction and planning** – what can you collect, where will you source it, how and when?

2. **Digital data collection** – the act of sourcing data, which may be an ongoing process.

3. **Data aggregation** – the organisation of data around selected key data elements, for example by aggregating or summarising all activity related to a particular account to show total numbers of events, total spend per month, and so on.

4. **Evaluation or scoring** – the assignment of some form of confidence score to events or aggregated results where an indication of risk or some other agreed criteria is required.

5. **Data analytics** – the conversion of processed data to digital intelligence, for example by linking scored data elements together

to form a chart revealing the likely source of a fraud or of an attack, or the use of geo-location to place message sources on a map. There are numerous possibilities here and the analytics facet of digital intelligence is an important growth area.

6.   **Dissemination** – the sharing of the digital intelligence product with those who have a need to know and who are also authorised to know in a form that they can easily understand.

The digital intelligence cycle

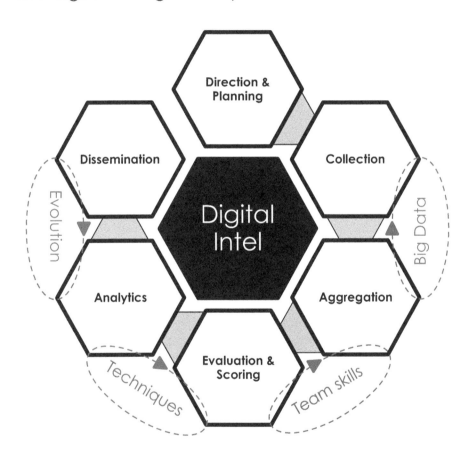

Figure 11.1   The digital intelligence cycle

As Figure 11.1 also shows, a few additional considerations need to be taken into account.

BIG DATA

Most digital data today comes in the form of Big Data. As you will recall, this refers to data sets that are too large to be efficiently processed by conventional data-processing platforms. So, right away, the digital intelligence team faces a challenge in terms of how best to collect, process and store data, how long to retain it and how to efficiently mine it.

Professor Paul Morrissey of the Tele Management Forum has identified four key issues that need to be considered during any Big Data project, all of which are relevant to digital intelligence investigators (see Figure 11.2). The comments included beside each issue are my own:

- **Volume** – Big Data is, well, Big.

- **Variety** – Big Data comes in a bewildering variety of formats and from an ever expanding set of data sources.

- **Velocity** – Big Data is being moved about at light speed and the window for collection and analysis can be very small.

- **Veracity** – just because it's big doesn't mean it's correct and analysts need to verify the relevance and veracity of each data source prior to basing their conclusions upon it.

Collecting, processing, storing and distributing data are all increasingly difficult tasks as the current growth in data volumes, speed of production (and hence the demands on timeliness of data), and the variety of forms continues.

Analysis organisations need to develop a comprehensive technology strategy to support Big Data management, whether this involves the creation of large data repositories (as in the data warehouse model) or the use of applications able to dip into multiple existing data sources simultaneously, without duplicating high-volume data storage.

Solutions must allow analysts to pull disparate data sets together, easily and without a requirement for them to handle the mundane tasks of mapping

The Big Data V⁴ Model

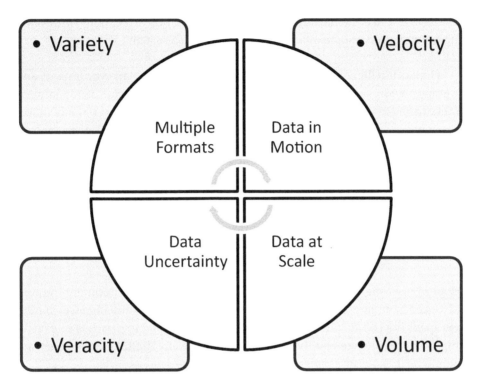

Figure 11.2   The Big Data V4 Model
Source: Adapted from figure by Professor Paul J. Morrissey.

fields and formats, to support reconciliations, geo-mapping, charting and link analysis, trending, queries and statistical reporting. This needs to be achieved with minimal latency so that the intelligence goal of providing accurate intelligence when it is needed can be met.

TEAM SKILLS

The words 'collect', 'process', 'store' and 'analyse' should immediately alert you to the fact that digital intelligence is as much a technical process as it is an intelligence process. The modern intelligence team is a data-processing and analytics team, as well as being an investigative and forensics team. Nevertheless, people's brains are always going to be more important than the technologies they interact with. The role of technology in intelligence is to facilitate the management of data and its conversion into more easily understood forms, but it will generally be human users who must interpret the results and make the most important decisions, handle exceptions or develop those innovative responses not programmed into a system.

Digital intelligence organisations need to invest in staff recruitment and training. A mix of skills is required including intelligence and data analytics, data management or database administration, statistical and mathematic, investigations, operational security, audit or enforcement, as well as managerial and leadership skills. Of equal importance is a clear career path within the organisation for digital intelligence recruits, either within digital intelligence itself, or across the wider organisation. Digital intelligence will struggle to attract and retain high-calibre professionals in the absence of such clearly defined paths and related personal development plans.

TECHNIQUES FOR ANALYSIS

Modern investigations and forensics in a Big Data environment require advanced software tools and techniques. The Business Intelligence market has spent the last few decades devising and perfecting approaches to exactly this kind of challenge and that is probably where any digital intelligence team should be looking for inspiration.

Digital intelligence teams need to move from simplistic trending and alerting models towards richer and deeper approaches to analysis that draw data from multiple sources to create new three dimensional views that would not otherwise have been available. Some of these sources may be non-traditional, such as open source social media posts or keyword strings in Blog comments. Some of the main techniques of relevance today include:

- Charting and link analysis;

- Geo-location analysis and mapping;

- Attribution of transactions to devices and people;

- Detection of markers in code;

- Device profiling;

- Web visit profiling;

- Capture and analysis of social media content;

- Image and reverse image searching;

- Steganographic analysis.

EVOLUTION

This arena is going to continue to evolve in line with the evolution of technology, services and user activities and awareness. All types of user are likely to become smarter about how they operate online and serious criminals will quickly become more adept at concealing their digital footprint. Digital intelligence teams need to evolve at the same pace if they are going to continue to be relevant and to deliver value.

Because digital intelligence is dependent on the Internet and database technologies as data sources and is required to identify threats and trends in a hugely complex and dynamic world, it cannot remain static. Those planning for or investing in digital intelligence will be doing themselves and their sponsors a disservice if they fail to design a model that will evolve and improve rapidly in response to daily changes in the environment.

Digital intelligence teams therefore need to develop iterative approaches to refine and extend their analytical techniques in the face of change and new data sources. As with any new intelligence function, sponsors should not expect results overnight and it may take years before this fledgling function fully matures.

Although the intelligence model on which my list has been based[2] is presented in different ways by different organisations, the principles it captures are universal; the collection, collation and interpretation of data, followed by its dissemination in the form of intelligence to those with a need to know. This process is an essential one that ensures that expertise is applied to raw data before conclusions are drawn by decision makers. The 'stove-piping' of raw data to leadership, without it having passed through the sanity checks

---

2   See Clive Hartfield and Karen Hartfield, 2008. *Intelligence,* Oxford: Oxford University Press, page 65.

imposed by this cycle, has often been a leading cause of business, political, diplomatic and military failure.

DIRECTION AND PLANNING

Online data sources are unimaginably vast and, as we will see when we look at the Deep Web, even the open source data can be relatively hard to get at, with many analysts remaining ignorant of the full range of available sources. There is a real danger that your digital intelligence project will end up being more about data collection and processing than it is about analysis and decision making. In my experience, many projects reach a point where 80 per cent (or more) of the effort and cost relates to data collection and storage and less than 20 per cent is related to actual analytics tasks and the intelligence product, with little measureable business value being realised because of this imbalance.

Most failures of this kind stem from poor direction and planning and the blame often lies with managers who underestimate the technical task and overestimate the value of the outputs from pure data processing – they forget about the role of the human brain in analytics and they don't invest in having the right kind of people in sufficient numbers to do the really valuable work. There really is no point in spending ten or 15 million dollars on data collection if you are then going to hire low-grade 'analysts' to perform the really difficult part of the job.

Some of the things you should consider when planning your project include:

- What are the top priority subjects, risks or questions you need to develop intelligence on? Make a list and refer to it often as you proceed.

- Where does the most valuable data sit and how can you source it and process it in a lawful and ethical fashion? Avoid being distracted by other opportunities to collect data that is of less relevance and value and make sure that you have a business case for every data collection activity.

- Once collected, what kinds of analysis will need to be performed to create valuable intelligence from the raw data? Plan the technical and human resource side of the analysis project in detail before you start the data collection activity.

- What will the recipients of the intelligence you produce do with it? Think about how your product needs to be presented and what forms of corroboration might be needed to support decision making.

- For Internet enquiries, what is your detailed investigation plan? (See the planning and guidance matrix provided later in this chapter.)

Handling Digital Intelligence Data

The data collection process occurs differently based on whether the data in question is open source or not, and on whether it is in storage, in memory or in transmission. The process is also affected by the identity of the organisation or individual attempting to collect the data and the identity of the target system holding the data.

These factors, acting in conjunction with one another, will determine where on the spectrum between investigative journalism and state espionage the data collection activity sits. Before you eagerly kick-off your own data collection project, you should place yourself on that spectrum and then evaluate how well your intended data collection techniques map on to your positioning.

STRUCTURED AND UNSTRUCTURED DATA

Source data may be either structured or unstructured. Structured data generally comes in table form or as delimited records with a fixed format, which is to say that the expert processing it knows what each field within a record should contain:

- Field 1 = Caller's phone number.

- Field 2 = Caller's SIM number.

- Field 3 = Caller's Cell Site ID, and so forth.

Unstructured data may contain a jumble of words or values, in no particular order. The contents of emails would represent unstructured data – we cannot predict what they may contain, what order the contents will be in, the language or spelling that will be used or even the meaning of particular words. Different kinds of analysis are required to process unstructured data, including key word searches and various heuristics but risks abound as reportedly shown in the case of the elderly lady who was arrested for emailing an account of the 'burning bush' from the Bible to a friend because an intelligence system determined that she was a threat to the life of then US President George Bush. There is a limit to what a rules based system can do.

Structured data tends to be easier to process and will often provide greater value in terms of assessing who sent which message to whom, from where, at what time and on what date. Unstructured data, while more difficult to process and analyse, will tend to offer much more value in terms of message content; what was said, felt, thought or believed, what a target's values and intentions might have been, or what their awareness of a third party's plans was:

- structured data is often more precise;

- unstructured data is often richer.

ENCRYPTED AND UNENCRYPTED DATA

A great deal of the digital intelligence data that might be gathered by an authorised body will be encrypted. For example, most telecommunications call records require decoding or decryption before they can be read by data analysis systems or with the human eye. This requires the creation of customised decoders or 'data readers' for every encoded data source. These data readers sit between the source and the analysis system and every new file containing collected data must be passed through them for processing before the main task of the intelligence system can commence. This can constitute an important bottleneck with strategic effects when decision makers fail to commit sufficient resources to what they regard as a mundane technical decryption task.

Many cases that come to the attention of the public, such as the recent *News of the World* 'phone hacking' scandal or the Climate Gate emails, actually involved unencrypted data that could be easily read by non-technical people. The forms of Big Data that are sometimes analysed by corporate security and fraud teams, or by employees of certain states, require much greater investments in software and hardware and the collection and reading of most of this data is not a trivial task, costing millions of dollars to achieve on an industrialised scale. Even within the competent bodies, there is a dearth of skilled people able to support the data collection and reading process and this adds to the intelligence challenge.

You should keep in mind two further categorisations, this time related to the form the source data might take:

- Relatively small volumes of un-encoded data that can be processed by anyone with a standard laptop.

- Large volumes of encrypted data that require serious IT skills and heavy weight computing systems normally only available to a business or the state, although a few independent actors will also possess these capabilities.

STEGANOGRAPHY

Steganography is the science of concealing messages within other media, such as images, video or sound files. This can be performed as an alternative to encryption, or it might be the case that the concealed message is itself encrypted, adding a second layer of security.

A simplistic example of this increasingly popular secret messaging technique involves editing the RGB (red, green, blue) value of given pixels in an image. The colour of the pre-defined pixels corresponds to a letter or number, but if the image is of sufficiently high resolution, the human eye will not detect the alteration. By this means, secret communications can occur in plain sight, for example via a Facebook photo album. Every digital intelligence team requires some familiarity with such forms of hidden text, of which there are many.

DATA AGGREGATION AND ENRICHMENT

One additional change that Big Data brings is the requirement to aggregate data before attempting many forms of analysis. Individual data records are now more granular than ever before (one part of a phone call, a data session record and so on) and a single file containing one day's communications data may contain billions of rows. Aggregation refers to the process of pulling like records together, based on a set of rules, so that multiple records can be expressed as a single row of data. For example, one might wish to aggregate all financial transaction data in a given data set, such that all transactions are consolidated at account level – one row per account in the aggregated table.

Data often requires enrichment before it can be effectively used for analysis. A typical mobile call record will include a record of the cell tower used to connect the call, but that might be expressed as a numerical value that has little meaning to an analyst. To address such a problem, a table that lists all numerical cell tower values and gives them a text-based name (as in '1234567 = Norwich Town Centre') is often used to 'enrich' the record. More aggressive enrichments involve the use of data in a record to calculate or insert a new value into the record, for example, adding a caller's name and address based on the SIM card number in a call record, or computing the cost of a transaction based on an external table of charges or on a pre-defined formula.

ENRICHMENT VS. TAMPERING

The line between data enrichment to support crime or intelligence analysis and tampering with evidence may be a thin one. Analysts are advised to:

- keep a detailed record of every step taken to adjust data records, with justifications;

- store backup copies of the data at every stage in the process, from raw data through each step of the aggregation and enrichment process, in order that the process can be repeated by independent assessors to validate that the final outputs were correctly arrived at.

This chain of evidence requirement only adds to the Big Data storage challenge.

Open Source Internet Investigations

The Web 2.0 is not fully machine readable and search engines use 'crawlers' or 'robots' to read and index hyperlinks and keywords. These crawlers need to be told what they should and should not index using inclusion and exclusion standards or protocols and their results are severely limited for a number of reasons. Search engines obtain their listings in two ways: either page authors submit their web pages to the engine, or search engine robots 'crawl' documents by moving from one hypertext link to another. This second approach returns the bulk of the listings. Robots work by recording every hypertext link and keyword in every page they index while crawling. Like ripples spreading across a pond, search engine crawlers are thus able to extend their indices further and further from their starting points.

The search results are compiled in indexes, with each search engine company (Google, Yahoo, Bing and so on) maintaining their own particular set of indexes. Users can search these indexes for keywords or word combinations, but the results of a Google search can differ from those of a Bing search because every index is unique. Each search engine actually maintains different indexes for different geographic regions and searches via the Google UK index will again produce different results from those obtained via the Google index in, say, Russia. So, contrary to the widely held belief that the whole world is connected to a shared data set, the reality is that Internet users in Russia, Europe, China or the USA may actually be reading very different content on the same topics, automatically or manually adapted to fit their perceived preferences, or possibly those of their respective governments.

INCLUSION AND EXCLUSION STANDARDS

Every website issues instructions to search engine crawlers on what should be included in its indexing search and which pages should be excluded. The two standards are:

1.   the Sitemaps Inclusion Standard or Protocol;

2.   the Robots Exclusion Standard.

The Sitemaps Protocol

The Sitemaps Protocol allows a webmaster to inform search engines about URLs on a website that are available for crawling. A Sitemap is an XML file that lists the URLs for a site and this allows search engines to crawl the site more intelligently. You can see an example of a simple sitemap by visiting my company's website at http://www.trmg.biz/sitemap.

Robots Exclusion Standard

The Robots Exclusion Standard takes the form of a text file named Robots.txt. This instructs crawlers to *ignore* named pages and it is used to hide selected pages or sites from search engines, preventing indexing, in theory. Compliance on the part of the crawler is by consent and the use of Robots.txt exclusions doesn't actually protect the excluded page. In fact, it can serve as a marker for a hostile search as to which pages might be the most interesting.

Page source and keywords

If you right click on a blank space on any web page a menu should pop-up and if your browser is set to display in English, 'View page source' will be one of the options shown. On most pages this source will include a set of keywords that are indexed by search engine robots when they visit that page. As explained earlier, this feature can be abused to pull people to the site, but the keywords used also give you vital clues about who the site is really meant for. For example, if what appears to be a real estate site actually contained keywords such as 'skunk' 'money' and 'cash', then all may not be as it seems.

The Deep Web

The main shortcoming of traditional search engines is that they are almost totally dependent on the Web's links to identify what data available online. However, less than 10 per cent of the open source data on the Internet is made available in this manner and only about 27 per cent of that is in English. This means that if you run an English Google web search on any given topic, you are likely to be searching only 2.7 per cent of the available data online at best, and even then you are further constrained by the fact that search engines limit the amount of data they bring back to you and that each index is also artificially limited in terms of what it holds.

There is tremendous value in the data that resides deeper in the Web than this very limited set of surface content; the information is there, but it is hiding beneath the surface of the Web. The Deep Web is that part of the Internet containing public data that is not indexed by conventional web crawlers. This deep or 'invisible web' is partly comprised of databases that sit below the hyperlinked web space and many estimates put the volume of data held in the invisible web at 500 times the 2.5 billion documents already held in hyperlinked surface web pages.

The main types of Deep Web data include:[3]

- web pages which are not linked to by other pages;

- public information held in large databases;

- scripted content accessible through links produced by JavaScript as well as content dynamically downloaded from web servers via Flash or Ajax solutions;

- private web password-protected data;

- content stored on other networks that run over the Internet;

- text content using the Gopher protocol;

- files hosted on File Transfer Protocol (FTP) sites;

- information hosted on networks, such as 'Tor' – The onion router.

There are commercial products available that have started to explore this new terrain. Pipl (http://pipl.com/help/deep-web/) claims to deliver much more data than standard searches, while Spokeo (https://www.spokeo.com) focuses on email names and social media searches. However, most Deep Web tools are still US and English language focused, although a Chinese firm is set to launch a new Deep Web search tool to address that huge market.

The Deep Web is an important area for online searching that must be incorporated into any serious open source enquiry, but traditional sources remain important because they are intended for publication and the quality and relevance of the information they contain will in many cases be higher than that held in Deep Web repositories. So, don't let the hype carry you away – search everything.

---

3   Ron Kelson, Pierluigi Paganini, Benjamin Gittens, David Pace and Fabian Martins, *The Malta Independent*, 14 October 2012.

The Multi-lingual InterWeb

Many in the west still tend to assume that the InterWeb is pulling the global community towards English as the common online language and that this has implications for a continuing spread of western ideals, ideas and culture. In reality, the fastest growing online language is Arabic, while Chinese now accounts for 24 per cent of web content. Forty five per cent of current Internet users live in Asia.

The Web is now truly globalised and when we search it we need to search it with a globalised mindset. In practical terms, this means searching in multiple languages, searching multiple indexes and using appropriate search terms, names and spellings in order to bring back truly relevant results. It is important, for example, to search international subjects using the appropriate languages; search where they live, work, travel or originate, as well as where they might be now.

Websites like Yamli (www.yamli.com) support Arabic-to-English searches and display Arabic text results alongside the English versions. 2lingual (www.2lingual.com) supports searches in two languages at once, including Chinese, Russian and many others.

Managing Your Online Search Footprint

The footprint left behind by your website visits is an important consideration because Google and other search sites track and store data on all of your searches, profile your activities and then deliver search results that match your profile. Website owners can often track who has visited, so if you are investigating criminal activity or the hacker community and you don't want to become the target of their counter-intelligence operations, you need to be extremely careful about how you go about things.

In addition to tracking your visit, sites also report what you are doing to other sites. The 'Collusion' plug-in (available for Firefox and Chrome at the time of writing) allows you to see which sites are reporting your activities and to whom in the form of a dynamic visual display.

If you wish to hide your IP address you have the option to download and use 'Tor', although this is not an endorsement and you must investigate the tool and the rules that might affect your rights to use it for yourself. Tor routes your online sessions through a relay of proxy servers and gives the impression that you are online in, say, Russia or the USA when you are in fact working from the UK. However, Tor also slows your browsing speeds down dramatically.

Viewing cached data whenever possible, rather than visiting the live page, can also help to lower your profile. The Internet Archive (http://archive.org/) is a privately funded repository that collects and stores web pages from across the Internet and allows you to search them historically. While this means that you won't be seeing the latest content, you will remain hidden from the page owner and you will also see content that might have since been removed. This last point is the real winner, although you should bear in mind the fact that whoever owns the archive can track and log your IP address and all of your searches.

Other techniques include the use of fake online identities for connecting or searching in social media and the use of a 'dirty' search PC that is not connected to the corporate network.

Effective Searching

Effective searches are totally dependent on users inputting appropriate search criteria because, as stated, each search engine uses proprietary web crawling and indexing criteria and indexes may also be distributed across numerous geographically dispersed platforms. Searching requires the use of multiple search engines in order to exploit the strengths of each and the use of advanced search 'operators' is also very important.

Note that search engine results can be very limited. For example, a search that claims to return 30 million results will only list ten–15 pages at ten items per page. In most cases, you cannot access the remaining 29.999 million 'hits'. Search engine results are also displayed by popularity, not merely by relevance to the search. From an investigator's perspective, this limits the value of online searches dramatically. Using different browsers and different search engines can help a little, but the main challenge remains and the only ways to dig deeper are to use more refined search techniques and Deep Web search engines, most of which are not free.

Some important additional search techniques include:

- image search filtering by type, colour, date and size;

- reverse image searches – searching online by using an actual image as opposed to describing the image with text;

- file type searches (for example, use 'filetype:xls' to search only for MS Excel files);

- searching by source to bring back only results from that source, as in 'source: Wikipedia';

- using wildcards.

Look at the search operators provided online by each search engine for more details. Twitter, Facebook and others also publish operators that help you to get a more valuable search result from their sites.

By combining the excellent resources freely available online from www.toddington.com[4] with my own research and experience, I have developed the Aide Memoire shown in Table 11.2 as a guide for Internet investigators. You will need to adapt this guide to suit your purposes and, more importantly, to match the legal, regulatory and corporate rules under which you operate.

Table 11.2   An Internet investigator's Aide Memoire

Activity	Tips and Advice	Investigation Plan	Investigation Notes
PLANNING	Determine the type of search you need to conduct. People search or company search? Subject or theme? Event or location?		
Rules	Confirm the legal rules you are working under.		
Surveillance	Consider whether undercover operations or surveillance (electronic or otherwise) and search warrants are required.		
Entrapment	Ensure correct legislation is followed regarding live communication (chat) with suspects or other parties.		

---

4   Accessed December 2012.

Footprint	Decide how you will conceal your search footprint if this is necessary for your own security (for example by using Tor or a Proxy Server).		
Proxy	If a proxy server is used, consider legal implications of changing your identity/location.		
Logging	Choose your search logging tool (for example, Zotero) or case management tool.		
Disclosure	Ensure FULL logging and disclosure of ALL steps taken, proxy servers used, communication with suspect(s) and authorisations received.		
Capture	Use plug-ins such as 'PDF It' or print screen/copy and paste functions to capture your findings.		
Capture	Consider capturing the whole search with tools like Snagit or Camtasia.		
Language	Determine the appropriate languages for your searches.		
Translation	Use translation tools to search for information in other languages if necessary.		
Engines	Decide which search engines you need to use and the optimum domains for search engine indexes.		
Meta search	Consider starting out with meta search tools for the first phase of the search.		
Filters	Adjust your search filters as appropriate before you commence searching.		
KEYWORD SEARCHES	Use the relevant search operators for each search engine.		
File types	Consider searching by file type, based on the type of data you are looking for.		
Advanced	Use advanced search techniques, including 'links' searching, Boolean or enforced term operators and forced-phrase searching.		
NAME SEARCHES	Use every possible name configuration and variation.		
Nicknames	Make guesses as to possible nicknames.		

Activity	Tips and Advice	Investigation Plan	Investigation Notes
WEBSITE VISITS	Conduct 'Whois' lookups on any IP addresses or domain names located.		
Accuracy	Always bear in mind the fact that IP address geo-location may be inaccurate or that it may be 'spoofed'.		
Traces	Ascertain physical server location using TraceRoute.		
Robots.txt	Examine robots.txt file exclusion standard to locate 'hidden' pages within a website.		
Page Source	Examine HTML for keywords, images and 'hidden text'.		
EMAILS	Trace emails to point of origin using most appropriate method.		
NEWS MEDIA SEARCHES	Search within news media sites using the site search functions normally provided.		
SOCIAL MEDIA SEARCHES	Search social networking sites and online communities such as Facebook, MySpace, Friends Reunited, Convicts Reunited, Bebo, and so on.		
Privacy	Respect privacy settings.		
Fake profiles	Avoid using fake profiles unless you have permission to do so.		
Communication	Unless otherwise advised, treat communications between site users as you would email traffic.		
Maps	Use tools like Geofeedia and Bing Twitter Maps or Flikr Maps to see geo-location mapping of social media posts for devices with location services enabled.		
CHATS, FORUMS AND ADS	Search message forums, groups and Usenet newsgroups.		
Community	Examine online classified and community sites such as Kijiji, Ebay, Craigslist, Listpic, using names, phone numbers and email addresses.		
Nicknames	Use nicknames as well as real names to search forums.		

BLOG SEARCHES	Search Blogs and free domain hosting sites such as Angelfire and Tripod.		
Themes	Search Blogs by theme as well as by user name.		
DEEP WEB SEARCHES	Search the Deep Web and locate relevant databases including electoral register, telephone directories, business databases, maps and genealogy sites.		
Geography	Use the Deep Web engines most appropriate for your geography.		
Associations	Also search in the geographic areas your subjects come from, visit or otherwise engage with.		
IMAGE SEARCHES	Search media sites such as Flickr, YouTube, Tineye, Webshots, Photobucket, Piclens, Pinterest, and so on.		
Search terms	Use a wide range of search terms as images might not be stored with the name of your search subject in the file name.		
Search options	Explore the available search options such as colour, file size, type of image, and so on.		
Exif data	Examine images for background information and explore Exchangeable Image File ('Exif') data for date, time, equipment specification and GPS coordinates.		
Reverse search	Use reverse image searches to search by image rather than keywords, meta-data or watermarks.		
Privacy	Before uploading an image for a reverse image search, consider whether you might be the first to put that image online and what the privacy implications of that act might be.		
VIDEO SEARCHES	Search for videos by subject, keywords, location, author and actors using both names and nicknames.		
Reverse Video	Stay in touch with the fledgling reverse video search sector and use that new technique when appropriate.		

Activity	Tips and Advice	Investigation Plan	Investigation Notes
INTERNET ARCHIVE SEARCHES	Examine the Internet Archive (www.archive.org) to locate antecedent information, previous site format and early associations.		
Bing cache	Use the green down arrow under Bing search results to review page cache.		
Footprint.	Remember that any update to page content (for example, to import images) may leave a footprint of your visit on the target webpage.		
SECONDARY SUBJECTS	Search for secondary targets such as friends, associates, family members, ex-partners, children, and so on.		
Peripheral info	Search for peripheral information such as vehicles, previous addresses, images or information referring to similar or past offences.		
Maps	Use tools like Google Maps, Bing Maps and Street View to gather more background details.		
FURTHER ENQUIRIES	Continually evaluate source and data for accuracy and show corroboration, links and locations.		
Forensics	If a suspect is located, consider whether a forensic examination of their computer system may be required and whether it is a realistic and permissible activity.		

The use of meta search engines can add a further enhancement to your work. Meta search engines execute a single search across multiple traditional search engine indexes. For example, www.dogpile.com simultaneously searches Google and Yahoo and eliminates any duplicates in the results. However, meta search engine results are even more constrained than conventional results and should be used only as a backup technique, or to get your search started as an initial tool of enquiry.

In summary, to execute effective online searches you need to:

- search ethically and within the law;

- search securely by hiding your footprint, if appropriate;

- use multiple search tools;

- use advanced search operators;

- search in multiple languages;

- use reverse image searches as well as text and file type searches;

- search the Deep Web AND the surface web.

Social Media as a Data Source

With over a billion people now communicating via social media services such as Facebook, Twitter and LinkedIn, the appeal of user posts and messages as sources of crime intelligence or evidence has never been stronger. The diversity of social media enhances its value as a source of information, but just as this vast seam of data is starting to be efficiently mined, a number of important inhibitors are also being identified. New US legislation in the form of AB 1844, questions about privacy and data protection, major flaws in the processes employed by social media providers for validating users' online identities, as well as attribution and geo-location challenges, may all conspire to undermine the reliability of social media evidence.

SOCIAL MEDIA COMPLEXITY AND VOLUMETRIC CHALLENGES

Legal and ethical thinking in relation to digital or open source online evidence and intelligence gathering is still playing catch up with the rapidly evolving social media product and service mix. One can spot this in the language used, for example in the way that social network services are generally treated as being homogeneous when, in fact, they have highly specialised characteristics.

Danah Boyd and Nicole Ellison defined social network services as 'web-based services that allow individuals to (1) construct a public or semi-public profile within a bounded system, (2) articulate a list of other users with whom they share a connection, and (3) view and traverse their list of connections and those made by others within the system'.[5]

While this definition is still heavily relied upon, it is already seriously outdated because the services have evolved. For one thing, social networking site members can now use privacy settings to create a non-public profile, limiting their connections to a very small group and possibly to a single contact. By so doing, they might claim that they are no longer networking but rather that they are communicating and that they therefore have an expectation of privacy. There are many differing views.

Secondly, social media has subsumed social networking. Social media is much richer and much more diverse than social networking, encompassing Blogging, micro-Blogging (for example, Tweeting), posting content, gaming and many other activities. Social media frequently includes a social networking component, but networking and communications within a group of contacts may not be the primary purpose of the user. In fact, many social media services are more akin to broadcast media than to networking. These distinctions are critical because of their likely impact on the value of evidence collected from social media sites, as we shall see, and this complex mix of services requires a finely crafted set of guidelines because each facet of social media has the potential to confront investigators and the courts with unique points for consideration.

Meanwhile, those who talk of capturing and analysing social media content in bulk might not fully appreciate the sheer scale of the social media data mountain. As mentioned, Facebook's data storage is growing by 0.5 Petabytes every two days and that firm, like its rivals, maintains vast data storage facilities consuming huge amounts of power and materials in their construction and operation. But how much of the data that they find themselves forced to hold is of any real practical value to firms or law enforcement? Very little, one suspects, and that value will decline further as users become more aware of monitoring.

PRIVACY AND USER IDENTITIES

Internet search engine provider Google has long been in the privacy spotlight and the company is not well served by recent missteps or by public statements by its CEO, Eric Schmidt. In October 2012 the firm admitted that its Street View vehicles had collected personal emails, passwords and other data by tapping into the unsecured Wi-Fi connections of private citizens. Why the cars would

---

5   http://jcmc.indiana.edu/vol13/issue1/boyd.ellison.html (accessed January 2013).

even be equipped to do this in the first place is unclear. Then in September 2012 the search giant confirmed that an employee had been fired for accessing the personal data of several users, four of whom were children, casting doubt on its internal security and data protection mechanisms.

Both users and watchdogs have long voiced concern about Google's control over users' online data and profiles. Schmidt has spoken to these concerns, but his predictions about the future of online data collection and use are worrying to many. This example, quoted in the *Atlantic*[6] in September 2010, is typical,

> *With your permission you give us more information about you, about your friends, and we can improve the quality of our searches. We don't need you to type at all. We know where you are. We know where you've been. We can more or less know what you're thinking about.*

Last year in the UK, the matter of Lord McAlpine's painfully public Trial-by-Tweet occupied much press time and it served to underline some important points concerning issues of online identity, privacy, journalistic ethics and defamation via social media which were widely ignored at the time:

- Social media is immensely powerful through its ability to influence opinions, but that power does not imply accuracy and, according to Jonathan Coad of the law firm Lewis Silkin, users have a clear legal and social responsibility to ensure that whatever they publish, regardless of the medium, is true and accurate if it infringes the human rights of others.[7]

- The complete lack of editorial control within the social media domain means that, at present, anyone can publish anything to a global audience without effective oversight.

- Establishing the identity of those posting on social media sites can be challenging. Well-known brands and high-profile individuals are the most likely to be correctly identified because they typically use their real names when setting up their accounts. Other users suffer from no such restrictions and accounts are regularly created using fabricated identities and random profile images found online.

---

6   http://www.theatlantic.com/technology/archive/2010/10/googles-ceo-the-laws-are-written-by-lobbyists/63908/ (accessed December 2012).
7   Interview with the author, 10 December 2012.

The true figure is unknown, but by comparing disclosures made by sites like Facebook with our own findings, I estimate that at least 5 per cent of all online profiles are wholly or partly fabricated and the total could well be higher. It is well worth bearing these points in mind as we consider the actual value of some of the data sourced from social media. It may well be that as awareness of the risk of monitoring by the state increases, only a diminishing minority of criminals will sign up for a social media account using their real names. In fact, far from being a vast bucket of reliable data, social media could just as easily become the most effective way to communicate and plan anonymously.

As outlined in another chapter, UK insurers Legal & General sponsored a series of experiments as an input to their Digital Criminal Report 2012. The fake Facebook profiles attracted hundreds of online friends. The most successful of these accounts now has over 950 such contacts and new friend requests are received daily, even though the accounts rarely engage in any activity at all. Fake accounts were also setup in LinkedIn and Twitter as a part of this trial and every one of these fake accounts remained live and unchallenged 18 months later.

While it is also true that pay-phones, pre-paid mobile devices and Internet email provide similar levels of anonymity, the degree to which new social media forms can be used for mass broadcast is unprecedented and this is what accentuates the problem. As we enter an era characterised by the 'news broadcast organisation of one', it becomes ever more important that we are able to validate the identity and credibility of each broadcaster. As Jonathan Coad rightly says, paraphrasing Lord Justice Leveson, we face the risk of mob rule online and our society needs to make a choice between responsible online behaviour governed by long-established legal principles for the protection of human rights, and the rule of the online mob.

The Possible Implications of US AB1844

On the other hand, while some push for greater accountability for what we post online, we are also seeing increasing pressure for better protection of online privacy. In September 2012 Sarah J. Banola and Stephen Kaus of US law firm Cooper White & Cooper published an online article[8] on the firm's website that addressed the possible implications of the signing into California law of AB 1844 on the same date.

---

8   http://www.cwclaw.com/publications/alertDetail.aspx?id=664 (accessed 5 April 2013).

AB 1844 prohibits employers from requiring job applicants or employees to allow access to their personal social media sites, except if access is reasonably required to investigate allegations of employee misconduct or violation of laws or regulations. Governor Brown announced his action on various social media sites, including Twitter, Facebook, Google+, LinkedIn and MySpace.

Specifically, the new law prohibits employers from requiring or requesting a personal social media user name or password, or requiring or requesting the employee or applicant to (1) access personal social media in the presence of the employer or (2) 'divulge any personal social media'. Presumably, the law could justify a legal action by the employee or an enforcement action by the Labor Commissioner, although a section added to the original text provides that the Labor Commissioner is not required to investigate or determine any violation.

'Social media' is defined as 'an electronic service or account, or electronic content, including, but not limited to, videos, still photographs, Blogs, video Blogs, podcasts, instant and text messages, email, online services or accounts, or Internet Web site profiles or locations'. The law prohibits retaliation against an employee who refuses to comply with a demand that violates the statute.

Important legislation such as AB 1844 can set the trend for legislation elsewhere, particularly if it originates in the US. It reflects the current direction of travel. AB 1844 may well herald a shift in attitudes towards the uses to which social media data may reasonably be put. Data that have hitherto been regarded as 'open source', and therefore fair game, may well come to be regarded as personal and private.

We should therefore not be taken by surprise if in the future we are required to clearly demonstrate that all social media data collection or monitoring activities are justified by suspicions that misconduct or a violation of laws or regulations has actually occurred. Simply sifting through public posts in order to detect evidence of previously unknown wrongdoings may come to be regarded as an unacceptable breach of privacy; while I may not have an actual expectation of privacy, I certainly do not have a reasonable expectation that the state is collecting and storing everything I say online.

BEYOND DEFAMATION TO INCRIMINATION

Twitter provides us with a perfect example of social media diversity. Unlike Facebook, where users 'friend' each other and form what can effectively become closed user groups, Twitter is by its very design a broadcast medium. The vast majority of Twitter's 100 million users fully expect to have their posts read by strangers and most seek the widest possible distribution. However, the failures of providers like Twitter to validate user identities allow users to create fictional or forged online identities with ease, not merely in order to conceal their true identity but occasionally in order to defame, impersonate or even incriminate others with impunity. This is something that cannot readily be done in the telecommunications or corporate email domains without the commission of acts such as credit card or identity theft, hacking or social engineering and this is another sense in which social media is different from traditional communications technologies.

In the absence of proper identity validation techniques for the whole of the user base, most social media evidence is potentially suspect and corroborating evidence is essential. However, even corroboration is becoming more and more difficult to achieve as users move away from the desktop computer with its hardwired connection and onto mobile devices, many of them using anonymous pre-paid SIM cards or operating across public WiFi networks.

A highly informative discussion of the issues related to privacy in the context of social networking is provided in a paper jointly written by UK lawyers Micheal O'Floinn and David Ormerod.[9] The authors raise a number of questions about expectations of privacy and the need for the authorities to the justify actions they may take to capture and record social network services communications, in particular when faked social media profiles are used as cover by investigators. Coad, on the other hand, contends that virtually all social media discourse is public, in the sense that it generally occurs between three or more people. The presence of that third party is the element required to make a defamatory remark actionable because it has been published. The question is whether the maker of a defamatory remark can simultaneously claim any expectation of privacy. Logic would suggest not.

This is all rather contradictory and confusing and it still leaves open the matter of messages sent between individual users of social media sites, which are not posted on the public 'wall' and which can only be accessed by

---

9   http://agc-wopac.agc.gov.my/e-docs/Journal/0000022421.pdf (accessed 1 October 2012).

logging onto the account of either sender or the receiver or via lawful intercept mechanisms. These would seem to be very similar to email messages and they might require different treatment. We therefore have a range of social media message formats to consider, including:

- broadcast messages, such as the McAlpine-related Tweets or unsecured Facebook posts;

- group messages within sites like Facebook, in those instances when privacy settings are activated;

- private messages sent one-to-one between individuals within sites like Facebook or Twitter, which can only be viewed by logging onto the account of one of the parties, or via lawful intercept.

Conclusion

Ethical questions, privacy concerns, identity validation flaws, technical data collection and retention challenges and the difficulties of corroboration outlined all raise serious questions about the practical value of social media evidence. This is not to say that those publishing defamatory remarks or plotting criminal offences via social media should not be held to account, but rather to acknowledge that as social media users become increasingly aware of official monitoring we can expect to see a corresponding increase in the use of fake profiles by anyone who fears surveillance, as well as increasing use of privacy settings or private messaging. Indeed, as I write, the WhatsApp messaging application is taking the market by storm, providing more secure messaging across devices such as the iPhone and Android handsets, and presenting investigators with a serious new challenge. Unless social media service providers take steps to strengthen their user identity checks (and here the horse may have already bolted) the value of social media and similar communications data as evidence is likely to decrease sharply over time.

My opinion is that the real medium to long term value of social media monitoring is likely to be found in analysis of the general, collective *tone* of communications rather than in individual message content. Social media can tell us what people are thinking and feeling, where they are statistically and how they might intend to behave as a group. In the longer term, social media is far more important as a source of *social intelligence* than as evidence and this is where the efforts of the authorities and large firms should be focused.

In Chapter 12, the final chapter in this book, we will take a quick look at what some of the other future changes in the ICT space might be, and what they could mean for risk, security and enforcement.

12

The Future of Cyber Security

Introduction

We have built the castle of our modern economic system upon the supposed bedrock of the information and communication technologies. Ours is now a duty of care and the task of ensuring that this rocky bed is not in fact quicksand is not one we can take lightly. However, the good news for some risk and security professionals is that the cyber security challenge *is* complex and that its complexity is increasing. Not every practitioner is able to get his or her head around the topic, but those who are able to do so, particularly if they are also able to explain the issues clearly to non-technical thinkers, will possess a real competitive advantage for as long as cyber security remains a central theme.

As shown in Figure 12.1 below, the proliferation of devices and Apps, plus new forms of use and mobility, leads to an increase in complexity. The resulting challenge is two-fold. IT teams are much more likely to bring their own devices into the workplace than any other group and these same teams often have exactly the type of data and systems access that criminals are interested in. It is also worth noting that these users have, on average, two to three different devices in their possession; think laptop, mobile phone or PDA and tablet.

Somehow, our security policies and guidelines need to address this diversity and the multi-threaded threats that go with it, while allowing for the fact that different job requirements and leadership requirements demand flexibility. The CEO is going to need his or her tablet and the marketing team will require social media access at work, regardless of what the security policy states, so policies need to be structured and updated with the emerging needs or demands of all categories of user in mind. This is necessary in order to avoid a need for the 'exceptions' that undermine security and render a policy meaningless due to a lack of consistency and the complexity of managing by exception.

Proliferation + Mobility = Complexity

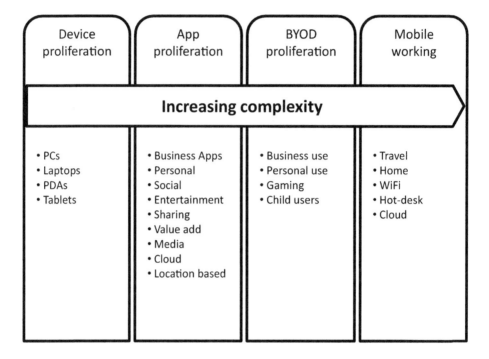

Device proliferation	App proliferation	BYOD proliferation	Mobile working
Increasing complexity			
• PCs • Laptops • PDAs • Tablets	• Business Apps • Personal • Social • Entertainment • Sharing • Value add • Media • Cloud • Location based	• Business use • Personal use • Gaming • Child users	• Travel • Home • WiFi • Hot-desk • Cloud

Figure 12.1   The proliferation of devices and Apps, plus the range of uses and mobility all add up to an increase in the complexity of the security challenge

Organisations must find ways of developing a balance between the needs of security and the needs of users that is acceptable to users. The reality is that users are, in the long term, far more likely to force their wishes on security than vice versa. So, security and risk teams need to learn to negotiate effectively and to engage with users constructively. For example, if it is known that a particular OS is the target of 70 per cent of malware attacks, the firm could consider advising users of this fact and prohibit devices running that OS while simultaneously negotiating a substantial volume discount for employees on devices from a supplier running a more secure OS. Likewise, when granting permission for employees to use social media via the secure corporate network (thus reducing their incentive to go across the street and use it insecurely in Starbucks instead) businesses can also agree a fair usage policy with users, but this must then be monitored and effectively applied.

Firms need to examine the App model and make a determination as to which Apps are allowed and which are regarded as a risk. This is a further BYOD compromise; you may bring your device to work but only if you run this email App, this calendar App, this Twitter App and so forth. All of this is possible if the conversation is handled in a mature way.

Ultimately, the solutions might lie outside the boundaries of the organisation and in the hands of network providers, Cloud service providers, equipment manufacturers and application developers. Is a time approaching when corporate liability for cyber security events will be pushed back up the food chain to these organisations? As cyber threats multiply, is it sustainable to hold each user and employer responsible for something that they were never really competent to deal with in the first place? After all, modern cyber security technologies have been thrust upon us – we didn't order them. So why should we now be held accountable for a security compromise that would never have occurred had we been left to our own devices? Increased corporate responsibility on the part of suppliers might well be the ultimate cyber security tool.

Cyber Security and the 4G Risk Landscape

Fourth Generation mobile technology ('4G') has arrived in all its glory and it is the time once again for myriad security consultants and some vendors to leverage change in order to scare their clients and win new business. The more things evolve, the more they stay the same.

In the simplest terms, 4G is merely the industry's response to the failure of 3G to live up to its over-hyped promise of a seamless, high-speed mobile data experience. Remember all the marketing that accompanied the 3G launch; the promise of high-quality streaming video on the mobile device, working from the beach, a future free of offices, no more face-to-face meetings and long journeys? Well, 4G is now supposed to deliver that 3G promise by providing a huge increase in bandwidth for users via an IP core and a next generation radio network.

4G isn't intended to provide a significant set of new services to users; the 3G service mix is already mature, possibly even saturated. And as fraud and other risks primarily follow the service mix, which is where the money flows, we probably shouldn't expect to see a huge short-term change in the risk landscape either. But one change is going to be hugely significant over the medium term and that is the transformation to a pure IP core.

With the IP approach there is likely to be an increasing 4G cyber security challenge as next generation devices continue to become nothing less than mobile computing platforms, connected to the Internet. The next generation cyber security matrix can be expected to represent a true convergence of traditional telecoms risks with cyber security risks and threat actors. A typical scenario is going to involve an access event gained through a cyber attack, followed by an exploitation event that takes the form of either financial fraud or data theft. This relationship between cyber access and fraud exploit will change the way operators need to address prevention, detection and the investigation of issues.

Revenue Assurance will also need to respond to some interesting new developments in the quality of service arena, depending on how operators choose to package and sell quality, but as is generally the case, the main task will be reading and processing the data for analytics purposes, rather than any particularly new complexity in the kinds of analysis that need to be done. Operators need to add new data sources and develop a holistic approach to risk that mirrors the convergence taking place on the service delivery side of the communications industry.

Cybernetics

Cybernetics refers to the merging of biological and computing systems. This is a highly advanced field and work has already been done to, among other things:

- incorporate animal tissue into computing devices, for example in the form of snail neurons that can transmit signals;[1]

- interface the human brain with computer devices in order to allow disabled people to control a PC or even to move a mechanical limb.[2]

Why is any of this relevant to cyber security? It seems very likely that this development path will lead us to a place where the digital and the biological are inextricably linked, meaning that, for example, the distinction between a

---

1   http://www.biochem.mpg.de/en/eg/fromherz/publications/01zecfro/index.html. (accessed June 2005).
2   http://research.microsoft.com/en-us/um/people/desney/publications/bcihci-chapter1.pdf (accessed June 2005).

computer virus affecting implanted computing devices and a biological virus affecting humans will become blurred. Similarly, an investigator seizing computer evidence might need to consider what to do about the chip embedded within the suspect's skull. In such a context, cyber security experts and medical experts will have to work hand-in-latex glove.

It reads like science fiction, but the Cyborgs (short for cybernetic organisms) are already here. Brain implants or neural implants are already being developed and trialled as a methodology for dealing with impairment or dysfunction in the brain. Implants for transmitting neurological signals around areas of spinal injury have already been successfully tested in large mammals like dogs. With the speed of modern medical advances, we can expect to see this area of development accelerate rapidly over the course of the next few years.

One logical next step will be to move from repairing brain or body function to enhancing perfectly normal functions, perhaps by improving sensory functions such as sight, hearing and smell, or by implanting wireless communications technology directly into the skull. Many of the early developments are likely to have military or security applications, but we should also be prepared to see high-end commercial products coming out, followed by offers for the bulk of the market within a decade or two.

The ethical and practical implications of these developments for cyber security practitioners, law enforcement and the legal system, as well as for the rest of society, are mind boggling. How, for example, do we define a person who has computer technology embedded within their brain? Is this a person, a computer or both? What are the risks of computer viruses afflicting these devices and how will we combine medical and cyber security practices to address such incidents? How feasible will it become to launch DoS attacks against such people and will those constitute a crime of violence or a computer crime? What procedures will the police need to adopt when reviewing or seizing computer evidence that includes data stored on technology embedded in the suspect?

Clearly, new areas of law, cyber ethics and best practice will emerge, as well as a whole range of new opportunities for cyber security professionals although we will no doubt come to terms with these emerging challenges just as we have done, or are starting to do, with the challenges of today.

Cyber Conflict

The complexity of cyber space isn't stopping the powers that be from preparing to fight their wars there. All of the major powers, and some lesser ones, are investing heavily in the development of both cyber defences and cyber weaponry.

THE PENTAGON'S FIVE STRATEGIC INITIATIVES

The US Department of Defence has developed and published its strategy for operating in cyberspace. The plan has five pillars:

1.   treat cyber space as an operational domain to organise, train and equip so that DoD can take full advantage of cyber space's potential;

2.   employ new defence operating concepts to protect DoD networks and systems;

3.   partner with other US Government departments and agencies and the private sector to enable a whole-of-government cyber security strategy;

4.   build robust relationships with US allies and international partners to strengthen collective cyber security;

5.   leverage the nation's ingenuity through an exceptional cyber workforce and rapid technological innovation.

The strategy is available at www.defense.gov/cyber[3] and although it is clearly a war-fighting strategy it does contain a number of references to defence, security and international cooperation. There is also recognition of the important role that non-state actors can play in the cyber arena and of the challenges facing anyone about to make a decision to launch a retaliatory cyber attack against another nation.

THE SIX AGES OF WAR

Convention defines five ages of war, but I like to list six, as shown in Table 12.1. Cyber warfare is broken out from traditional signals intelligence on the

---

3   Accessed 8 March 2013.

basis that cyber technologies and infrastructure are game changing, even revolutionary, and that they criss-cross civilian, governmental, military and corporate boundaries in a pattern so complex and variable that it is difficult, perhaps even impossible, to map it accurately. In a sense, we have returned to an age of warfare that predates the geological survey, with military forces operating in cyber space likely to find themselves as ill-informed and short on accurate, timely and complete intelligence as those of Napoleon, Kutuzov, Sun Tzu or Lee.

Table 12.1   The six ages of war

1st Age	2nd Age	3rd Age	4th Age	5th Age	6th Age
Land	Land	Land	Land	Land	Land
	Naval	Naval	Naval	Naval	Naval
		Signals	Signals	Signals	Signals
			Air	Air	Air
				Space	Space
					Cyber

One key differentiator that marks the cyber conflict challenge out from all others is the speed of change, both technological and infrastructural, compounded by the speed and volume of data processing. With hundreds of millions of users and millions of domains being added to the Internet over short periods of time, simply identifying new targets and keeping track of existing ones is a truly daunting task. Faced with such a challenge, a corporate body would immediately ask about the cost/benefit ratio and national governments should perhaps consider equivalent questions.

FACTORS AFFECTING CYBER CONFLICT

There is a presumption among a large proportion of those thinking about this topic that the conduct of cyber conflict between major powers is a given. At the very least, it is assumed that a failure to develop a comprehensive defence and retaliatory capability is a weakness that an enemy would naturally exploit, either in the form of a digital Pearl Harbor first strike, or as part of a wider conventional warfare strategy.

One consequence of this mindset has been the rapid development of the cyber conflict arms race, similar in many ways to the nuclear arms race that took place during the mid-to-late twentieth century and planning for cyber conflict could actually serve as a trigger for war in its own right, but this may be unavoidable given the obvious cyber security risks we face. Listed below are eight key factors that could combine to make a major cyber conflict between the world's great economic and military powers both complex and catastrophic for the global economy.

Globalisation

Twenty-first century globalisation rests on a technological foundation and we are all aware of how devastating even a short-term loss of Internet and communications services can be to corporate activity. However, we are less conscious of the impacts of such a technical failure on the globalised economy.

Consider a typical international bank along the lines of an HSBC. The bank's own marketing images depict a global network of banking hubs and national branch networks, all interconnected and interdependent, handling financial transfers across borders, managing the accounts of globalised corporate clients and individual account holders alike, all supported by outsourced cyber security, call centres in India, the UK and the USA, and massive Cloud service facilities.

This bank does not exist in any one country – it exists globally. Launch a cyber attack on any major economy and you risk bringing down the whole bank, not only in the targeted state, but everywhere. Target the Internet in India and call centres supporting half of the world's major firms may go down at the same time, which leads us into the next point.

Entanglement

Although the word entanglement is generally used to describe an inability to clearly separate legitimate military cyber targets from civilian ones there is an even closer correlation with the concept of quantum entanglement.

Quantum entanglement refers to the relationship between quantum particles that are so tightly interdependent that it is impossible to describe the qualities and behaviour of one particle without taking the other into account. This is a powerful metaphor and it captures the unpredictable and extremely complex interdependencies of modern cyber technologies.

The Internet today probably provides one of the best examples of chaos theory in action. Attempting to bring down the cyber assets of one nation without disrupting the whole system will be like trying to swat red butterflies in the dark without hurting the blue ones. In a wholesale cyber conflict we simply can't predict the cascade of effects emanating from a bilateral series of attacks on infrastructure, nor can we be certain about our ability to adequately control the attack tools used or to focus their energies with sufficient precision. Our response therefore has the potential to cause more harm than good.

Response

There are effectively two options for decision making and response in any high-technology risk environment:

- respond automatically in real-time based on a predetermined set of rules or some form of artificial intelligence; or

- provide information to a group of human decision makers and depend on them to respond as quickly as they can.

The problem faced during a cyber conflict is that the attack may be over in milliseconds, long before a human user even registers an alert on a screen, while automated responses are a very risky proposition, particularly if they include retaliatory strikes.

We have arrived at the age when technology, while not yet more intelligent than us, certainly outperforms us for speed of response and volumes of data processing and storage. The decision we will need to make is whether speed or reason are paramount, although if a major event does occur, this question may come to be purely academic. You can send me your answer then – by post. A big part of the problem is attribution.

ATTRIBUTION

Clever Internet criminals use a range of techniques to alter or conceal their email addresses, domain names, IP addresses or equipment identities and geographic locations. The most advanced criminal operations will daisy chain or 'trombone' traffic across multiple devices and jurisdictions to conceal their origin, so the notion that the cyber conflict unit of any modern state would attack another cyber-capable state and leave an easy to follow trail back to its own servers somehow doesn't add up.

It almost goes without saying that once detection has occurred, the really challenging part of the decision-making process will be attribution – determining who *really* attacked us as opposed to who appeared to attack us. This in turn breaks down into sub-questions such as:

- Where did the attack come from geographically?

- If it was a distributed attack (possibly involving hundreds or thousands of devices) can we identify its root?

- Was the attack government sponsored or encouraged?

- Was the attack launched from the territory of the sponsor or from that of an innocent third party?

- Should the government whose territory was used have been able to detect the attack, given their own cyber capabilities?

- Should that government have been able to prevent the attack?

- How is that government responding to the incident now?

It is difficult to envision this iterative decision-making process being carried out rapidly and it seems very probable that answers to some of these questions may never be had because false flag attacks are likely to be the norm rather than the exception.

False flag attacks

The previous paragraphs hint at the very real possibility of 'false flag attacks', these being attacks by party or state A against B that are deliberately designed to implicate C. There could be any number of motives for such action, ranging from the individual through the political to the corporate.

Just a few of the relevant questions that will need to be addressed before a rational and informed decision can be made about how to retaliate are:

- Are there non-state actors who would want us to attribute the attack to a particular state?

- Are there other state actors who would want us to attribute the attack to a third state?

- Are there citizens within our own nation who would wish us to attribute the attack to another state, possibly for ideological reasons?

Cyber conflict seems unthinkable, yet it is already a reality and attacks by nation states against other nations occur regularly. For us to assume that our political and military leaders know best is to fall into the same trap as those who marched under the previous century's banners of militarism. Let us hope that our economic livelihood is not put in jeopardy by big power politics and misguided war fighting strategies.

Conclusion

In examining the topics of cyber crime and cyber security, we have found ourselves focusing repeatedly on a few core topics; dependency on connectivity, the threat of large scale, sophisticated attacks, and the awareness challenge. To my mind, the first is paramount and the others are contributory. Many of the very knowledgeable and expert professional people I met during the course of this writing project tended to dismiss the more extreme risks, the most common refrain being that the Internet is simply too large, with too many redundancies built-in, for it to fail because of the actions of a few cyber criminals.

My view is unchanged, however. Large as the Internet is, it remains finite; mathematically speaking, there is an absolute limit to the number of processes and the volume of data it can handle at any one time. Double the size of the network, quadruple it, multiply it by a trillion and still it has an upper limit on processing. There is, on the other hand, no theoretical limit to the number of processes and the number of bits of data that could be generated by a cleverly devised and successfully executed cyber flooding attack, exploiting for example the one billion (and counting) user accounts on a social service like Facebook. In fact, because of the scale of its penetration of the user base, a service like Facebook is the most obvious channel of attack, yet, as we have seen, the evidence suggests that we should be highly skeptical about the quality of the security procedures in place at sites of this nature. A successful Facebook-type computer worm, attacking the capacity of the network to carry traffic, could very easily make manifest the central risk of our common dependency on connectivity. Without connectivity, everything else 'cyber' becomes irrelevant and you may find yourself reading this text by candlelight.

This is not scaremongering. As I explained at the outset, my business, my lifestyle and my children's education each depend entirely on having a secure and reliable Internet service. Without it, I will have to seek work on a local farm and I will be competing with thousands of other recently unemployed cyber workers. But ignorance of the risks and complacent managerial and governmental decision-making on both strategic and operational levels serve to make this a real, if remote, possibility. If we fail to educate both users and leaders in the ways of a secure network of networks, we face the almost inevitable consequence of an eventual failure of the one technology upon which we, our economy and our way of life depend.

Appendix
Sample Response Plan

The form overleaf represents a simple Incident Response Plan that can be used or adapted to fit the needs of any organisation.

Cyber Incident Response Plan

Organisation:

Dept. or Team:

Risk Level Evaluation

Level	Label	Risk character	Typical level of response
1	Strategic	The issues experienced or anticipated have the potential to halt all critical operations and processes for an extended period of time.	Board level involvement. Coordination with appropriate government agencies. Implementation of DRBC Plan.
2	Severe	There is likely to be an observable degradation of key services or operations with the potential to affect share value or reputation.	Board level involvement. Possible coordination with Police/other. Review of DRBC Plan. Execution of Media and Social Media plans.
3	Elevated	There is likely to be a measureable impact on internal operations and processes, but the risk to share value or reputation is considered low.	CXO involvement. Re-read and discussion of DRBC Plan. Coordination with PR team. Police involvement only if appropriate. No media contact made.
4	Operational	There is unlikely to be any measureable impact on internal operations or processes and no impact on share value or reputation is anticipated.	Appropriate C-level involvement or reporting. Departmental level operational responses and containment. Normal business processes continue.

Critical Infrastructure

Type	Location	Description

Emergency Key Contact List

Role	Name	Email address	Mobile Phone
Board level			
Chairman			
etc.			
C-Level			
CXO			
CFO			
CIO			
CTO			
COO			
Etc.			
Operational			
Security Head			
Risk Head			
Fraud Head			
Etc.			
External			
Police			
Information Comm.			
PR Firm			
Etc.			

Action Plan

Actions (all as per organisation's cyber security plan)	Risk Level				Locations	Remarks
	4	3	2	1		
Backup data to removable storage	x	x	x	x		
Move backups to DRBC site(s)		x	x	x		
Halt key processes				x		
Shut down equipment				x		
Recover log files	x	x	x	x		
Execute Contact Plan		x	x	x		
Etc.						

Recommended Reading and Online Resources

Publications

Clough, Jonathan, 2012. *Principles of Cybercrime*. Cambridge: Cambridge University Press.

Hartfield, Clive and Hartfield, Karen, 2008. *Intelligence*. Oxford: Oxford University Press.

Johnson, Mark, 2012. *Demystifying Communications Risk*. Farnham: Gower Publishing.

Naughton, John, 2012. *From Gutenberg to Zuckerberg*. London: Quercus.

Richardson, Louise, 2007. *What Terrorists Want*. London: John Murray.

Treverton, Gregory, 2001. *Reshaping National Intelligence for an Age of Information*. Cambridge: Cambridge University Press.

Websites and Reports

Serious Organised Crime Agency (SOCA)
http://www.soca.gov.uk/ (accessed: January 2013).

Professor Ross Anderson
http://www.cl.cam.ac.uk/~rja14/ (accessed: January 2013).

Fraud Intelligence magazine
http://www.counter-fraud.com/ (accessed: January 2013).

The Register
http://www.theregister.co.uk/ (accessed: January 2013).

US National Cyber Incident Response Plan
http://www.federalnewsradio.com/pdfs/NCIRP_Interim_Version_September_
    2010.pdf (accessed: January 2013).

PWC Global State of Information Security Survey 2013
http://www.pwc.com/gx/en/consulting-services/information-security-survey/
    index.jhtml (accessed: January 2013).

Ernst & Young Global Information Security Survey 2012
http://www.ey.com/GL/en/Services/Advisory/Advisory-Services_Information-
    Security-Services (accessed: January 2013).

McAfee Threats Report: Q2 2012
http://www.mcafee.com/uk/resources/reports/rp-quarterly-threat-q2-2012.pdf
    (accessed: January 2013).

Deloitte Global Financial Services Security Study 2012
http://www.deloitte.com/view/en_GX/global/industries/financial-services/2ac3
    00d256409210VgnVCM100000ba42f00aRCRD.htm (accessed: January 2013).

CyberSource White Papers and Reports
http://www.cybersource.com/cgi-bin/resource_center/resources.cgi (accessed:
    January 2013).

Anderson, Levy et al., 2012. *Measuring the Cost of Cybercrime*
http://weis2012.econinfosec.org/papers/Anderson_WEIS2012.pdf   (accessed:
    January 2013).

ENISA Threat Landscape, 2013
http://www.enisa.europa.eu/activities/risk-management/evolving-threat-.
    environment/ENISA_Threat_Landscape/at_download/fullReport (accessed:
    March 2013).

Social Media

Neira Jones
http://neirajones.blogspot.co.uk/ (accessed: March 2013).

Hayley Kaplan
http://what-is-privacy.com/home/#axzz2C7NtTfNr (accessed: January 2013).

Index

*For Product Safety Concerns and Information please contact
our EU representative GPSR@taylorandfrancis.com Taylor & Francis
Verlag GmbH, Kaufingerstraße 24, 80331 München, Germany*

T - #0023 - 290525 - C0 - 246/174/17 - PB - 9780367605469 - Gloss Lamination